POLICY ANALYSIS
and
POLICY INNOVATION
Patterns Problems and Potentials

POLICY ANALYSIS
and
POLICY INNOVATION
Patterns Problems and Potentials

Editors

Peter R Baehr   Björn Wittrock

SAGE Modern Politics Series Volume 5
sponsored by the European Consortium for Political Research/ECPR

 SAGE Publications · London and Beverly Hills

Copyright © 1981 by
SAGE Publications, Ltd.

For information address
SAGE Publications Ltd
28 Banner Street, London EC1Y 8QE

SAGE Publications Inc
275 South Beverly Drive
Beverly Hills, California 90212

British Library Cataloguing in Publication Data

Future Studies and Policy Analysis in the Political
  Process *(Conference), Brussels, 1979*
  Policy analysis and policy innovation. — (Sage
  modern politics series; vol. 5).
  1. Policy sciences — Congresses
  I. Title   II. Baehr, Peter R
  III. Wittrock, Björn
  300'.1   H61   80-41079

ISBN 0-8039-9809-0
ISBN 0-8039-9810-4 Pbk

Contents

Introduction

Björn Wittrock
University of Stockholm

and

Peter R. Baehr
The Netherlands Scientific Council
for Government Policy

The 1970s witnessed a growing interest among government policy-makers in the potential and impact of cross-sectoral and long-range oriented policy analysis and futures studies. This interest manifested itself in a number of Western nations by the creation within central executives of units specializing in this type of analysis and study. At an intellectual level much of the interest in policy analysis and futures studies emerged out of a tradition characterized by a highly rationalistic conception of the policy-making process. Policy-makers, objectives, alternatives, and the costs and probabilities associated with the consequences of different courses of action were assumed to be clearly definable and subject to an analysis that saw the policy-making process as one of a sequence of rational choices.

Some of the intellectual foundations of these activities have been increasingly questioned. The fuzzy nature of policy problems and policy objectives has been amply stressed. The complex features of a group of policy-makers are better understood — so the argument often goes — in terms of interconnecting networks than in those of a unitary 'planning subject'. And it seems to be an open question as to under what conditions various kinds of knowledge and policy analysis will actually be used and have an impact on policies. The connection between policy analysis and policy innovation is an

uncertain one. In the case of analyses ranging across traditional administrative boundaries and far into the future, this uncertainty is
even more pronounced. Hence, there is an obvious need to take
stock of practical experiences of cross-sectoral and long-term
oriented policy analysis and confront current and competing
models of policy analysis with these experiences. Against this
background the workshop 'Futures Studies and Policy Analysis in
the Political Process: Patterns, Problems and Potentials' was
organized by the European Consortium for Political Research in
Brussels in April 1979, in cooperation with the Netherlands Scientific Council for Government Policy and the Swedish Secretariat
for Futures Studies. It was attended both by political scientists with
a mainly theoretical interest in the subject and by individuals with
personal experience of various government forecasting and policy
analytical units. Papers and discussions at that workshop have
served as a point of departure for the present book, which is divided into three major parts.

In the first part the nature and conditions of linkages and barriers between research and policy are examined. In Chapter 1
Daniel Tarschys outlines the prospects of policy innovation in a
zero or low-growth economy. He emphasizes the different styles of
organizational development and policy analysis that are necessary
preconditions for bureaucratic change in a slow or zero-growth
economy. Andries Hoogerwerf (Chapter 2) identifies a number of
possible contributions social science could make to public policy.
He also outlines models of relationships between research and
policy-making. In Chapter 3 Sverker Gustavsson argues that a solution to the linkage problem is at hand. It requires, however, that a
distinction be made between the different bases of legitimacy of
researchers and politicians. While accepting the thesis of a
mismatch between policy-making and social knowledge, and questioning whether current planning bodies generally serve as bridges
rather than barriers between these domains, all three chapters
underscore the potentials of linking knowledge to action in such a
way that public policy innovation should also be possible in a zero
or low-growth economy.

The chapters in the second part of the volume review various national experiences of cross-sectoral and long-range oriented policy
analysis. In the workshop in Brussels discussions dealt with the
situation in the Netherlands, France, West Germany, Britain,

Canada, New Zealand and Sweden. This volume focuses on five of these nations.

William Plowden gives a thorough account of the origins and operation of the British Central Policy Review Staff (CPRS). Its changing role during the 1970s is outlined; the life cycle of the CPRS has coincided with a change in public mood away from one of expectations of steady economic growth and of confidence in a rational model of policy-making. The impact of the CPRS is analysed in terms of its effect on the climate of opinion among decision-makers and its ability to put issues on the political agenda. In Chapter 5 Peter Baehr presents the Netherlands Scientific Council for Government Policy against the background of the extensive Dutch planning tradition. The Dutch council has in several respects acquired a position that is unique in an international perspective; it has succeeded in gaining a central and respected position in the executive and has still retained independence and a high degree of openness in its style of work.

Björn Wittrock examines the role of the Swedish Secretariat for Futures Studies (Chapter 6). This body was set up in 1973 following the recommendation of a governmental commission headed by Alva Myrdal, then Minister of State. The Secretariat was located at the crossroads of ministries in the central executive and of parliament. Its work has been characterized by an ambition to clearly spell out alternative courses of action and to promote a public debate on options and developments. Thereby, it has been able to influence Swedish policy formation — mainly in the field of energy — in ways that indicate alternatives to those envisaged by most rational models of policy analysis.

In Chapter 7, Simon Miles reviews governmental futures studies and cross-sectoral policy analysis performed by various units on the Canadian scene. The author claims that what is lacking is not so much resources as the willingness of individual departments to go beyond their immediate territory; the existence of a truly comprehensive body responsible for assessing long-range societal developments is also lacking.

Juliet Lodge argues in Chapter 8 that a tacit premise behind the establishment of the New Zealand Commission for the Future was that the regular ministerial organization did not provide a suitable framework for long-term analysis and futures planning. The need for such activities was felt the more strongly as New Zealand's international position had to be reconsidered during the 1970s.

The third part of the volume is devoted to normative policy analysis and to an examination of the limitations and potentials of different models of political futures planning. Jonathan Gershuny outlines and confronts two basic models of normative policy analysis, the rational model and the incrementalist one. Gershuny's chapter is a succinct survey of the debate surrounding rationalism and incrementalism. It emphasizes the limitations of both models and accepts neither of the two. This conclusion is in a sense a pessimistic one. It does not prescribe a clear role for forecasters and policy analysts in the process of public policy-making except that they should not allow themselves to be mistaken as 'neutral instruments' in politicians' hands. But there are also three seminal implications of Gershuny's argument that are well in line with the contributions by Lars Ingelstam and Peter Self in Chapters 10 and 11.

Gershuny questions the incrementalist view of policy innovation as a process consisting of small and reversible changes as well as the rationalist view of it as a process involving comprehensive review of feasible options where the results of policy analysis are fed into a well-ordered system of policy-formulation and decision-making. But implicit in the criticism is the plea for alternative accounts of policy innovation.

Lars Ingelstam suggests that a sense of uncertainty and urgency among policy-makers might be necessary before they take real heed of analyses that propose wider margins for action than are normally considered feasible. Strategic policy innovation requires that policy alternatives have been elaborated so as to be available. But favourable external conditions are necessary if these alternatives are to affect policy-making and result in real change. Ingelstam puts forward the idea that the 'spirit of the age' is one important component in such an external setting. The 'spirit of the age' serves to define the limits of what is politically possible but also serves as a common perceptual basis for an informal coordination of small- and medium-sized decisions in the different sectors of contemporary society.

A second implication of Gershuny's argument refers to his observation that the rationale for a certain type and scale of decision-making depends upon the socio-technic substructure that underlies it. If this is so, then Ingelstam's views about the role of the informal economy are relevant to a discussion of models of normative policy analysis. Ingelstam contends that political futures planning so far has been largely confined to an analysis of the public service sector and the formal market economy, to the neglect of the informal economy and its interlinking with the money economy. Assessments of costs and benefits accruing from policies of various scale are thereby unduly influenced.

Thirdly, in his treatment of the rational model Gershuny does not discuss only the comprehensive or holistic version of it. He also deals with different proposals that involve a limitation of the scope of rationality to some limited set of options and effects, so-called bounded rationality. He identifies three types of problems encountered by policy-making according to ideas of bounded rationality. These concern the specialized or sectoral allegiances of individual administrative institutions, the personal and narrowly partisan ones of politicians, and, thirdly, the fragmented and departmentalized nature of social science. These various forms of difficulties might in turn promote 'issue dissensus' and 'process dissensus' and contribute to the erosion of the moral foundations of collective decision-making as the role of the state extends itself. Problems connected with the social sciences and their limited capacity to serve as a basis for policy-making are discussed in Chapters 2 and 3 by Andries Hoogerwerf and Sverker Gustavsson respectively. The difficulties of overcoming the strong sectoral feature of modern administrations are taken up by Björn Wittrock (Chapter 6) who searches for ways out of the dilemmas of comprehensive planning, and by Peter Self (Chapter 11) who emphasizes the need for planning units which can escape from the bureaucratic bias towards supposedly 'hard' data and from the day-to-day pressures of the political agenda. Such planning units should, Self argues, 'adopt a more imaginative and free-ranging but carefully objective approach to policy issues'. Thus, although the difficulties discerned by Gershuny involve a formidable array of problems, the volume also contains pieces which attack those very problems.

Peter Self's chapter, 'Planning: Rational or Political?', also epitomizes some of the main themes of the entire volume.
— More attention will have to be paid to cross-sectoral and long-range analyses because of: public pressures on limited — and on-

ly slowly growing — government resources; the pressures for comprehensive types of regulation; the fact that politicians are increasingly held responsible for a widening set of social consequences; increasing cross-national vulnerability to ecological and economic chain reactions; and because the negative side-effects of public policies become more visible. In sum this amounts to a need for cross-sectoral and long-range policy analysis as well as a justification for comprehensive planning. This need does not primarily derive from the existence of a large set of 'rational procedures waiting to be tapped . . . but because it is necessary for governments to tackle societal problems on the scale on which they occur, difficult though this is'. Self, and most of the other participants in the original workshop, thus oppose the claims of those modern welfare economists who argue that the problems of allocational, systemic, political and international overload can be solved only by strategies of deregulation and exclusive reliance on market mechanisms. Some form of comprehensive planning is called for to match individual preferences, social outcomes and the scale of social problems.

— Most contributors caution against a drift towards allocative, corporate planning of a hierarchical nature and argue for the future elaboration of other modes of planning, with less reliance upon numerical projections of current technological and economic trends and a more imaginative search for alternative options in public policy-making.

— An analysis of the explicitly political characteristics of forecasting, policy analysis, and planning is necessary. This kind of analysis will — many participants of the workshop emphasized — naturally widen into an examination of the role of the state in contemporary society and will have to pay attention to coordinated complexes of organizations with elements from all sectors of society, both private and public.

1 Research, Planning and Policy-making: Barriers and Bridges

1 Public Policy Innovation in a Zero-Growth Economy: A Scandinavian Perspective

Daniel Tarschys
Swedish Parliament

A hundred years or so ago the Scandinavian countries embarked upon a process of social and economic change commonly known as the industrial revolution. Our economy was remodelled in the course of only a few decades. Saw mills, factories and workshops shot up everywhere. Hundreds of thousands of people left farming to find jobs in the new industries. When the flight from the land was at its height in Sweden, in the 1890s, industrial employment rose by about 40,000 persons a year.

At only one other point in Swedish history have we witnessed such a transformation of the economy, and that is the expansion of the services sector since the second world war. Once again, a very large proportion of the population has transferred to new occupations, primarily in the public sector. In the last ten years, employment in the local government sector alone has increased by 40,000 people a year. But expansion had commenced way back in the 1950s and 1960s. Schools, hospitals, day nurseries and after-school centres were built all over the country. Small local government offices bulged, burst and were replaced with modern high-rise office blocks. This time the flight was from goods production to services and administration.

Membership of the Swedish Municipal Workers' Union recently

This paper was previously published in the *International Social Science Journal*, Vol. XXXI, No. 4, 1979, and is reproduced by permission of UNESCO.

surpassed that of the Metal Workers' Union, making it the largest trade union in Sweden. This is something of a symbolic confirmation of the upswing in the public services sector: suddenly it is no longer merely a supporting function in a predominantly industrial society but is itself becoming an increasingly dominant economic activity. Thirty years ago the small rural authority in Sweden had no more than a score or so employees. Today local authorities and county councils employ one in every five of Sweden's workforce, and in practically all districts it is local government itself which is the major employer.

The *public sector revolution* of recent decades is just as radical an upheaval in our social and economic life as the industrial revolution was at the end of the nineteenth and the beginning of the twentieth century — a process which has fundamentally transformed our daily life (see Tarschys 1978). Tasks formerly carried out in the home have been transferred to communal organs. Public services have been extended and diversified, but so also have public controls. While we have become increasingly dependent upon one another in a closely integrated economy we have also a greater need of social control. The closer we live to one another and the more we develop trade and services, the more we are affected by the conduct of other people. Technical advances have also created new dangers which make it necessary to have stricter supervision. This is the Janus face of the public sector revolution: on the one hand, it creates greater freedom and opens up opportunities the great majority have never had before, and on the other, it demands a new readiness to adjust and conform. Every advance, every step forward has its unavoidable price.

In spite of economic recessions, the expansion of the public sector has hardly slowed down at all during the 1970s. This is partly due to the fact that a welfare state of the Scandinavian variety is programmed to promote high employment and, therefore, to increase its input of counter-cyclical resources when the economy weakens. But it is also due to the fact that the public sector has its own intrinsic dynamics. The volume of central and local government activity is not only affected by the decisions we make right now, but also by commitments made many years ago. With the type of reform programmes which started to be launched on a large scale during the 1960s — what I now have in mind is the growing amount of planning and longer-term programmes of various kinds

— one can actually say that we have become more and more governed by old decisions. The costs accruing from an ambitious and far-sighted policy are often not fully apparent when the decision is made, but make themselves felt as time goes on, when plans are put into effect. Here we have a paradox to which we should give a great deal of thought: even though the purpose of planning has been to create greater efficiency and freedom of action in the development of society, quite often policy-makers have found that it has eventually tied their hands and restricted their freedom of action.

Consequently, the prime problem of the 1970s for the public sector is the growing gulf between income and expenditure. On the one hand, public activities have continued expanding and transfers have increased substantially, partly on account of demographic factors. On the other hand, economic growth has slowed down. There are several reasons for this. In the international sphere, we have had the oil crisis and the economic disorders which have followed in its wake, particularly because of the inability of the oil-producing countries to use their newly-won purchasing power. We also have the industrial upswing in some developing countries which have started to be serious competitors to European industry. But the imbalance also has many indigenous causes. During the 1970s people have tended to enjoy the rise in their living standards in forms other than earnings: more leisure, less stress and better working conditions. It is also feasible that higher taxes have produced a growing volume of private transactions that bypass the tax system. For these reasons, the declining growth of GNP need not be a reflection of an equally strong slowdown in the real, qualitative rise in people's living standards — on the contrary, it is quite feasible that by these standards we have had just as rapid an improvement in well-being in the 1970s as we had in the 1960s. But, on the other hand, it is little comfort to the politicians who have to worry about making fiscal ends meet, as an increase in the tax-free joys of life does not result in the heartening jangle of revenues pouring into government and municipal coffers. No matter how false the much-disparaged GNP concept may be, it is a very real headache for ministers of finance.

And consequently, deficits on public balance sheets have been growing. In 1979 Sweden's budget was in the red by about 39 billion crowns, approximately one-tenth of GNP. The long-term

budget presented in April 1979 also foresees annual budget deficits
in the region of 50 billion crowns in the next five years. And what is
more, the long-term budget is based on fairly optimistic assumptions and makes no claim to be a forecast of probable trends in
state expenditure. One precondition, then, is that the government
will not suddenly be forced to pump in resources to save flounder-
ing industries, as has so often happened in recent years. Another
precondition is that politicians will refrain from deciding on new
undertakings and that government authorities will not request
higher appropriations than those already passed by the Riksdag.
So, even with these assumptions, the deficit on the Swedish budget
for the next five years will be about 200 billion crowns.

Recessions always breed a certain amount of pessimism, and I
particularly want to stress that we should not draw too far-reaching
conclusions from trends in the past few years. There is any amount
of discussion about how many of our problems are of a structural
nature and how many are due to temporary fluctuations in the
world economy. But let us put these discussions to one side for the
moment. The important point is that even if the most optimistic
forecasts for the next few years were to materialize, Sweden's state
finances would still not balance. Comfort can be sought in various
techniques of national accounting or in popular Keynesian
philosophy that says there is never any need to worry about budget
deficits. But for all that, there is no getting round the uncomfor-
table truth — the gap between revenues and expenditure persists,
and there are good grounds for presuming that it will grow.

What can we do about it? The classical remedy, of course, is to
raise taxes. But most people agree that it is going to be very difficult
to increase the tax burden to any effective extent within the
foreseeable future. Admittedly, that opinion has often been expressed before, but nevertheless ways have been found to draw in
more resources to defray public spending. The prophesies made
from time to time about an absolute tax ceiling have not so far been
fulfilled. In 1906, the French economist, Leroy-Beaulieu, maintained that the public sector could never appropriate more than 12-13
percent of gross national product and at the same time keep the
economy buoyant. Immediately after the second world war, Colin
Clark, the Australian economist, said that the magic limit was 25
percent. Today, some Scandinavian countries have already passed
the 50 percent mark, and our societies have not collapsed yet. But

the fact that old predictions have been off the mark does not mean that we can go on and on raising taxes. Even the tax pressure we have today is disturbing from many points of view, not least because it encourages invisible transactions, and thereby undermines the civic spirit and solidarity which keep society together.

As far as the purely economic outcome is concerned, the immediate effects of tax increases may have been exaggerated, but on the other hand, some of the more long-term effects have probably been underestimated. There is seldom an immediate reaction to raised taxes, but as time goes by people learn to handle the system and adapt their behaviour accordingly. We have seen in Sweden in the past few years how more and more people are discovering that a reduction of their working time by a few months a year, a day or so a week, or a few hours a day makes no major inroads into their take-home pay. When the entire workforce realizes these advantages we shall be well on the way to a part-time society — a society which in many ways is easier to live in and more humane but which in a narrow fiscal perspective seems somewhat difficult to manage.

The Scandinavian countries are not alone in their struggle to solve the problems of the high tax economy in the 1970s. The same trends are evident in many other industrialized countries. More and more literature has been published in recent years about the crises facing state finances and government (Boelsgaard 1975; Cornford 1975; Crozier et al. 1976; O'Connor 1973; Poulantzas 1976). We have also become increasingly interested in the legitimacy of government and in the difficulties associated with sustaining a sufficiently broad support for common tasks — that debate is particularly lively in West Germany where theorists like Jürgen Habermas and Nicolas Luhmann have taken up the cudgels. And, finally, there is a third major debate going on about the concepts of 'ungovernability' and 'government overload' (King 1976; Scheuch 1976; Rose and Peters 1978; Rose 1977).

The conclusion we can draw from all this is that it will not be particularly easy to restore balance to public finances by massive increases of income. A heavy increase of the tax burden would lead to such serious pressures — both political and economic — that it cannot be assumed that the net result would be beneficial. We already have a number of examples of raised taxes which have not had the desired result, because it has been difficult to collect them or the taxpayers have found one way or another to adapt their transactions so that they have not been liable to pay the new taxes. In all probability these problems will crop up in the future too. Theories about the 'absolute tax ceiling' may have a shaky foundation, but nonetheless it is obvious that within the foreseeable future it will be impossible to extract much greater resources to defray public spending without inflicting severe damage on both the national economy and the civic spirit.

It is against this background that we must examine the future of the public sector. We leave behind an expansionary phase which has fundamentally changed central and local government activities. The future presents new challenges: many old collective needs are as yet far from satisfied, and many new collective needs are emerging as a result of technological development, of structural changes in industry and of changes in the structure of the population. The political and administrative tasks we are facing are not less urgent than those we have had during the past few decades, but because of the more severe economic climate we shall have to tackle them in a new way. So far, it has been possible to carry out innovations in the public sector by mobilizing new resources. But now we have to release resources we already have at our disposal to a much greater extent than before. We must enlarge the scope for innovation and development by reviewing previous commitments. Only in this way can we pursue a dynamic policy in the future and reasonably satisfy the demands which are emerging in society. For if we fail, the alternative is total stagnation. We shall just be plodding along with already established activities as far as financially possible, and the 1980s will become the decade when we only implement the political decisions left over from the 1960s and the 1970s. And as everyone knows, it is by no means a light kitbag we have packed for ourselves and our children to shoulder. For one thing, the pensions we have so generously promised ourselves will be an extremely heavy burden for coming generations.

Demands for 'reviewing old decisions' and 'new priorities' have already begun to appear in political discourse. They appear fairly often in committees' terms of reference and in instructions. But so far these demands are more a matter of principle than a genuine readiness to review the basis on which practical decisions are made. When from time to time policy-makers are forced to economize and make reductions, they usually follow the line of least resistance and cut down on the expenditures nearest at hand — these are often new investments or new recruitment or refresher courses for conscripts, or something like that. Accessibility is used as the primary criterion of choice. This is obviously an exceedingly primitive savings technique which sometimes hits really essential undertakings, but on the other hand consistently protects already established activities and older commitments which may sometimes be quite dispensable but which were impossible to survey and appraise when the original decision was taken. If the worse comes to the worst, this method can lead to absolutely idiotic economies for which the state and society has to pay dearly — while little justified functions continue to flourish and receive their annual increment.

Why, then, is it so difficult to reconsider old commitments and established activities? Well, if one wants to identify all the forces conspiring to maintain the status quo then the list will be a long one (Starbuck 1965). It is no exaggeration to say that the structure of our entire political system is such that, generally speaking, innovations only emerge through expansion and are very seldom the result of new priorities. There are, quite simply, no strong forces which call into question established fund transfers or public activities. On the other hand, there are many strong forces which constantly clamour for new expenditure. A few years ago, I had reason to study the budget estimates of Swedish authorities during various phases of the twentieth century, and I was struck by the fact that in the main the same old arguments were repeated from one decade to the next (Tarschys and Eduards 1975). It would not be difficult to compile material for a similar study of the requirements channelled via the organizations and the political parties. Policy-makers are bombarded from all sides by new proposals of what should be done. But suggestions for possible economies are fewer and farther between.

If we take a look at the rewards and sanctions system functioning in our political and administrative institutions, it is easy to understand why the system works as it does. There are many reasons why a local politician or a member of parliament appeals for new benefits for neglected groups. There are also many organizations which try to influence politicians by informing them of the shortcomings in public activities. But usually there is little incentive to suggest reductions of government and local authority spending. Thrift of this kind usually triggers off outbursts of indignation from political rivals and angry protests or, at least, surly looks from those who may be affected.

In government administration, too, there is nearly always an inherent desire for expansive changes and a definite resistance to all thought of economizing. Business economists and sociologists can give a long list of reasons why the overwhelming majority of public organizations want to grow. These factors range over a broad field, from the most idealistic of convictions that public efforts must be stepped up in order to remedy serious shortcomings in society to the more personal ambitions for self-development, improvement and promotion. Most top executives would rather handle a growing organization than one that is stagnating or shrinking — as long as the organization is growing frictions between different departments and employees can be resolved by satisfying the requirements of both parties, and it is also easier to motivate employees if there is a promise of future rewards. There is also an element of prestige bound up with expansion. Anyone who is given more and more people to work under him is regarded as successful, whereas anyone whose staff is reduced cuts a poor figure. It would be easy to enumerate many more factors which help to promote an expansive line in politics and administration, but the ones I have given are sufficient. The trend is clear: there is very little incentive for administrators and our elected representatives to take a critical look at what they are doing or are involved in, but there are good reasons why they should strive for a more widespread public involvement.

This, of course, is a problem that the ministries of finance, ministries of the budget, local authority treasurers, finance departments, or whatever they may be called, have been grappling with for a long time. Many of the characteristics of public administration are due to the constant endeavour of the central policy-making authorities to curb the expansive inclinations of the agencies responsible for implementing programmes. One classical strategy is to draw up detailed regulations for how funds are to be used and insist on top-level decisions even for insignificant outlays. Another is to develop a sophisticated accounting system which gives a better overview of the breakdown of outlays by type of cost, cost centre, cost by product, etc. A third method is to develop the dialogue on the budget in such a way that the authorities allocating funds have access to better information about the priorities set up by the administrative authorities. The development of administrative techniques over the past few decades contains many experiments along these lines which are well worth discussing at length, but at this point I wish to make only one small but essential observation. And that is: none of the new methods used so far has been able to curb the expansive tendencies of the public sector.

Actually, the question we have to ask ourselves is rather whether they have not stimulated expansion. Various kinds of efficiency improvements have oiled the machinery of public administration and got the wheels turning faster. Performance has certainly improved and production techniques have become more sophisticated, but costs have not been reduced nor has the number of employees decreased. The same is true of the operational audits carried out by the National Audit Bureau, particularly since the end of the 1960s — they have resulted in greater efficiency and innovations, but seldom or never in economies. Max Weber once described bureaucracy as the most rational of all forms of organization, but nonetheless we have been working hard in recent decades to push this administrative rationality to loftier and loftier heights. And we have undoubtedly succeeded on the whole: today we have a government administration with a high degree of internal efficiency. The snag is, though, that all this effectiveness has become so expensive to run that we can no longer only be content with more effective methods for achieving objectives. The objectives themselves must be subjected to a strict priority grading, so that scarce resources are actually used for the purposes which are now considered most pressing. The internal rationality of public administration is not enough — we must also seek to achieve external rationality in the sense that the activities and performance of the public sector are really geared to the preferences of society.

We often hear that this is a political question, and not the business of civil servants. But I am not so sure about that. Now that the public sector is so large, it is practically impossible for politicians to keep themselves up-to-date on all the many issues authorities and agencies deal with. It would be absurd to put the whole responsibility for policy development on these bustling parliamentarians and at the same time sentence all the people who have personal experience of, and insight into, the problems to be passive practitioners. By this time I think most people realize that the doctrinal lines of distinction between politics and administration have become very blurred. Now we have to develop political theory so that we are not held back by obsolete ideas. If we are going to breathe new life into the public sector under straitened economic circumstances, then we shall have to set free all the creativity and all the critical good sense there is, both among public officials and among the general public and their political representatives. And we shall have to create procedures for analysis, debate and decision-making which give scope for the reconsideration of former decisions and which do not only result in demands for more and more resources.

It is obviously an extremely difficult task to reshape the political system along these lines, and I have no illusions about getting very far very soon. But, nevertheless, I should like to suggest three goals we should try to attain if we want to create better prospects for a regrading of priorities. And these are: (1) a greater propensity to change in the corridors of public administration; (2) greater scope for the reconsideration of former decisions in the policy-making process, and (3) better background information on which to base political decisions.[1] I shall deal with these three goals in that order.

1. A *greater propensity to change* in public administration has for many years been one of the major objectives of the authorities concerned with improving operational effectiveness, and it is an objective they have tried to achieve in several different ways: by training personnel and by developing staff capability, by effectiveness audits which have increasingly been aimed at promoting change, by the elaboration of operational and long-term planning techniques, etc. My impression is that a good deal of headway has been made on all these fronts which has stimulated interest in development and innovations at the authorities. The only trouble is, however, that the exploratory processes set in motion in this way very soon develop into expansive courses of action. We search for new tasks and new markets when the old ones start petering out, but we seldom try to find ways of simplifying tasks and economizing. From the cashier's narrow and lofty look-out point, this hectic activity must seem no less than a threat. Or to quote a well-tried senior civil servant at Sweden's former Ministry of Finance: 'As soon as I hear the word "development" I know it's a case of more money'.

Of course, the search for new tasks and up-to-date methods is not to be despised — every energy must be put into this search in our present condition. But the new thing is that we must now put some dynamite behind efforts to identify the old functions which can be reduced or wound up. It is simply a matter of learning that authorities, unlike diamonds, are not for ever. Just like firms, they can come into being, grow, stand still, shrink and disappear. In one sense we must also have less respect for the goals which the government sets up for public activities.

Policy-makers are setting up new goals all the time, but that is not to say that they are worth striving for ad infinitum. It must be legitimate, both within government administration and elsewhere, to question the assignments once given to authorities and to measure the performance of authorities, not only against the proclamations issued by the parliament and the government in the distant past, but also against the common sense of those carrying out the assignments and of other competent observers.

There are, of course, a good many obstacles in the way of this kind of self-examination in the various authorities and agencies. 'You don't saw off the branch you are sitting on yourself' as the Swedish proverb says. But this is perhaps not so obvious a truth as it seems. To be sure, people's interest in pruning varies a great deal. Anyone who has another branch to hop on to need have no fear about helping to work out an impartial and straightforward appraisal. Consequently, job security has a vital bearing on the sluggish propensity to change in government administration. Greater opportunities for circulating between different jobs, different departments, different authorities, perhaps also between government, municipal and private posts, would undoubtedly make people more willing to review existing activities. Personnel policy has a vital role to play here.

But there are also other ways. An important factor is the structure of organization. If we want to retain a large measure of flexibility it is generally advisable to avoid permanent solutions. By entrusting more tasks to temporary organizations, one creates a psychological preparedness for change — those concerned are aware of the fact that their occupation is not for ever. The difference between a head of division and the leader of a project is that the head of division is considered to be a success if his division gets bigger and bigger, whereas the leader of a project is considered a success if the project can be wound up in good time and with reasonably good results. This seems to be an excellent reason for establishing fewer divisions and more projects. On the other hand, there are many problems associated with temporary organizations, and not least of these is the sense of insecurity the personnel have and the consequent difficulty in recruiting qualified manpower. The matrix organization offers an interesting combination of advantages: here we have both the stability desired by the employees and the mobility desirable for the review process. The same effect can be achieved by authorities lending their officials for other assignments without depriving them of their basic appointments. For example, Olof Palme, Sweden's former prime minister, was an executive officer in a Swedish defence agency for quite a long time while he filled various other posts in government administration.

A lot can be done to incorporate procedures for reviewing established activities in public administration. In the United States, research has been commenced recently on these questions, and a quantity of extremely interesting literature has emerged that deals with the concept of 'policy termination', giving not only empirical material on successful and unsuccessful termination processes, but also theoretical generalizations and good advice for hopeful terminators.[2] The Swedish Agency for Administrative Development has published an investigation of a dozen or so authorities which have reduced or wound up some of their activities.[3]

2. The other area where I believe changes are necessary is *the political decision-making process* in general and the budget process in particular. Theoretically, these processes allow substantial scope for the review of policies, but in practice there is very little scope. Theoretically, the annual process of preparing the budget permits very far-reaching changes, but shortage of time, political ties and the material available means that in practice it is quite impossible to do anything more than an 'incremental' examination, a marginal examination. Efforts have been made in various parts of the world to solve this problem by introducing different kinds of programme budgeting, priority-graded financial requirements and, most recently, zero-base budgeting, but with little success. The annual examination of the budget is, and will remain, a purely formal procedure in the case of the overwhelming majority of items making up the Budget Bill.

No radical changes can as a rule be made in the Swedish system nor in those of the other Scandinavian countries without the setting up of a governmental commission of inquiry. But commissions of inquiry are also on the increase, even if their terms of reference attempt to delimit their areas of study. There are comparatively few examples of government commissions which have been able to pinpoint suitable ways of economizing or which have demonstrated how urgent needs can be satisfied without inputs of new resources. If we want government commissions to produce results of this kind they must be told to do so by the government, and even then it is not certain that they would succeed. The ten or so commissions appointed in Sweden since the seventeenth century charged with the specific task of finding ways to economize have not bequeathed any particularly impressive catalogues of feasible economies.

One suggestion which may be worth thinking about is the 'sunset legislation' passed three years ago in the State of Colorado and which has since spread rapidly to about half of the states of America (Adams 1976). This prescribes quite simply that on a certain date, five or six years hence, the 'sun will set', i.e. the mandate will expire, for a large number of primarily regulatory authorities. Unless the state congress then decides that the activities of the authority are to continue, its activities will be terminated. In other words, the idea is that administrative authorities, like some foodstuffs, are to bear the label 'not to be used after...', and recently, some laws have started to be labelled with sunset clauses. As a general measure this may seem a trifle complicated if the real intention is to attain a policy review involving something more than a purely ceremonial reaffirmation, but the philosophy underlying the proposal is attractive anyway. In Sweden we have a rather too carefree habit of making decisions with a limitless validity. Every month the Riksdag passes a great number of proposals for guidelines applicable in one area or another. In many cases, it would undoubtedly be a benefit to decide on a checkpoint from the start: that at such and such a time the initial decision will be reviewed for the purpose of making sure that it has had the desired effect.

It is possible that we should also go a step further by introducing a system whereby all or most public commitments are subjected to a more thorough review at appropriate intervals. One suggestion that has often been put forward recently is a more summary treatment of budget issues every year to allow an in-depth examination of certain specific areas. For example, once during every electoral term the Riksdag should do a thorough stocktaking in every major sector, but in between, should make do with merely recording the year-to-year changes.

The reorganization of work on the budget along these lines presents a good many problems and would be ineffective unless it were accompanied by the compilation of more detailed background material on which decisions can be based. That brings me to my third point.

3. Political decisions are seldom better than the *information* on which they are based. One reason why it is so difficult to reconsider previous decisions is that the policy-makers often lack two kinds of knowledge. In the first place they do not really know what is wrong with the activity they are required to judge, and in the second place, they are not sure what to do about it. In other words, they cannot make a diagnosis and they know little about alternative treatment — particularly non-expansive alternatives.

The flow of information in every large organization is very selective. The information that finds its way up through the hierarchy to top-level management has passed through many filters and been coloured by many personal aspirations. Therefore, it is not to be wondered at that the executives know little about what is going on and often have a different and usually brighter picture of the actual situation than the people at the bottom of the pyramid. Nor is it surprising that the type of knowledge which could build a foundation for decisions on reductions and economies rarely finds its way automatically up through the organization's information system. The management which wants to know more about the actual situation cannot sit with its arms folded waiting to be fed with the facts, they must try to get hold of the information themselves or detail someone to do it for them.

The sultan in *The Arabian Nights* used to disguise himself and mix with his subjects to find out how they were getting on. Frederick the Great, who set Prussian bureaucracy in motion, also set up a secret police force to check up on his civil servants. In our day and age, potentates have generally resorted to less picturesque methods for getting the information they want, but there is no denying the need.

If we are going to devote more time and energy to the reconsideration of old public undertakings, then the analytical work done both in the authorities and elsewhere will have to be improved. Greater efforts will have to be made to get the collaboration of those immediately concerned in working out constructive measures, a search for the kinds of improvement which can be carried out within the limits drawn by economic restrictions. But at the same time, we must initiate R&D work which is not bound to the internal interest of public authorities. This is where, for example, operational audits and sectoral research come into the picture. We have a great deal to learn in this field from the policy analysis and policy research now emerging in many countries. We need more comparative studies of how one and the same problem is being tackled in different countries, in different provincial governments or local authorities. We also need effectiveness studies which show what results the chosen solutions have achieved so far. And we need constructive development work which produces alternatives.

Follow-up, evaluation and applied R&D are necessary requisites if the review of existing decisions is to have any effect. When the government and parliament have to make decisions about the police force or the upper-secondary school or shipping policy, it is essential that they should not only have at their disposal the monologues of the authorities pleading their case in budget estimates, but also have access to background material which gives them a broader survey of results achieved, shortcomings and alternative lines of development. And we need not only written documentation but also workable procedures for dialogue and debate. Anyone who has something worth saying must have a chance of saying it, and different opinions must be able to match themselves against one another before decisions with long-range effects are made. Long-time observers of bureaucratic organizations have few illusions about their ability for radical adaptation and change. 'Regrading priorities' is an attractive catchphrase, but in the real world it means challenging vested interests. As long as the costs of suggested policy changes fall on people other than those who reap the benefits, we can always expect resistance to innovation. The impressive array of tools and methods for more rational management and policy-making that have been developed in recent decades — systems analysis, PPBS, ZBB, etc. — have not meant much in this context. For a number of reasons that at least intuitively are perfectly clear to their members, most organizations seek to eschew reductions in their functions and revenues.

Yet if we accept all our old priorities in an economy of slow or zero growth, the inevitable outcome will be stagnation and standstill. This is why the review and reexamination of established policy programmes and institutional reforms aimed at facilitating resource transfers will become ever more important. Unless they are justified by consumer demand, public undertakings should be no less mortal than private enterprises; but we have little experience in putting an end to government activities. If reformism is to survive in an era of slow growth, that art must be mastered.

NOTES

1. Suggestions as to how these goals might be advanced are presented in the report of the Swedish Government Commission on Public Policy Planning (Förvaltningsutredningen) headed by the author. The title of the report is *Förnyelse genom omprövning* (SOU 1979: 61). An English summary of the report, *Policy Innovation through Policy Reappraisal,* may be obtained from Budgetdepartementet, S-103 10, Stockholm.

2. See the special issue of *Policy Sciences*, Vol. 7, No. 2 (1976) on policy termination. Cf. also de Leon 1977.

3. *Nolltillväxt, avveckling och förändrad inriktning — erfarenheter från elva myndigheter.* Statskontoret, Rapport 1978: 24.

REFERENCES

Adams, Bruce (1976) 'Sunset: A Proposal for Accountable Government', *Administrative Law Review*, vol. 28, No. 3.

Boelsgaard, Kurt (1975) *Den ustyrlige stat*, Copenhagen: Børsen Bog.

Cornford, J. (1975) *The Failure of the State: On the Distribution of Political and Economic Power in Europe*, Totowa: Rowman.

Crozier, M., Huntington, S. P. and Watanuki, J. (1976) *The Crisis of Democracy: Trilateral Task Force on the Governability of Democracies*, New York: New York University Press.

King, Anthony et al. (1976) *Why is Britain Becoming Harder to Govern?* London: BBC.

Leon, Peter de (1977) *A Theory of Termination in the Policy Process*, Santa Monica: Rand P-5907.

O'Connor, J. (1973) *The Fiscal Crisis of the State*, New York: St Martin's.

Poulantzas, N. (1976) *La Crise de l'Etat*, Paris: PUF.

Rose, Richard (1977) *Ungovernability: Is there Fire behind the Smoke?* Glasgow: Studies in Public Policy No. 16.

Rose, R. and Peters, G. (1978) *Can Governments Go Bankrupt?* New York: Basic Books.

Scheuch, E. (1976) *Wird die Bundesrepublik Unregierbar?* Cologne: Arbeitgeberverband der Metallindustrie.

Starbuck, William H. (1965) 'Organizational Growth and Development', in: James G. March (ed.), *Handbook of Organizations*, Chicago: Rand McNally.

Tarschys, Daniel and Maud Eduards, Petita (1975) *Hur svenska mydnigheter argumenterar för högre anslag,* Uddevalla: Liber.

Tarschys, Daniel (1978) *Den offentliga revolutionen,* Falköping: Liber.

2 Planning Agencies: Bridges or Barriers between Research and Policy Processes?

Andries Hoogerwerf
University of Twente

1. THE PROBLEM

In the period after the second world war many efforts were made to prepare public policy in a scientific way. Organizations were set up for planning, policy analysis, forecasting and scientific policy preparation (Roes 1978). The intention was that these bodies should function as a bridge between science and policy by delivering a scientific contribution to public policies. The high expectations with which these bodies were initially welcomed now seem to have given way to some disappointment. In an increasing number of publications the activities and products of planning agencies and similar organizations are criticized, sometimes quite sharply (Bierman et al. 1978). In the beginning these publications were largely normative or theoretical but in the last few years empirical research on policy preparing organizations also seems to have been emerging. Shortly summarized, the tendency of these publications seems to be that planning agencies and similar agencies function not only as a bridge, but also as a barrier between citizens and scientific research on the one hand, and public policy on the other. Part of this problem is a central theme in this chapter. We shall attempt to give a tentative answer to the following questions:

1. To what extent do planning agencies of the central govern-

ment in the Netherlands function as a bridge or a barrier
between the process of scientific research on the one hand,
and the policy process on the other?

2. Which factors concerning planning agencies, policy processes and research processes explain the role of planning
agencies as a bridge or barrier between scientific research
and public policy?

The analysis is intended as an exploration of empirical research on
the role of planning agencies in the policy process in the
Netherlands. In order to answer the above questions, we shall compare an outline of their activities with their task descriptions and
with a number of possible contributions social research could make
to public policy.

2. THE CONCEPTS

The concept of barriers in policy processes has so far been used
mainly for analyzing the distance between citizens and government
and the related phenomenon of non-decisions (Bachrach and
Baratz 1970). In this connection barriers can be defined as all situations in which the conversion from one part of the policy process to
the next fails to come about. The barrier concept applies to all processes that can be distinguished in a policy process (Hoogerwerf
1978a).

Besides, another dimension can be distinguished, namely the barriers between the policy process on the one hand, and the process of
scientific research on the other. This chapter will deal with this last
dimension. The analysis will be limited to barriers that appear in
the stream from social research to public policy.

According to our operational definition a barrier exists as far as
a planning agency does not fulfil its official tasks or does not make
the possible contributions of social research to public policies as
formulated below. A bridge exists as far as a planning agency actually fulfils its official tasks or makes the possible contributions of
social research to public policies as formulated below.

3. THE TASKS OF PLANNING AGENCIES

The differentiation between sector planning, facet planning and comprehensive planning might serve as starting point for a description of the tasks of Dutch planning agencies. Sector planning includes the planning of one branch of governmental activities, generally coinciding with a governmental department. This kind of planning, that is partially related to budget preparation, is made by the departments themselves. It falls beyond the scope of this chapter. Facet planning is directed at coordinating all governmental activities in one aspect (facet), such as the economic, the social-cultural and the physical facets.

In the Netherlands the Central Planning Bureau has been studying the economic facet since 1947. Its main task is to prepare a central economic plan, which as a matter of fact is not a plan but a prognosis. For the scientific preparation of public policy this bureau furnishes information on the economic aspects of measures in different policy fields. Within that framework, a macro-economic survey and a central economic plan are published yearly.

Since 1965 research on the physical facet has been undertaken by the National Physical Planning Agency, which was set up in 1941 under a different name. Its task is to assist the minister of public housing and physical planning in preparing policy regarding physical planning; to do research and to advise on physical planning; to contribute to the general supervision of compliance with the law on physical planning and with the regulations based on this law.

In 1973 the Social and Cultural Planning Office was established to study the social-cultural facet. Among other things, its tasks are:

1. to prepare scientific surveys in order to obtain a coherent description of the condition of social and cultural well-being in the Netherlands and of the expected developments in this area;

2. to contribute to a responsible choice of policy objectives and to point out advantages and disadvantages of the different ways to achieve these objectives;

3. to gather information regarding the implementation of interdepartmental policy in the area of social and cultural well-being in order to facilitate its evaluation.

For comprehensive planning, at least in some measure, the Scientific Council for Government Policy was established in the

Netherlands in 1972. Shortly summarized, the tasks of this advisory organization are:

1. to present scientific information for the benefit of public policy on long-term developments in society, at the same time mentioning problems in time;

2. to develop an integrated long-term framework that the government can use to decide on priorities and to make a coherent policy;

3. to propose activities in the field of forecasting and long-term planning that can be undertaken within as well as outside the central government.

The task of the Committee for Development of Policy Analysis, dating from 1971, is also important for planning. The tasks of this committee can be shortly summarized as follows:

1. advising and reporting to the government on the meaning and usefulness of policy analysis;

2. stimulating the application of policy analysis in the ministries by providing information and documentation and by indicating possible improvements;

3. coordination of the development and expansion of policy analysis;

4. developing appropriate methods for policy analysis and keeping up with scientific developments in the area of modern budgetary systems.

These task descriptions show that each of the above-mentioned agencies for planning and policy analysis have, at least partially, the task of functioning, in one way or another, as a bridge between scientific research and public policy, especially by means of doing research and/or by giving scientific information and advice regarding public policy. According to the budget of 1979 the personnel of the planning offices was as follows: National Physical Planning Agency 315, Central Planning Bureau 158, Scientific Council for Government Policy 52, Committee for Development of Policy Analysis 34, Social and Cultural Planning Office 27.

4. POSSIBLE CONTRIBUTIONS OF RESEARCH TO POLICY

We shall start our analysis by differentiation between five possible contributions of the social sciences to public policy in order to get a better insight into the idea of barriers.

A first possible contribution is the analysis of social problems. A problem exists if there is a discrepancy between a goal or some criterion and the perception of an existing or expected situation. Research can provide more knowledge and insight regarding existing situations, expected situations (both with their causes and effects) and criteria for the evaluation of existing and expected situations.

A second contribution is the analysis of existing policy. Policies are concerned with the achievement of certain ends with certain means and in a certain time sequence. In the first place, researchers can analyse the means-end-structure of policy (empirical policy analysis in the narrowest sense). In the second place, the underlying causal theories (policy theories) can be analysed and then compared with scientific theories or with research results. Finally, researchers can compare a policy (policy content) with one or more other policies. The analysis of policy content can be carried out in terms of finality, level of abstraction, priorities and time sequences (see 4.5).

In the third place, research can concentrate on the analysis of policy processes. This involves the analysis of the preparation, determination, implementation, evaluation and adaptation of policies.

Then, there is the evaluation of policy, policy processes and policy effects. Evaluation research is dominated by the demand for policy effects and particularly by the demand for effectiveness. That is to say, the main question is: to what extent do policy instruments contribute to the achievement of a certain goal? In other words, effectiveness research is an empirical test of the theory behind the policy.

Another possible contribution of the social sciences is the design of policies (policy development). Policy-makers and their advisers, including planning agencies, deal, among other things, with the designing of policy: formulating the policy that is to be pursued. Here four types of policy design can be distinguished.

A policy design can be formulated in terms of a final sequence, i.e. a scheme of one or more final goal(s), intermediate goals, and instruments. A final goal is a goal that the actor intends to achieve via one or more other goals. An intermediate goal is a goal that an actor intends to realize in order to achieve a further-reaching goal (Kuypers 1973). Designing a policy in a final way is deriving the means and intermediate goals from the final goals (deduction) or vice versa (induction). However, such a final derivation assumes an empirical causal theory. Even if such a theory exists, final derivation is not easy.

A policy design can also be formulated in terms of ordering goals according to the level of abstraction. An example of such an ordering might be the division into main goals, sub-goals and singular goals. A main goal is the ultimate situation or development that is strived for in a certain policy area. In the process of goal analysis, sub-goals intervene as transitions from abstract, main goals to concrete singular goals. They give a further specification of the main goals in terms of functions (e.g. preventive vs. curative), of reference groups (e.g. youth vs. senior citizens), of geographical dispersion, etc. Singular goals are deducted from sub-goals and characterized by the fact that there is a direct relation between this type of goal and the various (combinations of) instruments used (*Beleidsanalyse* 1976). The development of such a design can also be performed deductively or inductively. A design in terms of the level of abstraction requires, most of all, insight into the extent to which processes are related. This is not only a matter of logic but also of empirical knowledge. Then there are policy designs in terms of priorities. Priority means here that the achievement of one goal is more important for the actor than the achievement of another one. A priority goal is a goal that the actor considers more important than other goals of a given instrument. A subsidiary goal is a goal that the actor considers less important than the main goal of a given instrument. Policy design in the sense of ordering priorities assumes insight into the actor's (designer's) scale of values, but also empirical insight into the expected costs and benefits of this policy; for the actor will give priority to goals that yield larger returns to him than other goals.

Finally, a policy design can be formulated in terms of a time sequence. In terms of a time sequence a differentiation can be made between primary, secondary and later goals. A primary goal is a goal that the actor wants to achieve earlier than the others (secondary, tertiary, etc.). Secondary goals are goals the actor wants to achieve later than one or more other (primary) goals. A policy design in terms of a time sequence assumes not only insight into the time preferences of the actor, but also empirical insight into the order and pace of the existing and expected changes. In a lot of social science research, these aspects of change receive little or no attention.

Other policy designs are possible, for example in terms of single and iterative goals, endogenous and exogenous goals, internal and external goals and instruments and still more (Zandstra-Andela 1978). The point to be made here holds that all those designs assume empirical knowledge. In principle for each policy designers can start from one or more vague goals or instruments and develop an elaborate policy design with a well-considered and explicit structure. Moreover, they can try to base the end-means relationships in policy as much as possible on causal or other relationships that are found in empirical research. With respect to each of the described possible contributions of research to public policy, possible barriers can arise. To give some idea of this we will first roughly sketch to what extent planning agencies in the Netherlands actually contribute the possible knowledge to the policy process.

5. ACTUAL CONTRIBUTIONS OF PLANNING AGENCIES TO PUBLIC POLICY

5.1 The Analysis of Social Problems

This is included in the tasks of each of the aforementioned institutions, with the exception of the Committee for the Development of Policy Analysis (COBA). As a matter of fact, they study the existing as well as the expected situation. Examples of research on existing situations and developments are the business cycle questionnaires, the information system on physical planning in the Netherlands, the social and cultural reports, the work on the development of social indicators and the research on social inequality. Research is also done on expected situations. Illustrations are the macro-economic surveys and intermediate term prognoses, scenarios for the urbanization report, certain elements of the social and cultural reports and a report on the next 25 years.

The planning agencies do not pay special attention to the criteria for the evaluation of existing and expected situations. The analysis of policy goals by the COBA, however, moves in this direction.

Sharp criticism is often levelled against the analyses of existing situations. Forecasts, as formulated by planning agencies, receive less criticism. This may be partially due to the fact that university researchers see the formulation of such forecasts as a specific task of these planning agencies, and partially to the fact that few university researchers are specialized in forecasting. Researchers specialized in this field tend sometimes to make very critical remarks on the forecasts formulated by the planning agencies (Darsono 1977; 1979).

A point of criticism is also the fact that planning agencies sometimes let normative elements permeate their analysis of existing and expected situations.

5.2 The Systematic Analysis of Existing Policy

This is only to a limited extent undertaken by planning agencies. On the other hand, for the COBA the analysis of existing policy is an important part of its activities. However, in the so-called deductive goal analysis, this is combined with and woven into a normative analysis. The beginning of the analysis is empirical, starting from opinions and statements of cabinet members. From an abstractly formulated and complex main objective this deductive approach then derives a singular and concrete objective via intermediate sub-goals. But the objectives developed in this way are adjusted — and that is a normative procedure — on the basis of comments from the political leaders and top civil servants in the department. In other words, unnoticed, policy analysis changes here into designing policy.

Through its work, the COBA has contributed an important stimulus to a more goal oriented way of thinking in the departments. However, the COBA does not analyse the ends in relation to the means.

The instrument analyses, e.g. the analysis of the subsidy instrument, are separate from the departmental goal analysis. Moreover, the COBA does give a division of objectives in terms of the level of abstraction (main goals and sub-goals), but not in terms of finality (final goals and intermediate goals), priority (priority goals and subsidiary goals), and time sequence (primary and secondary goals). The COBA also pays little attention to the empirical basis of the policy theories (assumed causal relationships) that form the basis for policies. In addition, the objectives are generally described in an abstract way. This all tends to make this kind of policy analysis a defective basis for evaluation research, focused on policy effects. It should be noted that systematic and empirical analysis of existing policy is also scarce and weakly developed in research undertaken outside the COBA, so that there is little research on which the COBA can build.

5.3 The Analysis of Policy Processes

Up till now Dutch planning agencies have tended to be very little occupied with the analysis of policy processes. There are, however, some notable exceptions. The Scientific Council for Government Policy devoted a great deal of its energy to policy organization and policy processes in, among other things, reports on the organization of the public sector and on the external and internal advisory organizations of the central government.

The Social and Cultural Planning Office pays attention to policy processes through, among other things, studies on participation (in the social and cultural reports) and on social planning. In the analyses of goals, instruments and costs and benefits, the COBA, on the other hand, does not go into the questions of policy preparation, determination, implementation and evaluation processes (*Beleidsanalyse* 1972, 11).

The other planning agencies give little attention to policy processes in their publications, except to the extent that they themselves are involved in policy preparation.

5.4 Policy Evaluation

Up till now four types of policy evaluation performed by planning agencies in the Netherlands can be distinguished.

First of all there are cost-benefit analyses. A social (comprehensive) cost-benefit analysis is defined as a type of policy analysis in which, as far as possible, a quantified survey is given of the social advantages and disadvantages of alternative policy measures during a longer period of time.

Secondly, there are reviews of policies and policy proposals on the basis of not always equally explicit objectives and other criteria.

The central economic plan is an example which, among other things, presents information about the expected economic effects of measures proposed by the government.

Thirdly, there are descriptions and analyses of the extent of goal-achievement. In the central economic plan, for example, systematic information can be found on whether or not the goals of economic policy are achieved. The social and cultural reports contain information about social developments which are important for the knowledge of goal-achievement by social and cultural policies.

Planning agencies are practically uninvolved in empirical research on policy effectiveness, in the sense of ex post research of the extent to which certain instruments contribute to the achievement of certain goals. Such research is performed almost entirely outside the planning agencies and the governmental apparatus.

Policy experiments form a different category. These are policy activities that are carried out in an experimental way. They have a temporary nature and are generally limited in scale. Their purpose is, at minimum, to investigate the effects of a policy (or of a part of it). Recently 73 policy experiments of the Dutch central government were identified. In hardly any of them were planning agencies involved (Hoogerwerf 1978b, 3-20). This is remarkable precisely because policy experiments — in which variables can be manipulated — are of great importance for scientific policy preparation and for the development of future policy.

5.5 Policy Design

The design or development of policies (Kuypers 1978) constitutes an important part of the activities of planning agencies. This results from the advisory task that these organizations have regarding public policy. It is amazing, however, how little Dutch planning bodies publish about methods and norms for developing policies.

Research on the policy thinking of planning agencies has, in some instances, resulted in sharp criticism. In a policy analysis of what had been reported on urban renewal in eleven annual reports of the National Physical Planning Agency the analysts concluded that there was no traceable coherent policy vision on urban renewal, either at one point, or through time (Bierman et al. 1978;

Faludi et al. 1979). It should be emphasized, however, that this analysis was based only on annual reports. There are many other and even more promising sources available for obtaining an insight into the policy vision of this planning agency.

6. THE USE OF RESEARCH BY PLANNING AGENCIES

Planning agencies not only undertake research themselves, they also grant research contracts to external institutions. Examining the nature of planning agencies, one would expect them to have a clear policy as to research. However, this is not always the case. On the basis of the analysis of a series of annual reports mentioned above, the researchers drew the conclusion that no clear criteria for the choice of research objects were traceable. Previous policies are hardly ever evaluated. There are quite a few connections between the research objects, resulting from a lack of programming. People within the agency have proportionally more problems in finishing their research than researchers outside the agency. To a certain extent the research has no visible policy implications. The large increase in the total number of personnel during the investigated period, without a proportionate expansion of the research staff, creates the impression that policy preparation is less and less supported by research activities (Bierman et al. 1978, 34, 35).

In order to get an impression of how scientific studies interweave with the activities of the National Physical Planning Agency, an analysis of footnotes in eleven annual reports was made. It appears that more than half (52 percent) of the footnotes refer to policy publications from national political sources. Only a quarter refer to scientific research in a broad sense (scientific research in the Netherlands 14 percent, foreign research 5 percent, studies by civil servants 4 percent and by the agency 2 percent). The most important trend is the relative increase of subsidiary sources of national political origin as against the relative decrease of the various categories.

The researchers conclude that for an agency that pretends to have as its task the scientific preparation of policy, a stronger orientation on scientific publications would not be unbecoming. The National Physical Planning Agency seems to find itself in a relatively closed circuit, in which political signals are predominant

(Bierman et al. 1978, 35, 69-71). Again we stress our earlier point that these conclusions are based on only one possible source for an analysis of footnotes. But a similar analysis applied by us to some recent publications of other planning agencies indicated the same kind of conclusions.

7. EVALUATION OF PLANNING AGENCIES

In the previous sections the actual contributions of planning agencies to public policy (section 5) and their use of research (section 6) have been sketched. We are now able to evaluate these contributions and the use of research. The criteria for this evaluation are the task descriptions of the planning agencies (section 3) and the possible contributions of the social sciences to public policy (section 4).

The task descriptions of the planning agencies are quite vague and broadly defined, so that it is difficult to use them as evaluation criteria. Nevertheless, it seems quite clear that planning agencies spend a varying amount of energy on certain tasks that appear in their task descriptions or that can be derived from them. Given its tasks description, the Central Planning Bureau could be expected to pay more attention to policy design than it has so far. Similarly, the National Physical Planning Agency could be expected to pay more attention to policy preparation and research. Looking at its task description the Social and Cultural Planning Office seems to show a rather limited interest in cost-benefit analysis and the valuation of policy implementation. The Scientific Council for Government Policy is relatively little involved with proposals regarding forecasting and long-term planning, but it has done a lot of research on policy organization, at least compared with its task description. The Committee for the Development of Policy Analysis keeps to its tasks in the field of policy analysis but its activities are concentrated on policy analysis (and policy development) in terms of levels of abstraction.

The task descriptions are so broad that they can be considered to include what we called in section 4 the possible policy contributions of the social sciences. If we test the actual contributions of the planning agencies against the possible contributions of the social sciences to policy, we can draw the following tentative conclusions, based on the sketch presented above.

Until now, the policy contributions of planning agencies have mainly been concentrated on the analysis of existing and expected social problems and on policy design. They tend to pay much less attention to the analysis of existing policy, to policy organization as well as the policy process, and to policy evaluation, at least in terms of empirical research on policy effectiveness.

Furthermore, it is noticeable that all the planning agencies play an advisory role, but that they give little explicit attention to problems of policy design, to the question of with what norms policy advice should comply, and to the methodological aspects of policy-advising. The methodological questions around the formulation of social problems also receive little attention (*Beleidsanalyse* 1978).

A reasonable interpretation of these facts seems to be that planning agencies, though intended to be a bridge, function partly as a barrier between research and policy processes.

8. FACTORS INFLUENCING THE BARRIERS BETWEEN RESEARCH AND POLICY

In the literature various explanations are given for the distance and barriers between research and policy. The recent literature survey by Patton on possible factors explaining the (non) use of evaluation research is illustrative. These factors include the different values, languages, reward systems and reference groups of researchers and policy-makers; the different relevance of research results for the various levels of a policy programme; the degree of dispersion of research results; the communication patterns in organizations; the positive or negative nature of research results; the reputation and legitimacy of the researcher; the methodological quality of the research. Based on his own research on factors influencing the use of evaluation research by policy-makers, Patton concludes that none of these factors are important all the time. According to him, only two factors are consistently important for the explanation of the use of evaluation research: first of all, political considerations and secondly, the 'personal factor', that is to say the presence of one or more persons who personally feel that the research and its results are important (Patton 1978, 63, 64).

Inspired partially by these findings, we shall set up our own analysis of these factors in terms of a number of assumptions that can be tested in more detailed empirical research. Explanations of the barriers between the research and policy processes are looked for in three areas: in planning agencies, in the policy process and in the research process.

8.1 Planning Agencies

In planning agencies various factors are present that can lead to barriers between research and policy. First of all, the task of the planning agencies is inexactly defined. Partly because of vague task definitions planning agencies have a large policy discretion and are subject to little control and correction. Indeed, these definitions indicate that planning agencies should stimulate a certain transfer of research to policy, but insufficient differentiation is made between, for example, research on the existing social situation, the expected situation, criteria for evaluating both of these, existing policies, the policy process, policy effects and policy designs. In some cases task definitions are one-sided: e.g. the Committee for the Development of Policy Analysis has the task 'to keep up with scientific developments in the area of modern budgetary systems' (*Beleidsanalyse* 1972, 38, 39). As if only this field were relevant to policy analysis and not, for example, political science or the administrative sciences!

A second important factor is the fact that the sub-culture of the planning agencies seems to be determined more by the culture of the political system than the culture of the scientific system. The agenda of the planning agencies is determined more by developments in the policy process than by developments in the scientific process. Scientific researchers have little influence on planning agencies. Some of these agencies have some kind of advisory board. However, these committees deal more with attuning the planning agencies to policy than to developments in the sciences. The composition of the boards already points in this direction.

Again in the policy process, some factors can be discerned which may lead to barriers between research and policy. Many policy-makers have little susceptibility to scientific information and planning. Politicians and government employees receive most of their information from sources other than scientific publications. The dominant political culture in the Netherlands is different from the scientific culture. Important criteria for policy-makers are power, support, attainability, publicity and sometimes effectiveness and efficiency. For the researcher, on the other hand, criteria like objectivity, systematics, validity and reliability are decisive. Moreover, the dominant political culture is different from that of planning. Politicians and policy-makers generally are inclined to think in terms of incremental policy-making, short-term and sector policies. Comparatively, planners think more in terms of synoptical policy-making, long-term and facet or comprehensive planning.

There is still another important factor. The degree of dogmatism, that is to say the extent to which one is susceptible to information, varies between policy-makers. There are policy-makers who are afraid of an empirical test of their policies and, more generally, of their subjective opinions. Such a test is quite often considered to be a threat to established opinions, power positions and career perspectives. This is connected to the fact that the present Dutch policy-makers have generally received an education (often in law or economics) in which little or no attention was given to scientific policy preparation based on the use of empirical research.

Policy-makers generally do not think systematically enough about their own policies. Often they do not succeed in articulating their research needs. Their goals and means are often not very explicit, specific, operational, or coherently formulated (Baars et al. 1974). Partly because of this, their policies are difficult to analyse, to develop and to evaluate. At the same time, part of the policy determination is left to the planning agencies. There are reasons to believe that what has been said about the City Development Section of the Public Works Department of the city of Amsterdam also applies to some degree to planning agencies on the national level: it has become an independent organization that chooses its own direction, almost independently of those who (are supposed to) direct it, namely the city council and the mayor and his alderman (Meijer 1978).

In the research process there are also factors that can lead to barriers between research and policy. Much of the research in the social sciences is little oriented to policy. Research that deals with policy and the future is very scarce. The planning agencies possess almost a monopoly in their field.

The organizational place of the research is also of importance. Van de Vall and Ghosh have, among other things, concluded that in-house research is superior to external or commissioned research as an 'agent' of organizational change and policy innovation as measured by the actual influence on decision-making (Van de Vall and Ghosh, 1974). However, the question can be raised whether the place of the researcher within the organization is not detrimental to the quality of the research. Moreover, such a stationing does not seem to be a necessary condition for a policy orientation.

The resources available for social science research are very limited, at least compared with those of the natural and technical sciences. In the so-called first stream of money, i.e. the normal university budgets, the social sciences work with a substantially less favourable staff-student ratio than the natural sciences. The situation of the second stream of money, consisting of subsidies, is as follows: the Dutch Organization for the Advancement of Pure Research (ZWO) gives yearly to astronomy alone more money than to all the social sciences together (in 1978 respectively 6.6 and 4.3 percent). In the third stream of money (research contracts) it appears that those Dutch government departments that mainly grant contracts to the natural sciences spend substantially higher absolute amounts and percentages of their budgets on research than do departments that work mainly with the social sciences. For example; Agriculture and Fisheries 13.6 percent, Economic Affairs 11.9 percent, the Home Office 0.1 percent and Social Affairs 0.1 percent (Hoogerwerf 1979).

9. CONCLUDING REMARKS

Regarding the relationship between science and politics, Habermas has made the well-known distinction between the technocratic, decisionistic and pragmatic models (Habermas 1963). According to the *technocratic* model — somewhat freely translated — the politician is dependent on technical and scientific specialists. Political decisions are the result of technological laws. Political goals are determined by technical instruments. In the *decisionistic* model, on the other hand, the power lies mainly in the hands of the politician. The specialist provides the technical knowledge and the politician makes the decision. Science can only point out alternative means for the politician's goals. According to the *pragmatic* model that Habermas prefers as a code of conduct, there is a critical interaction between scientists and politicians. Science not only provides means for the given goals, but also brings up the goals for critical discussion. For his part, the politician does not uncritically accept the scientific contributions either.

Given a choice between these three models, many planners in the Netherlands today would probably prefer the pragmatic model. This matches the preference for so-called communicative planning that sees as a central problem the creation of communication channels which give citizens access to political decision-making. In other words, the legitimacy of the planning is at least as important as the effectiveness and the efficiency of government action.

The author of this chapter agrees with the need for a critical interaction between science and politics. With all respect for the work done by the planning agencies, their contributions to this critical interaction are probably still open to improvement.

On the basis of our analysis, the following tentative conclusions about the role of planning agencies in the Netherlands can be formulated. Planning agencies deal to different degrees with the analysis of existing and expected social problems, the analysis of existing policies, the analysis of policy processes, policy evaluation and policy design. In view of this, planning agencies make use of scientific research and knowledge to different degrees. Planning agencies, though intended to function as a bridge, function partly as a barrier between research and policy processes.

Some hypotheses for further empirical research can be formulated as follows: Planning agencies will function more as a barrier and less as a bridge between research and policy processes as

1. the tasks of the planning agency are less precisely defined;
2. the sub-culture of the planning agency is more one-sidedly defined by that of the political system;
3. policy-makers are less susceptible to scientific information;
4. policy-makers think less systematically about their policies;
5. the research process is less oriented towards the policy process;
6. fewer financial resources and less manpower are available for social science research.

REFERENCES

Baars, J. et al. (1974), *Ruimtelijk beleid in Nederland*, Ijmuiden.

Bachrach, P. and Baratz, M. S. (1970) *Power and Poverty: Theory and Practice*, New York.

Beleidsanalyse, 1972-1.

—— 1976-2, Handleiding voor de departementale doelstellingenanalyse.

—— 1978-1, Het formuleren van der probleemstelling.

Bierman, M., Hol, P. J. H. M. and Verdenius, J. R. (1978) *Van gissen naar beslissen: Verkenning van nationale beleidsvoorbereiding inzake ruimtegebruik en verstedelijking*, Amsterdam: SISWO.

Darsono, A. (1977) *Futurologie en prospectief bestuur*, Voorschoten.

—— (1979) 'Beleidsprognostisch onderzoek: Naar aanleiding van een WRR-rapport', *Beleid en Maatschappij*, VI (1), January 13-22.

Faludi, A. et al. (1979) 'Is "Van gissen naar beslissen" toch meer gissen?, Een kort commentaar ', *Stedebouw en volkshuisvesting*, February, 91-94.

Habermas, J. (1963) *Theorie und Praxis*, Neuwied.

Hoogerwerf, A. (ed.) (1978a) *Overheidsbeleid*, Alphen aan den Rijn.

—— (1978b) 'The "Experimenting" State', *Planning and Development in the Netherlands*, X (1), 3-20.

—— (1979) 'Wat kunnen de maatschappijwetenschappen doen voor het openbaar bestuur?', *Tijdschrift voor openbaar bestuur*, 5 (5), March, 83-87.

Kuypers, G. (1973) *Grondbegrippen van politiek*, Utrecht/Amsterdam.

—— (1978) De ontwikkeling van het overheidsbeleid', in: A. Hoogerwerf (ed.), *Overheidsbeleid*, Alphen aan den Rijn, 108-21.

Meijer, Q. (1978) *Woningdifferentiatie en stadsvernieuwing in Amsterdam*, Amsterdam.

Patton, M. Q. (1978) *Utilization Focused Evaluation*, Beverly Hills/London, 179-98.

Roes, Th. H. (1978) 'De voorbereiding van overheidsbeleid: Planning', in: A. Hoogerwerf (ed.), *Overheidsbeleid*, Alphen aan den Rijn, 61-86.

Vall, van de M., and Ghosh, P. K. (1974) 'Sociaal onderzoek en beleid: De interveniërende variabele "onderzoekstructuur"', *Sociologische Gids* (5), 289-301.

Zandstra-Andela, B. G. (1978) 'Rationalisatie van de beleidsbeslissing bij de overheid', in: A. Hoogerwerf (ed.), *Overheidsbeleid*, Alphen aan den Rijn, 248-68.

3 Where Research Policy Erred

Sverker Gustavsson
University of Uppsala

Research as an intellectual matter is one thing. Research as a social matter is another. If we distinguish between the internal and external aspects of research, it becomes easier to see what the policy implications are. The failure to make this simple distinction explains why research policy has become such a difficult task. That is the contention of this chapter.

For a long time, theoretical education was based on what Aristotle and Thomas Aquinas had said. Actions people undertook in their everyday lives were based on various rules of thumb. As late as the eighteenth century, criticism of these traditional authorities and rules of thumb was something that amateurs did, cloaked in the protection of academies and patrons. Only during the latter part of the nineteenth century was such criticism institutionalized. Governments and firms established laboratories and institutes. Soon, parties and organizations also began to make use of research. The purpose of all this was to get better data for making and implementing decisions. The right to criticize began to be seen as a duty. This took place to the extent that principles of logical thought began to be included in school curricula for children. Our entire modern worklife is today based on that idea. To an increasing extent, we live in a society based on research and education.

During the interwar period, the political consequence of the conclusion that criticism of authorities and rules of thumb was socially useful was drawn. The idea of a conscious *research policy* was born. People began to ask what principles should guide the search for knowledge and understanding. What is the proper domain for research? What should its direction be? And how should it be organized in relation to the democratic political system?

TWO PRINCIPLES

For those who first began to argue for a conscious research policy there were chiefly two different desires that had to be balanced. One was that research should be free and independent, that it should be done for its own sake (Polanyi 1941). The other was that research should be directed, practical, and useful (Bernal 1939).

Neither principle was permitted to dominate the organizational structure for research policy in the democratic countries. A compromise was achieved. The content of the compromise is illustrated by the situation in Sweden, where approximately 35,000 people are involved in the five billion Swedish crowns spent in structures designed to produce critical studies of our preconceived notions, our policies, our production methods and our work organization in various areas.

Of these 35,000 people, about 5,000 (with access to about one billion crowns in funds) are doing *academic* research. They work at colleges and universities, and they get their money through the budget of the Ministry of Education — in the form of positions, buildings, and grants obtained by application to the various research councils. The other 30,000 (with access to four billion crowns) are doing *sectorial* research. They get their money from the budgets of ministries of agriculture, defence, energy, housing, etc., as well as from private industry. Those who do not work for firms work either at special branch or sectorial institutes, or in academia.

Thus, both academic and sectorially initiated and financed research occurs in academia. Companies, national agencies, government commissions and local authorities receive contracts for research purposes. And scholars apply for — and, to an increasing measure, receive — grants from the sectorially organized research councils for housing, energy, agriculture, social research and technical development.

On the other hand, there is one research-related activity which occurs only in academia, i.e. training of future scholars. Owing to this fact, the base for both academic and sectorially organized research is the same. For both groups of researchers, contacts with the international, more theoretically oriented debate about research theory and methodology come through the universities.

THE NEED FOR COORDINATION AND OVERVIEW

Since the end of the 1950s there has been a steady stream of complaints about the ever-increasing difficulty in getting an overview of how the two basic principles of research policy are being applied in practice.

The coordinating task forces whose only function is to put various parts of society and of the research community in contact with each other are innumerable. And many researchers are constantly thinking about their position and their responsibility in society, both on a personal level and in their professional associations. Nevertheless, it is clear that something is wrong. There are hundreds of thousands of well-educated people in and around research in our democratic societies who have not succeeded in finding a role for themselves in modern society. Everywhere we meet people who have all the tools, all the time and all the personal security they could want — but who are still not happy. 'There's something wrong with the system', they say. 'What I want to do, I'm not allowed to. And when I do something I'm allowed to do, nobody pays any attention to it. It seems as if society sees research and higher education as a form of detention camp, where they keep us so we don't go around disturbing the production process'. At the same time government agencies, as well as private firms and organizations, cry out for new ideas and initiatives.

Evidently, something must be done. But what? How shall we together be able to expand our ability to influence our future — democratically, and with the help of research? And according to what principles should the contacts of scholars and of the research community with the rest of the social world be developed and deepened?

WHAT IS THE ERROR?

Let me start with a few words about what, in my opinion, will *not* get us anywhere: seeing restlessness and anti-intellectualism as attitudes which simply come and go. During certain times, it is noted, rational discourse is treated with contempt. In other periods, people are more oriented towards scholarship and technology. During the last ten years, anti-technology and 'back to nature' sentiments have gone like an epidemic over the Western world. All this is true, of course — but only as a description of the symptoms, not as an explanation of anything. And this view does not help us to determine what we should do about the problem.

If we want to get somewhere, we have to go to the roots. And the roots are the research policy doctrine we have followed. We must bear in mind the problems research policy seeks to solve. Perhaps the mistake was to make the distinction between academic research and sectorial research in the first place — that distinction which was made in the international discussion of these issues during the interwar years and which has continued in practical policy ever since.

This is the thought that suggests itself after reading several recent Swedish reports which describe the growth of sectorial research organizations in Sweden since the 1930s (see for example Stevrin 1978). All these studies emphasize the need for coordination. But they all take the interwar distinction for granted. None questions the basis of the established research policy.

That is precisely what we should be doing, in my opinion, i.e. questioning the basis of our research policy! Only in that way will we be able to master the tasks which lie ahead of us. And only in that way will we be able to create the enthusiasm for our own tasks which is now so often lacking among scholars and researchers.

THE DISTINCTION BETWEEN THE INTERNAL AND EXTERNAL ORGANIZATION OF RESEARCH

As I see it, the error stems from the failure of the present research policy to make a very important distinction, i.e. between the *internal* and the *external* organization of research. Included in the internal organization of research is the question of which intellectual rules should apply for research activities. What kinds of problems should research pose? What should standpoints look like? And how should researchers argue for and against different types of standpoints?

The external organization of research includes the question of which administrative rules should apply for research activities. Who should take the initiative? How should the research be financed? And who has the responsibility for determining to what extent and in what manner proposed changes in research policy, production, or professional rules should come about?

In practice, a research policy must of course take a position on both of these questions in a unified context. But standpoints as well as arguments in both questions become easier to understand if we treat them separately.

The Internal Perspective

From an internal point of view, the choice concerns two kinds of intellectual efforts: those oriented towards description and explanation, on the one hand, and those oriented towards practical decision-making, on the other.

To describe and explain is to answer questions about how things are, and why they might be that way. Political and ethical values of course play a large role for the choice of problems. But it is not these values which are under debate. It is those assumptions about the real world which our values point to.

Research oriented toward practical decision-making, on the other hand, tries to answer questions about how things should be, and what might or should be done to make them that way. What is central is the presence of actors who must choose among various alternative courses of action. It follows from this that intellectual efforts come to be directed in somewhat different directions. An interest in the choice of goals and means takes precedence over an interest in pure science. To the extent that the practitioner — the midwife, the doctor, the union official, the manager, the local politician, the auto mechanic, the dental technician — is interested in how things are or why they might be that way, he or she does so within the framework of an interest in what should be done, what can be done and what has been done.

The External Perspective

The external perspective on the organization of research, however, is of greater interest here. Discussions about research have over the years come to take place in an atmosphere of resignation. Social criticism has gone off in other directions. In my view, the road we started travelling at the beginning of the 1960s was correct. The mistake was that the new ideas in programme budgeting and other forms of evaluating public policy were greeted with too much enthusiasm. Those who were interested did not distinguish between difficulties in principle and difficulties in practice. And — as I would especially like to emphasize in this connection — no distinction was made between those difficulties relating to the internal organization of research, and those relating to how it is and should be organized externally.

What gives researchers and investigators, paid by taxpayers' money, the right to put into question, during working hours, the correctness of democratically made decisions? Regardless of how research is organized internally, it is a normative problem of the first order to make publicly supported social criticism compatible with the principles of political democracy. In trying to answer this question, we have to distinguish clearly between two different arguments for autonomy within the framework of the larger, all-inclusive democratic system.

The General Self-Management Argument

The first argument has as much (or as little) to do with any social activity as with sectorial research or within-government policy analysis and evaluation. As a general point, autonomy is a way to increase participation by those most directly affected by something. It vastly increases the opportunities citizens have to participate in society's governance. But the 'popular will' in more narrow associations can easily come into conflict with the popular will in the larger association. On the basis of a judgement about this conflict, societies have balanced application of the principle of autonomy on the one hand, and the principle of representative democracy on the other. This is what both the debate over the guild system in an earlier epoch, and the more recent deliberations about workplace democracy (in both factories and government agencies) have been about.

The Paradox Argument

Of greater interest in this regard is the second argument. It takes special aim at the fact that those concerned are involved with criticism of our preconceived notions, our policies, our production methods and our practices in every imaginable area of life. The argument has the character of a paradox.

The paradox takes the following form: the aim of criticism is clarification and demystification — *Entzauberung* as Max Weber once put it in German. Its intention is to promote responsible action. Political and other social action, on the other hand, claims to *be* responsible action. Critical activities therefore, cannot themselves be subject to the demand for responsible action, at the same time as they are themselves bound by a demand to demystify. For it is by no means clear that it is responsible to offer new interpretations and perspectives. In order to promote responsible action, critical activities must be irresponsible as far as their external consequences are concerned. Therein lies the statement that seems to say something opposite to common sense, but which nevertheless is true (for a closer analysis see Gustavsson 1971, 44ff. and 172ff.).

In my view, it is possible, within the framework of democratic political doctrine, to use these two different arguments — the general self-management argument and the paradox argument — in support of the view that people *with public financial support but without political responsibility* can and should devote themselves to criticizing the ends and the means which guide public activities. All other arguments — different variants of the idea that one takes responsibility before God, or before History rather than before the people's elected representatives — presuppose that the social critic possesses some form of higher insight.

FREEDOM AND RESPONSIBILITY IN THE CRITICISM OF SWEDISH HOUSING POLICY

Based on my own knowledge of the Swedish sector for housing, building and physical planning, I will now try to answer the external organizational question as far as that sector is concerned. In order to make the answer as interesting as possible, I will ignore the general trend towards increased workplace democracy which has occurred in recent years. For the sake of argument, I will assume that this trend applies to the same extent for those involved in social criticism as for those involved in other activities.

Our attention is thus concentrated on the question of which institutional arrangement the paradox argument might justify. What recommendation regarding the external organization of evaluation activities can we make consistent with democratic doctrine? What is, in principle, the difference between having an evaluation of housing policy conducted by the National Housing Board (a government agency), a government commission, the National Swedish Audit and Accounting Board, the National Swedish Institute for Building Research, or a university department?

The basic idea behind the paradox argument is that there should be a balance between two different viewpoints. On the one hand, researchers should be free to choose what problems to analyse, to choose what views they wish to defend and to judge the scientific validity of the arguments other researchers have made. On the other hand, politicians are responsible for the practical consequences of having posed the problem in a certain way, of the viewpoint presented, and of the correctness or incorrectness of the arguments. The closer the evaluative work is to political responsibility, therefore, the more important it is to those in political charge to have the problems posed exactly the way they desire.

According to normative democratic theory there are four countervailing groups. It thereby challenges all sorts of technocratic ideas. The politically relevant spectrum is not from physics to theology but from 'truth' to 'power'. Along this continuum there are four groups. At the poles are the politicians and the researchers, and between them are two mediating groups, the administrators and the professionals.

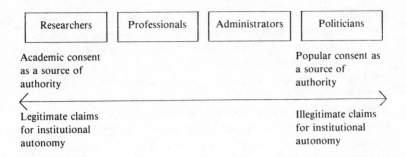

Figure 1
**Relations Between Researchers, Professionals,
Administrators and Politicians According to Normative
Democratic Theory**

The relations between these four groups are governed by 'the twofold principle of freedom and responsibility' (Price 1965). This means two things: (1) the nearer the 'truth' pole, the more legitimate are the claims for institutional autonomy and the researchers are thus 'established dissenters', responsible only to their equals, and (2) the nearer the 'power' pole, the less legitimate are the claims for institutional autonomy and the greater is the responsibility in relation to the voters.

The majority of members of Parliament would probably like to know to what extent governmental money for housing construction has the desired effect. Indeed, many of them would probably even wish for an investigation of the question as to what extent housing policy as a whole has a progressive, regressive, or neutral effect on the distribution of welfare in the housing sector. But few, if any, are prepared to accept the political consequences of formulating directives to a governmental commission to that effect because the expressed intention to find out how things are would be interpreted politically as almost taking a position for a redirection of current policy.

In a situation where the politicians probably do think the way I have suggested, researchers at the National Swedish Institute for Building Research hesitate about whether they have a right to pose questions of the sort outlined above. Many of them believe that

such questions lie outside their legal mandate to engage in 'research
and experimental activities designed to promote rational development of planning, production, and administration in the construction field'. This wording in the statute of the institute implies, according to many, that means and goals may only be questioned up
to a certain point. The passage about 'rational development' is interpreted by these researchers as if it were only the degree of effectiveness of the means chosen, and measurements against goals
already established through the political process, which may be
undertaken. The general effects of the means chosen, the reasons
for the goals chosen, and an evaluation in relationship to goals
other than those officially decided upon is seen as lying outside the
statutory realm of sectorial research, according to this widely accepted interpretation of Swedish research policy doctrine.

   In debates on this point I have defended the opposite view. If one
looks at the various institutions involved in criticism and research, I
believe that sectorial research institutions have an *obligation* to do
what those closer to political responsibility cannot; i.e. critically
question views held by participants in the housing policy process.

PROPOSED PRINCIPLES FOR THE EXTERNAL ORGANIZATION OF RESEARCH

The further the formulation of a given research task occurs from
the seat of political responsibility, the greater the responsibility, in
my opinion, to make the formulation according to the researcher's
own judgment. This is not an invitation to act arbitrarily. The
guiding sense of responsibility comes, not from a relationship to
democratic political institutions, but from the norms growing out
of scholarship as a profession. Thus is the balance between
freedom and responsibility retained.

   If we take the paradox argument as a point of departure, the
solution to the problem posed here could be formulated as follows:

Activity	Rule
Governmental Commission	Problem posed in political context; solution based on rules for scholarship as a profession
Implementation of Public Policy	Problem posed in administrative context; solution based on rules for scholarship as a profession
Official Programme Evaluation	Problem posed in official evaluation context; solution based on rules for scholarship as a profession
Sectorial Research	Problem posed in terms of responsibility to build up a systematic picture of the public policy in question; solution based on rules of scholarship as a profession

Figure 2
Proposed Principles for the External Organization
of Research in Swedish Housing Policy

Conditions in the housing sector are probably no different in any important way from those in other sectors. In fact, I would imagine that conditions in this sector — regardless of how we evaluate them — are representative of a major tendency in twentieth century political development — the tendency in democratic welfare states to attempt, through a large and rather complicated machinery, to combine a high standard of living for all citizens, an equitable distribution of the costs for this standard of living, and a large degree of participation. Thus, how a society organizes to criticize itself is fairly important.

BOTH SIDES IN THE DEBATE HAVE BEEN GUILTY OF THE SAME ERROR

In the light of this distinction between internal and external perspectives, there is one thing which stands out clearly, i.e. how misdirected the debate about the status of research in society has for a long time been. During the entire period of time during which we have failed to make this distinction, both sides in the debate have been guilty of a basically similar error in reasoning.

What representatives of academic research have wanted to defend is the *independent status* of research from an *external* perspective. They have wanted to defend their right, guided by their responsibility as professionals, to criticize and to pose questions. But the conceptual error they made has prevented them from using the right arguments in support of this point of view. Instead of arguing in terms of the paradox they have been enticed into rejecting normatively oriented research problems. As if that is what the question is all about.

And what representatives of sectorial research have wanted to advocate is *normatively oriented* studies from an *internal* perspective. They have wanted to defend their rights to support, criticize and refine policies, methods and practices in various substantive domains. As society has become more dependent on research, this has become all the more important. But the conceptual error they made has prevented them from using the right arguments to support training and theory development in the normative area — training and theory development which would be subjected to the rules of reasoned discourse for practical decision-making. Instead, they have attacked the freedom of scholarship in the external sense. As if that is what the question is all about.

All this is the result of our failure during the interwar years to distinguish between the internal and the external perspectives. This failure has haunted us ever since.

ELIMINATING THE ERROR — AND AFTER

If we distinguish between the internal and external perspectives, it becomes easier to see what we ought to do. That is the basic idea of this chapter. From an internal point of view, research policy ought to devote considerably more attention to training (and to methodological development) in the area of normatively oriented studies. Attention should be given, both in the academic and sectorial research areas, to theory development and training in the art — neglected for fifty years — of investigation and evaluation. If we take areas directly related to practical questions of public policy and its formation, the only ones where we have systems for training scholars are in law, medicine and technology-related fields — that is, the practical subjects which gained a toehold at university before the increasing role of the government in society. Those practical disciplines which appeared after the democratic breakthrough — social policy, housing policy, energy policy, environmental policy — do not enjoy corresponding university-based training programmes or disciplined channels for theoretical debate. Everything is handed over to the sectorial bodies, with all the obvious disadvantages in terms of quality and continuity which this implies.

Decades of sins of omission must be made up for. This does not mean that research oriented towards pure description and explanation should cease. What deserves to be defended is the freedom of scholars to freely choose problems and methodologies, not the right to avoid working with normative problems.

From an external point of view, research policy ought to devote considerably more attention to systematizing and clarifying the formal rules for research in government commissions, for self-criticism in government agencies and private firms, for official programme evaluation, for institute-based and university-based sectorial research. Currently there is great confusion both among politicians and among researchers. A consistent application of the paradox argument would be able to stimulate all these activities.

In this area as well, there are decades of sins of omission to be made up for. The growth of anti-intellectualism all over the Western world during the last ten years has made matters worse, to be sure. But the crisis goes deeper. If rules are established in line with the paradox argument, nobody should be able to say that the sovereignty of the political system is being questioned. For what deserves to be advocated is normatively oriented social criticism, based on the rules which apply to scholarship as a profession — not that problems necessarily need to be posed in exactly the way those with political responsibility desire.

Taken as a whole, even relatively moderate measures in both these key areas should be able to create quite considerable long-term effects in bringing about a better debate — from all points of view — about our preconceived notions, our policies, our production methods and our practices in every imaginable area of life.

REFERENCES

Bernal, J. D. (1939) *The Social Function of Science*, London: Routledge & Kegan Paul.

Gustavsson, S. (1971) *Debatten om forskningen och samhället*, Stockholm: Almqvist & Wiksell.

—— (1977) 'Forskningens inre och yttre organisation', *Vetenskapsmannen i samhället*, Stockholm: Almqvist & Wiksell, 1977, 41-47.

Polanyi, M. (1941) 'The Growth of Thought in Society', *Economica*, Vol. 8, 428-51.

Price, D. K. (1965) *The Scientific Estate*, Cambridge, Mass.: Harvard University Press.

Stevrin, P. (1978) *Den samhällsstyrda forskningen*, Stockholm: Liber.

II Policy Analysis and Futures Studies in Central Executives: Patterns and Problems

4 The British Central Policy Review Staff

William Plowden
Royal Institute of Public Administration,
London

INTRODUCTION, ORIGINS AND ACTIVITIES

Introduction

This article describes the origins, objectives and activities of the
Central Policy Review Staff (CPRS), from its establishment in
1970-71 till the present. It considers the different ways in which the
CPRS has carried out its tasks, and some of the issues which have
been raised in the course of this — issues which are likely to be confronted by virtually any analytical or advisory unit operating with
the same kinds of terms of reference as the CPRS. Finally, it tries
briefly to assess the success of the CPRS, though acknowledging
the great difficulty of doing this.

Origins and aims of the CPRS

The CPRS is a small (fifteen-twenty professional staff) advisory or
analytical unit attached to the Cabinet Office, working for the
Prime Minister and Cabinet. Several separate, though closely
related, streams of thought contributed to its creation. First, while
the Conservative Party was in opposition after 1964 its leader,

Edward Heath, set up an elaborate series of studies aimed at identifying not only the policies but also the procedures to be followed by a future Conservative government. One of the main themes to emerge from this work was the need for some kind of integrated 'central capability' at the heart of the government machine which could draw together the several functions then distributed between the Treasury (particularly control of public expenditure), the Civil Service Department (management of the civil service) and the Cabinet secretariat (running and servicing the Cabinet and its subordinate committees). Second, various senior civil servants wanted to see a new dimension added to the services provided by the Cabinet secretariat — that dimension being a more explicit concern with coordination and planning. A third influence was the thought that both the Prime Minister and non-departmental Ministers (and to a lesser extent all Cabinet Ministers, whether heads of departments or not) needed an expert staff to brief them on the merits of the proposals and policies of individual departments; these ought to be related to some conception of the objectives of the government as a whole, especially in the longer term. (A job of this kind had been done for Mr Churchill as Prime Minister during the war by the so-called 'Statistical Section' under Professor Lindemann. A special 'Economic Section' to do the same job in relation to economic matters was attached to the Cabinet Office between 1943 and 1952.)

A final powerful but less well-defined thought underlay all the others. In British central government Ministers, whether they are heads of departments or not, are politicians virtually isolated among civil servants. (Only recently have Ministers other than the Prime Minister started to have one or two personal advisers chosen by themselves.) Even Prime Ministers work in an environment where there are few counter-checks to civil service advice. This relative organizational and intellectual weakness of the politicians reinforces the inevitable tendency for governments, even if they have been able to define and agree on some reasonably clear objectives, to be deflected — not only by the pressure of events but also by the inertia of the bureaucracy. A 'counter-bureaucratic' presence at the centre, working for the Cabinet, would help Ministers in defining their objectives, making operational sense of these and coping coherently with new developments.

The new unit which was announced in October 1970, to achieve these complex objectives, was fairly modest in scale — much smaller, in particular, than would have been the projected 'central capability' mentioned above. The government 'white paper', *The Reorganisation of Central Government*,[1] spoke mainly in terms of the fourth argument summarised above. There was a need, it said, for

> a framework within which the government's policies as a whole may be more effectively formulated. For lack of such a clear definition of strategic purpose and under the pressures of the day to day problems immediately before them, governments are always at some risk of losing sight of the need to consider the totality of their current policies in relation to their longer term objectives; and they may pay too little attention to the difficult, but critical, task of evaluating as objectively as possible the alternative policy options and priorities open to them.

The government therefore proposed to set up 'a small multi-disciplinary central policy review staff in the Cabinet Office'. It would work for Ministers collectively, under the supervision of the Prime Minister; its task would be to enable them to take better policy decisions by helping them
— to work out the implications of their basic strategy in terms of policies in specific areas;
— to establish the relative priorities to be given to the different sectors of their programme as a whole;
— to identify those areas of policy in which new choices could be exercised;
— to ensure that the underlying implications of alternative courses of action were fully analysed and considered.

Activities

This outline was surprisingly closely reflected in the main activities of the CPRS as they developed over the next few years. It was in fact the only formal guide available to the CPRS and its first director, Lord Rothschild, in deciding how the CPRS should be composed and what it should do; in characteristically British style the CPRS had no legal basis or detailed terms of reference. The whole development of the CPRS has depended on how the director and his staff have interpreted their functions in the light of political and other constraints, and have been able to apply their interpretation in practice. The constraints themselves have varied over time, in nature and intensity, with sharp discontinuities when Rothschild himself retired and when a Conservative government was replaced by a Labour one in February 1974, and vice versa in May 1979.

Policy on staffing the CPRS developed slowly and informally. Lord Rothschild, who largely determined the style and content of CPRS activities not only during his period of office but for some time thereafter, had not had previous experience of government. He had just retired, aged 60, from the post of head of research at Shell. He was a scientist of distinction, a man of strong, even eccentric character and strong views, and of considerable personal wealth — in many senses, a thoroughly independent person.[2] He was given the rank of permanent secretary (i.e. equivalent to the permanent head of a major ministerial department); he started work with a young administrative civil servant as his private secretary and, as the nucleus of his staff and liaison officer with the rest of the Cabinet Office, an able middle-ranking official who had previously been working there, and who had helped to prepare the white paper on the reorganization of central government.

The CPRS started work in February 1971. Rothschild recruited the rest of his staff more or less equally from inside and outside the civil service. The civil service members were nominated by their departments but needed Rothschild's approval. The outsiders were recruited solely by him. (The CPRS was thus unique in British central government in that all its staff were selected by its head.) Several of the first members of the CPRS were open supporters of the Conservative Party; one later became a Conservative member of Parliament, another the chief policy adviser to the Chancellor of the Exchequer in Mrs Thatcher's government. Although one or two later members of the CPRS were equally active members of the Labour Party, the staff as a whole has always had the status of civil servants; the practical effect of this has been that even those temporarily recruited from outside are not necessarily expected to leave when the government changes.

The staff rose over the first year or so to a total of about eighteen professionals; it has never been larger than this. Civil service members of the CPRS have always been drawn from a range of departments. One or two departments — Treasury, Foreign and Commonwealth Office, Department of Defence — have almost always been represented. Outside members have come from the business sector, especially the oil companies, from banking, the universities, consultancy. Of academic backgrounds other than the liberal arts, the most commonly found has been economics. At different times the CPRS has also included a sociologist, a political scientist, a demographer, a biologist and others. A typical snapshot of the staffing of the CPRS at a particular moment is given by its composition on 1 March 1977. The six members who were seconded from government departments came variously from the Department of the Environment, the Inland Revenue, the Foreign and Commonwealth Office, the Department of Employment, the Department of Health and Social Security and the Ministry of Defence. One government economist was in his first government post after leaving university, and was to go on to the Treasury. The previous employers of the eleven non-official members had been Essex University, the London School of Economics (three), British Petroleum, the West Indian Sugar Corporation, Bowater, the London Business School, the World Bank, OECD and the British Treasury. Six of the total were economists.

Rothschild himself was replaced in October 1974 by Sir Kenneth Berrill, an academic economist who had been bursar of a Cambridge college, chairman of the University Grants Committee (an independent body responsible for distributing government funds to the universities) and, briefly, Chief Economic Adviser in the Treasury. He retired in March 1980, and was replaced by Mr Robin Ibbs, a board member of ICI with particular responsibility for planning, and at that time virtually unknown in government circles.

From the start the CPRS was physically located in the Cabinet Office, among the members of the Cabinet secretariat and, like them, close to the Prime Minister's office at 10 Downing Street.

The output of the CPRS has taken several quite distinct forms. The first derived from the CPRS concern with the government's 'strategy'. It consisted of regular attempts to make a reality of this elusive concept by organizing meetings at which the Cabinet were invited to think, and talk, in broad 'strategic' terms; they were presented with wide-ranging papers produced by the CPRS, looking beyond the current detailed problems of the day to deal with major issues in fairly comprehensive and long-range terms. Sometimes the same papers would be discussed at later meetings of more junior Ministers. These strategy meetings were launched with some enthusiasm in the early days of Mr Heath's administration. They became less frequent during the developing crisis of 1973-74.

Although the CPRS was involved in occasional activities of this kind under the subsequent Labour government, these do not seem to have been — even in intention — nearly as systematic. CPRS based strategy meetings do not seem to have been revived by Mrs Thatcher.

However, secondly, the CPRS also took the chance to contribute to ministerial discussions of day-to-day issues, arguing that broad agreement on strategic objectives must not be eroded by incompatible decisions in specific cases. The normal way for a Minister to raise an issue, or make a proposal, in the Cabinet or one of its committees is to circulate a paper in advance. Any other closely interested Minister may also circulate a paper (if there is time: it is an all-too-common trick for officials and ministers to try to 'bounce' their colleagues by presenting 'urgent' recommendations at the last possible moment). The discussion will be based on these written materials. One or two other Ministers present may have a departmental interest in the subject; if so they will be briefed on it by their officials. The chairman will usually have a neutral and mainly procedural brief provided by the Cabinet secretariat. Other Ministers round the table, who are in constitutional theory 'collectively responsible' for the decisions whether or not they take any part in discussing them, may be completely unbriefed.[3]

The CPRS soon developed the practice of contributing on its own account to some ministerial discussions, especially when it felt that proposals were not being properly presented, or that decisions might be taken without being properly thought through. The CPRS contribution usually took the form of a 'collective brief' directed at Ministers in general; it might sometimes consist of a note or memorandum sent to the Prime Minister alone, or even simply a few paragraphs inserted in the Cabinet secretariat's brief. Ideally the CPRS contribution would be more concerned with the merits of proposals than was a secretariat brief, more concerned with the 'total picture' and with the interests of the government as a whole than would be the papers circulated by ministerial heads of departments, and better informed than whatever material might have been provided for the other Ministers present. Of course not every ministerial discussion seemed to call for a CPRS contribution; and even where such a contribution might have been helpful there might well be no time or no relevant CPRS expertise. As a result, over the years collective briefs have been prepared on only a small proportion of subjects discussed by Ministers — about 50 a year.

The third main form of CPRS output was periodic self-contained reports on major topics. About half a dozen such reports have been produced, on average, a year. Only some of these have been published; even the existence of the others has been kept secret. Published reports have dealt, for example, with government policy for scientific research and development, energy conservation, policy towards the motor industry, overseas representation, the heavy power plant industry, the coordination of social policies, relationships between central and local government and the long-term policy implications of population change.[4] Unpublished reports have covered, among other subjects, Concorde, energy policy, policy towards the computer industry and race relations policy.[5] The decision whether or not to publish a report has usually been taken fairly late in the course of a study; it has depended on the political sensitivity of the subject matter, the content of the report itself and of its conclusions in particular, and so on.

The CPRS has also always been liable to be used as a coordinator or troubleshooter in interdepartmental activities, for example in chairing and/or providing the secretariat for joint committees tackling some sensitive issue. Effective coordination can and indeed should rest on detailed analysis and understanding of the policy areas concerned; but in practice this role is possibly one of the least analytical of all those played by the CPRS. The case for it is presumably that no major department could be relied on to produce a disinterested chairman and that the Cabinet secretariat, concerned to be neutral, might not do the job purposefully.

The CPRS also played a part in the now defunct British variant of PPBS, known as Programme Analysis and Review (PAR). Like the CPRS itself, PAR was introduced by the Heath government in 1970. Despite some crippling flaws in conception and execution, its principles were sound enough to be worth recalling. The basic aim of PAR was to review both the scale and the content of particular spending programmes, relating them to expenditure constraints and, where possible, to the government's wider objectives.[6] With the Treasury, the CPRS was involved in choosing the programmes to be reviewed and, intermittently, in the review process itself. It also, when the final report came to Ministers, regularly provided a collective brief commenting on the report and on the programme in question. The ultimate failure of PAR had no connection with the CPRS contribution, which was quite consistent with the CPRS general tasks and, as a whole, was well performed.

One type of activity worth mentioning here, but about which there is little to say, is long-term studies. The CPRS has done one or two pieces of work with a really long-term focus, notably the study of population change mentioned above, and several of its major reports have looked further ahead — ten or fifteen years — than do most internal government documents. But generally the CPRS has operated on very much the same time-scale as the rest of government.

Finally, one specific group of activities, though based in the CPRS, are something of an anomaly. The presence in the CPRS of the post of Chief Scientist is perhaps the best single illustration of the somewhat haphazard way in which the CPRS has taken on functions during its lifetime. This is not the place to tell the story of British governments' attempts to develop a 'coordinated science policy', but the story has intersected with that of the CPRS since 1977. In that year the Cabinet Office unit responsible for advising members on science and technology aspects of government policies was dissolved and its main functions transferred to a newly-created post of Chief Scientist, located in the CPRS.

The first and so far only holder of this post is a former Professor of Biology from Essex University. He has a range of functions; his working relationships with other parts of Whitehall are equally varied. In some respects he acts simply as any other expert CPRS staff member. In addition he is responsible not only for general coordination and 'trouble-shooting' in the science and technology field, but also for some genuinely executive functions in the area of international scientific relations. His coordinating activities are supervised by a standing committee of permanent secretaries, under the Secretary to the Cabinet; he is advised on the industrial applications of science by a specially created Advisory Council for Applied Research and Development. In his international capacity he is virtually independent. Undoubtedly his presence and his activities contribute valuably to CPRS thinking; but taken as a whole they do not fit very comfortably with the rest of the CPRS programme.

Working Methods

The activities which have related and contributed to these outputs have also taken several forms. The CPRS has always had regular contacts with the Prime Minister — its proximity to 10 Downing Street has helped here — and other Ministers. These contacts have been both informal and, more formally, through the attendance of a CPRS representative (usually the head or his deputy) at Cabinet committee meetings. (The only other civil servants normally present at ministerial meetings are the secretariat, who do not take part in discussion.) For reasons too arcane for explanation, this privilege did not extend to meetings of the Cabinet itself. The CPRS would normally be represented whenever it had put in a collective brief, or when one of its own reports was being discussed.

There is naturally also a great deal of formal and informal contact with civil servants, at all levels. CPRS members sit on interdepartmental committees of officials. They meet and consult with officials in departments, especially when a major CPRS report is being prepared or discussed. The working relationship with the Cabinet secretariat is important, since it helps the CPRS to know when and how issues are coming up for discussion among Ministers, and to time and shape its interventions accordingly.

Outside the government, the CPRS naturally needs to consult experts on many topics, since its own resources are so limited. It has indeed tried to make a virtue of necessity, deliberately extending its contacts as far as possible beyond those normally used by civil servants and Ministers. In all the major CPRS studies a great deal of evidence has been taken, usually in private, from people and organizations inside and outside government. In the review of overseas representation, described in detail below, the CPRS team took written and oral evidence from literally scores of people. Occasionally these consultations have been formalized, by the placing of contracts with firms or individuals — for example, McKinseys for the motor industry study mentioned above, academics for more limited pieces of work.

The CPRS has rarely appeared in public; the two most conspicuous occasions have been its two examinations by parliamentary select committees — once giving evidence about its activities in general, once defending its report on overseas representation.[7] Ar-

ticles and stories about it appear fairly regularly in the press —
usually not outstandingly well informed.

SOME ISSUES

Any advisory unit, such as the CPRS, must be extremely sensitive
to the environment in which it operates — the CPRS perhaps particularly so, lacking as it does any formal definition of its role or
any statutory basis.[8] What it does must depend largely on what its
clients are prepared to accept; it can survive only as long as it remains generally acceptable. (If the Prime Minister so wished, it
could be abolished literally overnight.) The CPRS has survived
some fundamental changes in the operating environment of
government as a whole, especially the world-wide shift from the
growth oriented attitudes of the early 1970s; far more attention was
then given to ideas of planning, goal-setting, priorities or coordination, than in the more pessimistic second half of the decade. The
CPRS has also seen major changes in its own immediate environment, with two changes of government and three changes of Prime
Minister. It is not a trivial achievement to have survived all these
changes (unlike its Australian equivalent).

Identifying the Client

But if the CPRS has needed to be sensitive to its clients' needs, it
has needed first to have a clear idea of who these clients are. The
original white paper announced that the CPRS was to work for
Ministers collectively. In practice it has largely done so: collective
briefs and major reports, even if commissioned by an individual
Minister, have been presented to Ministers in general. But the collective nature of this clientele presents problems. It is arguable that
for most British Ministers, most of the time, their role as departmental head takes precedence over that as member of a government
(Dell 1979). They are mostly more concerned with the affairs of
their own Ministry and their own position than with the position
and interests of the government as a whole. As a result they will
often either resent CPRS advice — if it threatens their own objectives — or ignore it — if it is not relevant to these. There will always

be some exceptions: one or two Ministers who are temperamentally less preoccupied with their sectional interests, and those who are professionally more detached because they do not head departments. These few are extremely important to a body like the CPRS as a potentially receptive audience for its advice, and as potential spokesmen for it at Cabinet.

Easily the most important Minister in this category is the Prime Minister. He or she is the one Minister whose job not only enables but requires him to think in 'governmental' terms. More importantly, it is the Prime Minister who sets the tone and directs the general course of a government — at least while things are going well. With these powers of initiative are linked the administrative control of the government; the Prime Minister makes and approves ministerial and senior civil service appointments respectively, and determines the procedures of the Cabinet and its committees.[9] The ways in which issues are handled in government, as elsewhere, often crucially affect the outcomes. In this context the other key figure is the Secretary to the Cabinet, who on these procedural matters is usually the Prime Minister's most frequent adviser.

For the CPRS, since its earliest days, a central question has been how far to exploit its physical proximity to the Prime Minister, and its potentially close relationship; or how far to try to act as the Cabinet's advisory staff, with a collective clientele, even at the cost of sometimes finding itself at odds with the Prime Minister and/or without any acknowledged ministerial supporter. Some supporters of the CPRS principle argue that in practice the CPRS can be really objective only if it openly becomes and operates as the nucleus of a Prime Minister's department. The relevant arguments are both constitutional and political. In the British constitution, both the convention of collective responsibility and the myth of prime ministerial equality work strongly against the setting-up of a Prime Minister's department. Moreover, given that British governments can and do survive the loss of reputation and influence by a particular Prime Minister, or his resignation and replacement, it would for the CPRS be a high-risk strategy to identify itself too closely with the Prime Minister and to neglect his colleagues. From the viewpoint of 'better government' it is probably also important to have a unit nominally independent of the Prime Minister and thus able to challenge prime ministerial policies. For the CPRS, probably the most effective approach is to provide a fair amount of collective advice — which all Cabinet members can see — but also a steady stream of personal communications for the Prime Minister — of which the rest of the Cabinet will be unaware.

Programme of Work

The identity of the CPRS client clearly interacts with another issue: the ways in which its work programme should be determined, and the principles determining its choice of tasks. It was originally envisaged that Ministers, as the clients of the CPRS, would put together and steer its work programme. A standing Ministerial committee was created for this purpose. Individual Ministers were asked to suggest problems which might be suitable for the CPRS. These two approaches did produce some fruitful suggestions. Others have been made by individual Ministers without prompting, or have emerged spontaneously during ministerial discussions. ('This is too difficult to settle now; let us ask the CPRS to have a look at it.'). A few proposals have originated with officials. Sometimes they have wanted to raise issues which, perhaps for political reasons, they cannot discuss in their own departments. Sometimes they have seen the CPRS as a useful ally in an argument with another department.

As a whole, though, much of the CPRS programme over the years has originated with the CPRS itself, even if for presentational or political reasons it has been helpful to find ministerial sponsors for some proposals. Most Ministers, most of the time, have their own personal fish to fry, and tend to think in fairly narrowly departmental and often short-run terms. The ministerial steering committee found that it had little to do, and was abolished after a couple of years.

Welcome though ministerial interest is, ministerial proposals for projects can occasionally cause problems — especially if the proposals are of the unpremeditated kind mentioned above. The project may be unsuitable for the CPRS (for example, calling for too many resources, or for expertise which the CPRS lacks), or the topic may raise virtually insoluble problems. If the CPRS reluctantly decides that a project would cause it difficulties it must be able to offer a convincing and undamaging excuse for declining it. For an organization like the CPRS, the skills essential for survival must include the ability to decline the 'poisoned chalice'.

Whatever the origins of proposals for CPRS activities, the question arises of how to choose among such proposals. This can be looked at from two rather different points of view: first, that of the contribution that the CPRS *ought* to be making to governmental decision-making. This might mean choosing projects which, say, fell in areas to which nobody else in government was giving enough attention, such as energy policy at the time when it had no separate department or Minister of its own; or which called for a 'central' contribution which no single department or Minister could be expected to make, for example the balance of legislative programme (Heath and Barker 1978).

But possible projects also can, and sometimes must, be judged in terms of what they might contribute to the effectiveness, standing and perhaps the survival of the CPRS itself. Here one test might be the degree of interest in the subject shown by the Prime Minister and/or senior Ministers. On a rather different level, the test might be whether the subject would draw on existing CPRS expertise or, if not, whether the expertise generated would be applicable and useful for some time to come. (Energy would again be a good example.) The case for any project, and indeed the need to find ministerial sponsors for it, also depends on its political sensitivity. At one extreme, a rapid small-scale critique of a programme which nobody regards with great favour obviously creates no problems. At the other, a major survey of one of a senior Minister's largest and most cherished initiatives, calling for a great deal of cooperation on the part of his officials, clearly needs to be set up with some care, and support for it canvassed in advance. If another equally senior politician can be persuaded himself to suggest that the CPRS should make this survey, its legitimacy will be all the greater. Sometimes the actual or expected opposition to a project will prevent it altogether. Topics which cross departmental boundaries, and which can thus be said to call for a detached and comprehensive view, have always seemed more appropriate and plausible candidates for CPRS attention than topics for which a single Minister or department are wholly responsible.

In practice it has not been possible to discern any very clear principles behind the work programme of the CPRS. It seems to have been essentially opportunistic and, as a result, eclectic. Its content and balance has varied over the years, influenced largely by the interests of the head of the CPRS and of his staff, by the current preoccupations of the Cabinet and by chance. In the early years of the CPRS a lot of work was done on energy policy, mainly as the result of Lord Rothschild's background and interest in the oil industry. During the Labour government of 1974-79 a lot of work was done on interdepartmental aspects of 'social' policies.

Role of the CPRS

Questions about the proper content of the CPRS work programme are inseparable from a complex of questions about its objectives, role and style of operating. Underlying them all is the basic question, 'What is the proper contribution of the policy analyst in government?' In particular, how far can or should he have a defined and explicit viewpoint of his own? How far, consequently, should he make firm recommendations about policy as opposed to simply analysing and setting out alternative options? Lord Rothschild, the first head of the CPRS, used to quote with approval the description of the CPRS role given by one of its members as 'Sabotaging the otherwise over-smooth working of the government machine.' This might be called the 'seismic' conception of the role: taken to its logical extreme it implies that the CPRS job is simply to cause some sort of disturbance so that the widest possible range of policy options can be given an airing. In this case perhaps the CPRS should be disinterested towards the ultimate outcome.

But Rothschild also always insisted that all the CPRS analyses should end with firm recommendations; they should press some course of action on Ministers. This might be called the 'advocatory' conception. It may be inevitable that policy analysts should develop and advocate their own points of view. Certainly the development of a 'CPRS view' seemed to follow inevitably from the nature of the CPRS programme, in several ways. Firstly, if an analytical unit is making major studies of contentious subjects it is almost bound to reach some firm conclusions, explicit or implicit, during the review. The CPRS from the first did so. If these conclusions are endorsed by CPRS management, and especially if they are then at least not dismissed by Ministers, they are likely to remain as the basis of the CPRS 'house view' for some time, and almost certainly for as long as those who prepared the report remain on the staff.

Secondly, the CPRS is in effect making judgements of a kind about
existing policies and programmes when it decides to cover them in
its work programme. (It would hardly have chosen to review race
relations policy if it had felt that the Home Office — the department
nominally responsible — was giving an adequate lead in this field.)
Thirdly, when a group of talented and ambitious analysts (some
drawn from outside government altogether) contemplates the inevitable follies and short-sightedness of a large bureaucracy, its
members will find it almost inhumanly hard not to make and express some firm judgements.

But however natural it may seem for analytical units like the
CPRS to express strong views on policy, this raises a variant of a
classic dilemma. It is that of the permanent official facing the
elected representative. How far does or should he insist on his own
point of view, and at what point accept that an issue has been settled against him? How does he justify his views? In the case of the
CPRS this issue arose during a protracted disagreement with the
then Energy Secretary, Mr Tony Benn, about the choice of nuclear
reactor for electricity generation. Mr Benn complained, loudly and
publicly, that in advocating its own views on this, and trying to persuade his colleagues and their officials, the CPRS was trespassing
on his territory; it was arrogating to itself functions which should
have been reserved to a department of state and its elected head.[10]

Mr Benn's complaint may perhaps be seen as largely the natural
reaction of a powerful politician irritated at being obstructed. But
it should not be dismissed. Particularly in British central government, the formal role of the civil servant is as the reasoning but
ultimately neutral adviser and agent of elected politicians. The latter are responsible for the policies which the civil servants carry
out. This allows a new Minister, or a new government, to take over
existing officials with the assumption that they will not work
against him. It is accepted that all members of the CPRS, including
those brought in from outside government, are civil servants who
are not expected to change with governments. But if the CPRS
strongly espouses a particular line of policy under one government,
what does it do when the government changes? In practice the
CPRS seems to have side-stepped this problem by lying discreetly
low when governments have changed, but the issue remains basically unresolved. In general, though it is obviously tempting for the
CPRS to label a department's policy as simply 'wrong', it is hard to

see how such labelling is justified unless the CPRS can show that the policy is at odds with the government's overall strategy or other policies.

Some commentators have suggested that one way out of this dilemma is to have the CPRS headed not by a civil servant but by a politician, who as a member of the government would normally share its views — not least because he would also be in closer contact with the Cabinet than a British civil servant can be.[11] But if this meant that CPRS advice was tailored to fit current political sensitivies, the CPRS would be failing to do a large part of its job as originally conceived. (The values, attitudes, beliefs and [sometimes] conclusions of the policy analyst are, and should be, distinctively different from those of his client.) The CPRS has never resolved this problem. Although in principle the 'seismic' and 'advocatory' conceptions of the analyst's role are barely compatible, in practice the CPRS has tended to espouse both at different times — and sometimes simultaneously. As a result it has sometimes found difficulty in defending either.

Involvement in Policy-Making and Implementation

A further question about the proper activities of the CPRS derives at least partly from the previous one. It relates to the stages in the policy-making process in which the CPRS should be involved. In principle CPRS contributions should be oriented towards Ministers, its primary clients. This means, most obviously, that the CPRS should play an active part at the moment when an issue is before Ministers, individually or in Cabinet — hence, for example, the 'collective brief', discussed above. But is this enough? First, if the CPRS intervenes only when officials have finished processing an issue and are ready to put it to Ministers, many of the available options may be closed, time for a decision may be short and a CPRS contribution may be either too late or genuinely disruptive. (A common complaint by civil service line managers against the CPRS is that it is 'irresponsible' in this sense.) There is therefore a good case for the CPRS to get into the act much earlier, when options are still being canvassed and positions have not yet hardened. This means sitting in on interdepartmental working parties and the like, and inserting views on behalf of the CPRS or, notionally, of

Ministers. Sometimes the CPRS has invited itself to such meetings, where it was itself interested in the subject. Sometimes departments have invited it — either, one may surmise, because they wanted to draw on CPRS expertise or because they hoped, by involving the CPRS in the earlier stages of policy-making, to lessen the chance of a possibly disruptive CPRS intervention later on.

This kind of pre-emptive intervention may make sense, but it is very time-consuming; it also raises yet again the question of for whom the CPRS is speaking. What kind of viewpoint should the CPRS representative express on an issue which Ministers have not yet considered at all? An example such as the protection of official information can be used to illustrate the point. If this topic is being discussed on its way to Ministers, should the CPRS do its best to counter the almost inevitably restrictive attitudes of the bureaucracy on the grounds that Ministers may wish to take a liberal position on this question? Should it be neutral? Should it, with regret, reflect the realization that Ministers may be as restrictive as their advisers? These are general questions which have not been answered.

No conclusive answers have been given, either, to the question of how long the CPRS should remain involved with an issue once this has been considered by Ministers. This question can arise when CPRS advice on the issue has been accepted, or when it has not. All too often, even though top decision-makers have agreed on a course of action, the inertia or resistance or both of their subordinates prevents or greatly distorts its implementation. If Ministers have decided to accept CPRS advice on an issue — or indeed if they have made a decision of any kind at all — should the CPRS help to follow up that decision, to ensure that it is implemented? The CPRS has done this from time to time, particularly when following up its own major reports. The most immediate objection to this is, of course, that the CPRS is an advisory and not an executive body, and that it has too few resources to pursue more than a very small number of subjects in this way.

A rather different question arises where the CPRS advice has been rejected. Should the analyst persist in urging his views on his clients, even though they have been rejected? How intensive a campaign should he wage in support of his points of view? Mr Benn's view, in the reactor case mentioned above, was that the CPRS had gone far beyond the proper limits. On the other hand, the

bureaucracy will use all the weapons at its disposal to resist un-
congenial proposals, and it is perhaps unnecessarily idealistic for
the proposer, alone, to rely on the unsupported power of reason.
The intensity and the effectiveness of CPRS campaigning has
varied between issues. In general, though, the CPRS has been rather
more engaged with the fate of its advice, and with subsequent action thereon, than has the Netherlands Scientific Council as
described by Dr Baehr.

The weapons used by the CPRS have not included appeals to support outside the government, tempting though this tactic is. But
there is no doubt that in the conservative and secretive British central government system, the would-be radical analyst on the inside
is at a disadvantage. He is surrounded by people who see their interests as threatened by change. He is constantly being told, in the
most reasonable tones, that his proposals are unoriginal, naive, unnecessary, irresponsible or disruptive. He is prevented by convention and by the law from openly canvassing support for change
where it is most likely to be found — outside the executive
altogether. Least of all is it open to him to look for allies in Parliament, whose links with the government are, Ministers themselves
excepted, almost non-existent. In this respect there is a striking contrast between the CPRS and the Scientific Council. Automatic
publication of the Council's reports allows outside support — and
opposition — to develop around their proposals, and also obliges
the government publicly to explain and to justify its reaction to
them. This difference may perhaps justify the CPRS' more activist
approach to its own proposals. It is worth observing that, despite
the severe temptation for the CPRS to 'leak' its proposals to outside interests and so to generate support for them, there are no
signs that it has ever done so during its nine years of life.

Relationship with the Client

The last major issue I want to discuss brings me back to the question of the relationship between the CPRS and whoever is deemed
to be its client. Whoever the client may be, what should be the
relationship between his views or interests and the activities of the
CPRS? In what precise sense does or should the CPRS work 'for'
the Prime Minister, the Cabinet or the permanent bureaucracy?

Should the consultant always serve the client's interests as perceived *by the client*? Thus, if the client were taken to be the Prime Minister, should any internal intervention by the CPRS necessarily support the Prime Minister's case? Or, if the Cabinet, should no CPRS report be published which was even implicitly critical of current government policy? The Rothschild conception of 'sabotaging the machine' implies that somewhere in the machine there will often be an interest which feels that the CPRS is 'rocking the boat'. This interest will sometimes include at least some members of the bureaucracy, since on most issues there will be some sections with whose views the CPRS will disagree. For the same reasons it will often include some members of the Cabinet. One can imagine issues on which the CPRS would be at odds with the whole Cabinet. In principle, this brings us back again to the notion of 'the CPRS view'. If the analyst is felt to be entitled to a view of his own, he presumably ought to put that view forward whenever it seems relevant. But if he is seen as totally neutral, even his analysis should be couched in terms which do not challenge his clients' policies.

How the CPRS has dealt with these dilemmas over the years seems to have been determined by a mixture of principle and expediency. Both, perhaps, have prevented any rocking of the government boat in public. The single celebrated exception to this in CPRS history was when in 1973 Lord Rothschild gave a public lecture in which he warned that Britain was becoming a relatively poor and uninfluential nation and should act accordingly.[12] This led to a major row with the Prime Minister, Mr Heath, which seems to have been at least partly instigated by senior officials who resented Rothschild's influence and disregard for some of the minor conventions. It was made public that he had been reproved by the head of the civil service and the Secretary to the Cabinet. As Mr Heath said some years later 'I don't think you can have somebody in that position and not just stick by the normal rules of the Civil Service...(Heath and Barker 1978).

In general, continuous private conflict with a majority of the Cabinet, or with the Prime Minister, is almost certainly just as inadvisable as public dissent. The clue to tactics here is to keep a fair balance, over time even if not at any moment, between opponents and allies. (In the British system the Prime Minister, in this respect among others, is probably equivalent to at least half a dozen average colleagues.) An apt commentary on tactics is provided by

Richard Crossman, reflecting in his diary about the defeat, instigated by himself, of a Cabinet colleague on a particular issue:

> Well, I won. But what did I gain by it?...All I've done is to make an enemy...I
> realise something now about Cabinet government: one should always be looking
> for friends and allies, not making enemies. That's why a Cabinet Minister is
> reluctant to weigh in on too many things...(Crossman 1975, 47)

This principle has underlain much of the CPRS' approach to its
work. In this context, the most appropriate metaphor to explain or
guide the actions of a body like the CPRS is that of an individual's
bank balance. Credits and debits can be incurred in many ways:
from a report which is well-argued, or ideologically acceptable, or
the reverse; or from a politically helpful, or unhelpful, action; and
so on. They can be in several different currencies — official as well
as ministerial, and with sub-categories of each kind. The CPRS account was opened with a generous payment in by Mr Heath, whose
creation of and support for the CPRS gave it an initial political
credibility within Whitehall which enabled Lord Rothschild to survive the first problematical months. Lord Rothschild spent, in
'Heaths', almost the whole of the CPRS' accumulated credit
balance as the result of his 1973 speech. Three months later,
Rothschild fell ill and was away for several weeks. The absence of
its head at a moment of government crisis greatly weakened the
CPRS' ability to contribute to events and thus to restore its credit
balance. Soon afterwards, the government had changed. This was
helpful in that it meant a change of ministerial currency; but the
accumulation of 'Wilsons' was a slow and painful business.

One other damaging run on the CPRS bank was caused when
Rothschild allowed himself, his colleagues and the CPRS as a
whole to be 'profiled' in a Sunday colour newspaper.[13] The
somewhat sensational, indiscreet and gossipy tone in which the
resulting article was written raised hackles all over Whitehall,
where civil servants were not accustomed to talking to the press
about their jobs and their relationships with their colleagues and
with politicians. The article made it possible for critics of the CPRS
to point to it as 'unprofessional', almost unethical, and its credibility was damaged accordingly.

One of the most difficult dilemmas for the CPRS, pursuing the
same metaphor for a moment more, has been how much of its

credit balance to hold in ministerial and in official currencies. Rothschild's own personal tendencies, and the circumstances of the CPRS' birth, led at first to close working relationships with Ministers. Many people regarded the CPRS as largely an instrument for carrying out specifically Conservative policies; the feelings and interests of civil servants were not always treated by the CPRS with great respect. After Rothschild was replaced by Berrill in 1974, the balance was felt to have swung the other way. Berrill's own temperament, background and skills, combined with the initial difficulty of establishing a rapport with the new Labour government, led to a much closer working relationship with the permanent civil service. The new Labour Prime Minister, Harold Wilson, had set up a small personal staff of outsiders in 10 Downing Street. This group inevitably met, for Mr Wilson, some of the needs that the CPRS had met for Mr Heath, and so helped to widen the gap between the CPRS and the Prime Minister. The official explanation that the Downing Street unit was to deal with short-term issues, the CPRS with longer-term ones, did not help; as the collective briefing activity had recognised, short-term tactical decisions can conclusively pre-empt long-term strategic ones. The two dimensions cannot logically be separated. It was widely reported at this time that the CPRS had been 'captured' by the civil service and inhibited from doing as radical a job as it had before. If Rothschild had rocked the government boat too much, it was said, Berrill had rocked it too little.

The contrast should not be exaggerated. Throughout its existence the CPRS has had perhaps surprisingly good relationships with the permanent civil service, even when disagreeing with the latter's views. It has had good access to departmental and other information, and close working relationships with officials at all levels. This can be attributed partly to the strong political support with which the CPRS started its life, partly also to the cultural and personal affinities with the civil service derived from its part-official membership. In the closed world of Whitehall, knowledge of the system, its conventions and its language (in the most literal as well as figurative sense) are invaluable aids to understanding and operating effectively within it. Since allies cannot usually be sought outside the system, they must be found within it; it follows that the conciliatory approach is often more effective than the abrasive, the oblique than the frontal.

Two Case-Studies

Before an attempt is made to summarise the development and effectiveness of the CPRS, two of its major reports may be interesting to consider as case-studies.

Review of Overseas Representation

This major study and report was probably the most controversial of all CPRS activities to date. It started when at the end of 1975 the CPRS suggested to the Foreign Secretary (then Mr James Callaghan) that the overseas representation of the UK should be looked at, to see if it had adjusted enough to the great changes in the UK's general circumstances and international role since 1945. Early the following year the Foreign Secretary formally asked the CPRS

> to review the nature and extent of our overseas interests requirements and in the light of that review to make recommendations on the most suitable, effective and economic means of representing and promoting those interests both at home and overseas. . .

The review was to cover the diplomatic service, overseas cultural and information activities (specifically, the British Council and the external services of the BBC) and those parts of the home civil service concerned with overseas interests. The CPRS had for some time been interested in trying to analyse and make more explicit the objectives of Britain's overseas services, and in the contribution and relevance to these objectives of the activities, structure, staffing and style of the diplomatic service. It was also interested in the working relationships between the Foreign and Commonwealth Office and other parts of Whitehall. (In short, the questions were whether the foreign service was trying to do the right job; and whether it was doing it effectively. Many thoughtful observers would have answered both questions negatively.) The cultural and information services were included for the sake of comprehensiveness.

The CPRS formed a small review team from its existing staff. This team was led by the head of the CPRS, Sir Kenneth Berrill; it included two people seconded from the Foreign Office itself and the Ministry of Overseas Development, a former member of the World Bank with considerable experience of developing countries, a man seconded from the Ministry of Defence, an economist and a sociologist. A liaison team was set up by the Foreign Office.

The study took seventeen months. The CPRS team took oral evidence from 50 individuals and organizations, and written evidence from many more people and organizations outside government. It talked to the staff of the FCO and of at least a dozen home departments with overseas links and concerns, and visited embassies and consulates in 27 countries.

When in 1977 the final report was presented to Ministers, and shortly afterwards published, it contained some sharp criticisms of existing arrangements. It concluded, among other things, that neither the UK's overseas policies nor its overseas services had adjusted enough in response to the decline in the UK's world status since 1945; that a lot of work done by the overseas service was ineffective, or of an unnecessarily high standard, or could be better done by others; that foreign service staff were not specialized enough. Its recommendations included closing many overseas posts, merging the home civil and the diplomatic services, pruning the overseas broadcasts of the BBC and cutting the activities of the British Council.[14]

The report aroused predictable opposition among the foreign service, the cultural bureaucracy and the large number of influential people in British public life associated with one group or the other. The Foreign Office had been systematically generating press opposition to the study and its likely outcome while it had been going on. A strident campaign of denigration and ridicule reached its climax in a debate in the House of Lords in which most speakers, some prompted or briefed by the Foreign Office, asserted roundly that the British diplomatic and cultural services had always been and still were the best in the world and criticized the impudence of the CPRS for suggesting otherwise.[15] (Perhaps the single most ridiculous comment on the report was an article by an academic which among other faults in the review team's approach singled out their impertinence in sending such young people to interview such distinguished old public servants.)[16]

The whole episode painfully illustrated the British governing establishment at its reactive worst. Whatever one's judgements of the review's conclusions, the quality of the arguments brought against it showed very clearly the need to develop analytical skills in Whitehall and Westminster. The CPRS also learned some lessons. At least for the time being, its credibility had been severely damaged. One strategic, and several tactical mistakes had contributed to this. There is no doubt that evaluating established institutions and redefining their objectives was an appropriate matter the CPRS. But it was a strategic error, and one which led to an extremely inefficient use of resources, to accept the whole of the very detailed terms of reference set out in the Foreign Secretary's invitation. Minute scrutiny of the foreign service's use of official cars and entertainment allowances was not, as many people including Edward Heath pointed out, what the CPRS was for. The opportunity costs of the review were great, since it tied up much of the time of nearly a third of the CPRS staff throughout the review.

The tactical errors included, first, accepting the Foreign Office's suggestion to visit so very many overseas posts; the effects of this were to overwhelm the team with repetitive detail, and to reduce the time available for thinking about fundamental questions and for drafting and presenting the completed study. Secondly, agreeing to cover the cultural and information services as well, a move which ensured that large parts of the media and the intelligentsia joined the campaign against the review. Thirdly, failing to counter the Foreign Office's propaganda campaign and so allowing them to dictate the terms of the public debate (which, to caricature it only slightly, revolved round the propriety of allowing a team mainly composed of young female radical academics to spend the taxpayers' money counting the cost of diplomatic cocktail parties in Ulan Bator.)

The report undeniably had weaknesses, including its overemphasis on economic criteria for evaluating the need for and success of diplomatic and other overseas activities. It also had great merits and raised some major issues which much of the debate simply side-stepped.[17] The skilful propaganda of its opponents had the double effect, in the short term at least, of defeating most of its proposals and lowering the reputation, effectiveness and morale of the CPRS. But in the longer term, the outcome has been much less clear-cut. There is little doubt that the report has helped to change the climate of thinking about overseas activities, and has sharpened the debate about their value. More specifically, when Mrs Thatcher's government was looking for cuts in public spending two years later, some of the economies proposed by the CPRS team were implemented, for other reasons and without acknowledgement, by some of the politicians and administrators who had so loudly dismissed them earlier. (The overseas services of the BBC once again vigorously defended themselves, with partial success.)

A Joint Approach to Social Policies

A second interesting case was the group of studies commissioned under this title, inevitably shortened to JASP. From the earliest days of the CPRS its private list of possible projects had included a reference to 'Interdepartmental aspects of social policy'. The issue seen here was simply expressed, but extremely complicated in application: that the policies and programmes of different 'social' departments, such as those concerned with social security, health or housing, were planned and managed in isolation from each other, and often in isolation from other activities not usually seen as 'social' at all, such as taxation. They were linked to no common scale of priorities or plan of action, although they often bore upon the same individual clients — upon whom their cumulative effects could be unpredictable and capricious.

The problem was clearly enormous. So, too, was the task of finding any practicable way of tackling it, including the secondary but crucial problem of persuading the several 'social' departments concerned to let the CPRS discuss and perhaps influence their priorities. The CPRS took on, part-time, a consultant from McKinseys to help in working up and presenting its analyses. The first approach suggested by the CPRS, for coordinating clusters of programmes aimed at particular 'client groups', was rejected by departments as too ambitious and, perhaps, too threatening to their autonomy. The second approach was deliberately much more gradual and consensual: the basic element in this was a small interdepartmental group of officials, chaired by the CPRS, which discussed problems and possible solutions on the basis of analyses provided by the CPRS. This group were not expected or asked to agree on the details of the final report which the CPRS drafted by Ministers, but in fact gave it broad support.

The report recommended a programme of work aimed at

developing a 'joint approach to social policies'.[18] The elements in this programme included regular meetings of Ministers to discuss, not day-to-day problems, but broader questions of social strategy; systematic 'forward looks' at likely forthcoming events in the social policy field; improvements in the presentation and analysis of social statistics; and several studies of specific topics, such as aspects of policies towards financial poverty, the relationships between central government and local authorities, the links between housing policy and other social policies, and the longer-term implications for social policies of changes in population structure and distribution. This programme was accepted by Ministers more or less as it stood, and its various elements were set in hand. Work was done, but not published, on policies affecting financial poverty. Several other studies were published.[19]

There was some internal reorganization in the Central Statistical Office, which produced a series of summary reports aimed at presenting Ministers with facts about selected policy areas. The special ministerial committee, chaired by the Secretary of State for Education, met only occasionally and made little impact on governmental thinking. Later, some other interdepartmental studies were carried out.[20]

This 'JASP' exercise aroused a great deal of interest outside government; both the original report, and the later study of central/local government relations, were seen by many as aimed squarely at real and important problems. It is hard to deny the intrinsic importance of using resources more effectively in this area. But for the CPRS the problem was how to keep up the momentum of this ambitious programme without devoting to it too many CPRS staff resources, and without in effect drifting into a continuing managerial role towards the other departments concerned. Especially if Ministers were to lose interest in this work, it would be literally suicidal for the CPRS to invest too many resources in it; the opportunity cost of doing so would be to forego many other pieces of work which Ministers would value more highly. It seems fairly clear that in its later stages the Labour government, like other governments at a similar stage of life, was not interested in work with such a long-term and problematical payoff. There were no signs that Mrs Thatcher's administration was particularly interested. By mid-1979, therefore, the CPRS involvement in JASP, and indeed JASP itself, were apparently at an end.[21]

CONCLUSIONS: A TENTATIVE ASSESSMENT

Finally, what general conclusions can be reached about the CPRS and about its effectiveness? How far was the original conception realized and justified by events?

As pointed out above, the CPRS as it emerged from the 1971 white paper was on a scale much smaller than some of its earlier proponents would have wished. The balance of its activities has continued to change gradually. It has never acted as a planning unit; its responsibility for overseeing the government's strategy became increasingly intermittent and, since early 1974, it has concerned itself mainly with discrete and often unrelated topics. The Mark I, or Rothschild, CPRS was fairly close to the outline given in the white paper. This was during a period of strong and purposeful ministerial government; it was, moreover, the last period of confident expectation of continued economic growth, of belief in planning and, in this sense, in rationality in policy-making. In these Conservative years the CPRS was licensed to roam freely in Whitehall, to summon Ministers to special meetings and to lecture them on their strategy. Rothschild had a close working relationship with Mr Heath; the CPRS' somewhat flamboyant, not to say aristocratic style and the presence in the CPRS of avowed Conservative supporters probably reinforced the links between the CPRS, the Cabinet and indeed the government party as a whole. The credibility of the CPRS was high until the autumn of 1973, when Rothschild's unfortunate lecture and subsequent illness, the economic and political crisis and finally the change of government pushed it out of the centre altogether.

It took some time after February 1974 for the CPRS to make itself respectable in the eyes of the new Labour government. Personal factors, and the creation of the Prime Minister's own policy unit, combined to prevent the CPRS from ever establishing the same relationship with Mr Wilson that it had had with Mr Heath. For reasons not altogether clear much the same was true of the Cabinet as a whole. Sir Kenneth Berrill had had much more experience of the permanent civil service, and of its style of working, than had Lord Rothschild. He also took a more pragmatic view of the possibilities of making changes in Whitehall, preferring where possible to work 'with the grain' rather than through confrontation. His period of office saw the publication of some of the CPRS' best reports, and some of its more ambitious projects: the report on the motor industry, for example, and the work on a joint approach to social policy. It also saw the report on overseas representation, and the continued strengthening of the Prime Minister's policy unit. It was widely reported, or suggested, in the press that the Mark II CPRS had not proved to be a success, that it had 'lost its way', had been 'captured by the bureaucracy' and might not even survive.

In these matters there can be no single truth. In particular, 'success' and 'failure' are extremely complex concepts in which the time dimension is critical. Claims or denials of instant results are part of the currency of politics; but in fact causal relationships are much more prolonged and problematical than politicians or their advisers are usually willing to admit. In addition, hostile or dismissive comment about the CPRS made privately or in the press can be at least partly discounted as the more or less inevitable reactions of people either affronted by CPRS advice or dissatisfied with the amount of support given by the CPRS to their own interests. For example, much of the response to the report on overseas representation was of the former kind. That episode was a clear illustration of the CPRS doing one of the main jobs for which it was created: challenging established interests and viewpoints within government. It is a job which is bound to cause resentment among professionals who often sincerely believe that no different ways of doing their jobs would be practicable or useful.

The main achievement of a body like the CPRS is probably to change the climate of opinion among decision-makers — a process which at best will happen only gradually and in which the precise responsibility of everyone is likely to be blurred. The essential first stage of this process is simply putting issues 'on the agenda' of policy-makers. The policy analyst in government should not protest if his advice has no visible impact for several years; or if the impact takes the form of his ideas, sometimes disconcertingly modified, being claimed as their own by other people. This is the occupational deprivation of his trade.

Judged by these criteria the CPRS seems, on balance, and taken over the whole of its lifetime, to be succeeding. It would almost certainly have been more effective if its work programme had been more deliberately related to some coherent principles, and its staff selected accordingly. Its relationship with the government of the

day could at times have been closer, even if this meant a less comfortable relationship with the permanent civil service. Some of its
activities have been ill-judged and some quite ineffective. But the
quality of some of its major studies, in particular, has kept their
conclusions relevant long after their first presentation and, as a
result, influential. Although the immediate impact of the report on
the motor industry was small, the analysis in that report has
become basic to much informed thinking about the problems of
British manufacturing industry.[22] Much though the review of
overseas representation was criticized at the time, by late 1979 its
underlying analysis and some of its specific recommendations were
starting to emerge in policy. Even the unpublished report on race
relations suddenly resurfaced in a leading article in the *Guardian* in
December 1979, commenting on the government's current proposals to limit immigration.[23]

It is still too soon to say whether the work on developing a joint
approach to social policies will have any lasting impact; but its
general principles, and the conclusions of particular reports, have
been extensively discussed and refined outside government, and the
process may well not yet be complete. Comments made by former
Ministers about CPRS activities such as collective briefing suggest
that these, too, have been found valuable.

It may never be possible to say more than this. The least that can
be said is that the problems with which the CPRS was created to
deal are endemic in governmental bureaucracies in general and in
Britain in particular; that there is no evidence that a different kind
of organization would have dealt with them more effectively than
did the CPRS; and that, despite undoubted false steps and shortcomings in its advice, the CPRS has managed to preserve its place
at the centre of British central government, poised between the
Cabinet and the civil service. Its activities and effectiveness have
depended largely — perhaps too largely — on personalities and on
context: Rothschild and Heath in the confident climate of 1971-73;
Berrill and Wilson/Callaghan during the more pessimistic and dif-
fident governments of 1974-79. The combination of Mr Ibbs and
Mrs Thatcher, in the difficult world of the early 1980s, is certain to
lead to further changes.

NOTES

1. Cmnd. 4506 (London: HMSO October 1970).

2. See, for example, Angela Croome in *New Scientist* 27 April 1972; Lawrence Marks in the *Observer*, 30 September 1973; J. W. M. Thompson in the *Sunday Telegraph*, 4 July 1970. Also Lord Rothschild's own volume of autobiographical essays, *Meditations of a Broomstick* (London: Collins 1977).

3. For a comment on this recurrent situation, see Crossman (1975), 280. Also Dell (1979).

4. Rothschild (1971); *Energy Conservation* (London: HMSO July 1974); *The Future of the British Car Industry* (London: HMSO 1975); *Review of Overseas Representation* (London: HMSO 1977); *A Joint Framework for Social Policies* (London: HMSO 1975); *The Future of the United Kingdom Power Plant Manufacturing Industry* (London: HMSO 1976); *Relations between Central Government and Local Authorities* (London: HMSO 1977); *Population and the Social Services* (London: HMSO 1977).

5. The race relations report was extensively 'leaked' in *The Guardian*, 24 October 1977.

6. See Heclo and Wildavsky (1974); also Jay (1972); and Heath and Barker (1978.

7. Minutes of evidence taken before the House of Commons Expenditure Committee (General Sub-Committee) 6 December 1976; Cmnd. 7308, *The United Kingdom's Overseas Representation* (London: HMSO August 1978).

8. See Pettigrew for an interesting analysis of how this problem has been dealt with in business organizations.

9. There was an extensive, if inconclusive, debate in British academic circles during the 1960s about how far Britain now had 'prime ministerial' rather than 'Cabinet' government.

10. These views were later refined and elaborated by Mr Benn in a lecture given to the RIPA, London, 7 January 1980, and reported in *The Times*, *The Guardian* and the *Financial Times* the following day.

11. See, for example, 'Thoughts on a Think Tank', *New Society*, 1 November 1979.

12. *The Times*, 25 September 1973; *Sunday Times*, 30 September 1973.

13. *Sunday Times Magazine*, 25 March 1973.

14. *Review of Overseas Representation* (London: HMSO 1977).

15. House of Lords Debates 1977-78, Vol. 387, Col. 852-1018.

16. Max Beloff in *Public Administration*, Winter 1977.

17. See, for example, the thoughtful and well-balanced analysis by William Wallace in *International Affairs*, April 1978.

18. *A Joint Framework for Social Policies* (London: HMSO 1975). See also Plowden (1977).

19. For example, *Relations between Central Government and Local Authorities* (London: HMSO 1977); *Population and the Social Services* (London: HMSO 1977).

20. For example, *Housing and Social Policies: Some Interactions* (London:

HMSO 1978); *Services for Young Children with Working Mothers* (London: HMSO 1978).

21. See Malcolm Dean, *The Guardian*, 28 November 1979.

22. See, for example, Adam Raphael, the *Observer*, 6 January 1980.

23. 'Ask a Slovenly Question', *The Guardian*, 19 December 1979.

REFERENCES

Crossman, Richard (1975) *The Diaries of a Cabinet Minister* (London: Hamish Hamilton and Jonathan Cape).

Dell, Edmund (1979) *Collective Responsibility: Fact, Fiction or Facade* (unpublished lecture given to Royal Institute of Public Administration, London, 4 December).

Heath, Edward and Barker, Anthony (1978) 'Heath on Whitehall Reform', *Parliamentary Affairs*, Autumn.

Heclo, H. and Wildavsky, Aaron (1974), *The Private Government of Public Money* (London: Macmillan).

Jay, Peter (1972) 'PESC, PAR and Politics', *The Times*, 31 January.

Pettigrew, Andrew M. (1975) 'Strategic Aspects of the Management of Specialist Activity', *Personnel Review* Vol. 4, No. 1.

Plowden, William (1977) 'Developing a Joint Approach to Social Policy', in Kathleen Jones (ed.), *The Yearbook of Social Policy 1976* (London: Routledge and Kegan Paul).

Rothschild, Lord (1971) 'The Organisation and Management of Government R&D', in: *A Framework for Government, Research and Development* (Cmnd. 4814).

5 Futures Studies and Policy Analysis in the Political Process: The Netherlands Scientific Council for Government Policy[1]

Peter R. Baehr
Scientific Council for Government Policy,
The Hague

Whoever intends to present a society with long-term options for future policy decisions is bound to encounter a host of difficulties of both a theoretical and practical nature. These difficulties are likely to increase if the information is given not by an individual but by an institution that is specifically charged with that task. This may be even more the case if such an institution is financed from public rather than from private funds.

The purpose of this paper is to discuss some of the difficulties faced by such an institution, the Netherlands Scientific Council for Government Policy, and the ways by which it has tried to solve them during the seven years of its existence. The period of observation is admittedly rather brief. This may, however, have the advantage that the organization is still flexible enough to change its ways, if offered useful suggestions.

The paper is divided into three sections. Section I contains information about the organization and working of the council and its programme of activities. In section II some of the problems that have arisen in the fulfilment of its tasks are discussed. The third and final section contains a few concluding observations.

STRUCTURE OF THE SCIENTIFIC COUNCIL
FOR GOVERNMENT POLICY
AND PROGRAMME OF ACTIVITIES[2]

In the Netherlands there exists a long tradition of planning for public policy-making. Central planning agencies exist in the fields of economic policy (since 1947), physical planning (1941) and, more recently, in the social-cultural field (1973). Next to these so-called 'facet' planning agencies there are the 'sectoral' planning divisions within the various ministerial departments. In 1968 a national commission, Preparation Research on the Future Structure of Society, the so-called De Wolff commission, was set up. Its task was to prepare recommendations regarding the organization of a scientific basis for an integrated government policy directed at a long-term development of society. It recommended, among other matters, the establishment of a planning council to provide for a form of 'integrated planning' in order to create a synthesis of the different forms of sector planning and facet planning. After a second national commission had prepared a report, it was decided to establish a Scientific Council for Government Policy. The difference between this proposal and the original idea was that the newly-established Council did not get the responsibility of coordinating the activities of the existing sector and facet planning bureaus.

The Scientific Council for Government Policy was set up on a provisional basis by Royal Decree in 1972. In 1976 the Dutch parliament passed a law, which established the Council on a formal legal basis. According to the law, the Council is charged with the following tasks:

1. to supply on behalf of governmental policy scientifically-based information on developments which may affect society in the long run and to draw timely attention to anticipated anomalies and bottlenecks; it should also define major policy problems and indicate policy alternatives;
2. to provide a scientific structure which the government can use when establishing priorities and which would ensure that a consistent policy is pursued;
3. to make recommendations with respect to studies on future developments and long-term planning in both the public and the private sector on the elimination of structural inade-

quacies, the furtherance of specific research activities and the improvement of communication and coordination.

The tasks listed indicate that emphasis was placed on supplying information rather than on straightforwardly advising the government (although experience shows that in actual practice a sharp dividing line between the two cannot be maintained). It is definitely *not* the task of the Council to determine the longer-term objectives of Dutch society. The Council provides information about alternative developments in order that the government may determine its priorities and select its longer-term objectives.

The Council consists of a minimum of five and a maximum of eleven members. (There are nine members at present.) The chairman and the other members of the Council are appointed by the Queen on the recommendation of the Prime Minister. Members are selected so as to represent a wide spectrum of academic disciplines and of political and social-economic views. They are appointed for a term of five years and are eligible for one subsequent term. The post of chairman is a full-time function; the other members serve either on a full-time or on a part-time basis. So far, university professors and directors of research have mainly been appointed to the Council. The present chairman is a former secretary-general of a ministerial department.

In addition to the regular membership there are at present four advisory members: the Director of the Central (Economic) Planning Bureau, the Director General for Physical Planning, the Director General for Statistics, and the Director of the Social and Cultural Planning Bureau. The Council has a scientific and administrative staff of approximately thirty people at its disposal. The secretary to the Council also serves as staff director. The annual budget for research activities amounts to about $500,000. All government departments, institutions and local authorities are legally obliged to provide the Council with the information it may require. The Council may consult directly with experts in the private and public sector.

The Council reports directly to the Cabinet through the office of the Prime Minister. Reports of the Council are published after the Cabinet has taken cognizance of them. The Cabinet must react publicly within a period of three months to the reports of the Council. The Cabinet can suggest items to the Council, but the Council draws up its own programme of work. The Cabinet may ask the Council for advice on specific subjects. The Council is entitled to refuse to supply such advice. So far, four such requests have reached the Council. One related to structural problems in the coordination of education policy (*Comments on the White Paper on the Contours of the Future Educational System*, Report No. 10, 1976). The second request was for the Council's comments on the government's discussion paper on sectoral councils for science policy drawn up by the Minister for Science Policy (*Comments on the Discussion Paper on Sectoral Councils for Science Policy*, Report No. 9, 1976). In 1979 the government requested the Council to draw up a report on an integrated long-term policy with regard to the national communications network, including the role of the press, radio and television, especially relating to new technical developments. The Council has accepted this request and will issue its report before the end of the present term, i.e. before 31 December 1982.

Closely related to the tasks of the Council are the two main criteria according to which projects are identified, namely *a long-term view* and *an integrated approach*. With respect to the long-term view it is commonly accepted that society has for various reasons become more complex than it used to be, while at the same time it is changing much more rapidly than in the past. The lack of long-term views regarding plausible, probable and desirable developments of society forces the government to react to situations instead of anticipating developments. Through its activities the Council helps to change a re-active political behaviour into a more pro-active one. This is of particular importance if policy decisions are irreversible or only reversible at high economic and social cost.

Fear has been expressed by some commentators that the Council would develop into a group of technocrats which would design blueprints of the future, at the expense of parliamentary and public influence on governmental policy. The Council was considered to be an agency closer to the Cabinet than to parliament, which might even further disturb the balance of power between the two. As much as possible, efforts have been made to prevent such a development. The Council is charged with presenting information rather than recommendations; thanks to the public nature of its reports, it is possible for parliament, the press and overall public opinion to keep a check on its activities.

The use of the term 'Scientific' in the name of the Council refers mainly to the fact that the work of the Council should not be influenced by prejudices and party-political preferences. It refers, furthermore, to the fact that the reports of the Council should be based on scientifically sound information. The Council should not be influenced by accidental political power positions and political interests of specific groups. It should serve as a kind of bridge between the world of scientists and scholars on the one hand, and that of policy-makers on the other.

As a further check and in order to facilitate communication with parliament, contacts have been established between the two chambers of parliament and the Council. These contacts, which take place once or twice a year, are used to express parliamentary wishes or suggestions with regard to the Council's programme of work. Furthermore, in order to prevent an 'ivory tower' position, regular contacts have been established between the Council and various groups in society such as the press, big industry, employers' organizations, the labour unions and the research staffs of the political parties. This should help to ensure a two-way flow of communication between the Council and the rest of society. In spite of these efforts, however, the Council has functioned so far mainly within the governmental establishment.

The Council is independent in the selection of topics it wants to include in its programme of work. During its first term of office (1972-77) the Council was engaged in the following seven projects, some of which produced publications that are listed below:

A General Survey of the Future

In December 1973 the Council decided to carry out a general survey of the future with the aim of drawing up a coherent long-term picture of the future of the Netherlands — that is to say up to the year 2000 — based on the expected course of a number of elements. Though the original intention was to arrive at a single picture of the future, it was decided at a later stage to work with two variants: one with a consistently moderate economic growth of 3 percent per annum and one with an economic growth gradually declining to zero. The project was carried out by an ad hoc committee, composed mainly of people from outside the Council, notably from the staff of planning agencies, advisory bodies and universities. The members of the ad hoc committee prepared papers in which they expressed their expectations for the future in their respective fields of knowledge. These papers formed the basic material from which, with the aid of the Council's secretariat, a forecast was produced and published (*The Next Twenty-Five Years: A Survey of Future Developments in the Netherlands*, Report No. 15, 1977 — this report is also available in English).

Values and Norms

The development of a society is partly determined by the values and norms which the various groups in a society observe in their own behaviour and in their evaluation of social developments. The Council's aim in choosing this field of study was to stimulate a higher level of awareness among political, administrative and social organizations in their thinking about the direction in which they would like society to develop in the long run. To gain experience with this approach a pilot study was carried out concerning the concrete issue of women's emancipation (I. J. Schoonenboom & H. M. In 't Veld-Langeveld, *Women's Emancipation*, 1976). In collaboration with the research institutes of the political parties the Council is also engaged in a study of the long-term options as expressed in the programmes of the various political parties. The material collected in this study will be used in a new policy-directed survey of the future (see below, p. 101).

Developments Abroad

Policy-making in a small country such as the Netherlands is to a large extent influenced by developments abroad. The Council investigated the possibility of systematically gathering information concerning these developments and of analysing this information in terms of their long-term relevance. Two pilot studies were published: one dealt with the problem of international migration (*Foreign Influence on the Netherlands: International Migration*, Report No. 7, 1976); the other concerned the availability to the Netherlands of scientific and technical know-how (*Foreign Influence on the Netherlands: Availability of Scientific and Technical Knowledge*, Report No. 8, 1976).

Social Inequality

An effort was made to achieve a better understanding of the national distribution of income, wealth, education, power and labour. Such an understanding would make it possible to indicate the factors in the field of social inequality which in the long run exercise influence on relevant developments in society. Studies were published on inequality in the Dutch educational system, inequality in the distribution of income in the Netherlands and inequality in the labour system. These studies resulted in a report on the relevant distribution processes, their interrelations and their implications for social stratification (*On Social Inequality: A Policy-Oriented Study*, Report No. 16, 1977).

Relationship between Economically Active and Non-Active Persons

Attention was focused on the relation between the economically active and non-active sections of the population. The main subject of the investigation was the question of future developments in this area, the consequences of change in the ratio and the possibilities open to the government to influence it. Attention was given to the relationship between the social security system, sickness absenteeism and the present labour market policy. An important item concerned the desirability of job creation in the non-commercial service sector ('the quaternary sector'). (*Do We Make Work Our Business? An Exploratory Study of the Relation between Economically Active and Inactive Persons in the Population*, Report No. 13, 1977 — this report is also available in English.)

Public Administration

The Council embarked upon this study because it believed that in the administrative organization of the Netherlands there are various impediments to long-term planning and policy coordination. In its report the Council pointed to structural bottlenecks both in the formulation of government policy and relations between the central government and local authorities (*The Organization of Public Administration: Aspects, Bottlenecks and Proposals*, Report No. 6, 1975). The Council also paid attention to the problem of advising the national government. Two surveys were published (*Survey of the External Advisory Bodies of the Central Government*, Report No. 11, 1976 and *Survey of the Internal Advisory Bodies of the Central Government*, Report No. 14, 1977) and an empirical analysis was made of the system of external advisory bodies and their development (*External Advisory Bodies of the Central Government: Description, Developments, Recommendations*, Report No. 12, 1977).

Technical-Scientific Survey of the Future

In this project the Council aimed at an identification and analysis of important future developments in the field of technology. Simultaneously the possibilities of controlling the development and application of technology were studied. Preparatory work was carried out regarding technological innovation and the future structure of industry in the Netherlands. This study was carried over into the second term of office (see below, p. 102).

When the first term of office of the Council came to an end on 31 December 1977, this meant that the Council, in accordance with its legal provisions, had to be newly constituted. (Two members were re-appointed, six new members, including a new chairman, joined the Council; a ninth member was added later.) It also meant that a new programme of work had to be drawn up. The first six months of 1978 were spent in discussions between the members of the Council and the members of the staff about the contents of the new work programme. Lengthy deliberations took place on what interpretation should be given to the tasks of the Council as formulated by law and what consequences such interpretation should have for the programme. Advice was sought from the advisory members. By the summer of 1978 consensus had been reached on the general outline of a programme for at least part of the second term of office. The programme was presented for comment to the Cabinet, the ministerial departments, the two chambers of parliament, a group of about 100 selected experts and a number of institutionalized groupings such as the trade union confederations, the employers' organizations, the research divisions of the political parties, the National Council of Churches, etc. Comments were also elicited from the advisory members of the Council. By the beginning of 1979 comments had been received from most of the outside experts. A meeting had taken place with the Cabinet and meetings had been arranged with both chambers of parliament. The programme of work covered the following subjects:

A Policy-Directed Survey of the Future

Many commentators saw as a deficiency of the general survey of the future which was conducted during the first term of office of the Council, that it was too general and that it lacked in policy-relevance. It was argued that the report had been written on too abstract a level, which put the task of translating the report into policy into the hands of the policy-makers. In order to make its second survey of the future more policy-directed the council had three approaches in mind:

(a) a translation of the 'high growth' scenario developed within the OECD *Interfutures* study[3] into the Dutch situation; the 'high growth' scenario was chosen as being most representative of thinking in leading Western political and economic circles about the most desirable (but not necessarily most probable) developments;

(b) an analysis of long-term options posed by various groups in society, including the various political parties. For this purpose the material collected during the previous term of office within the project 'values and norms' will be used (see above, p. 98);

(c) a confrontation of the results of the analysis mentioned under (b) with the policy framework and political processes mentioned under (a).

This exercise should have at least the following two results:
— the presentation and evaluation of alternative images of the future presented in a manner that can be used by political parties, social organizations and policy-makers;
— the development of methods which can help to expedite the solution of middle-term problems.

Place and Future of Dutch Industry

The point of departure is the assumed desirability of economic growth, maintenance of the level of international competition and protection of the environment, as manifested in terms of goals by the intervention framework of the government. The question is asked as to what will be a desirable development of production and employment in Europe in general and in the Netherlands in particular. Is it to be expected that the total production of business is going to increase again, accompanied by absorption of labour instead of expulsion? And under what conditions may this development be thought feasible?

Further problems dealt with in the project are:
— What sector structure(s) may be realized in accordance with the desired long-term development, taking into account, among other things, the relative development of international demand and competition and the development of technology?
— How does the foreseeable or feasible long-term development relate to the actual situation and tendencies in the economy, projected to the year 1985?
— In case of serious discrepancies: What policy will be required to get the Dutch economy back on the road to long-term growth?
— What are the prospects for the regional economy structure in 1985, taking into account the regional profiles, including features like comparative advantages and traditions?

Labour

One of the central problems tackled in the labour project is the esteem which is going to be accorded to work in the long run. A number of suggestions has been raised in recent years, all geared to the idea of making long-term unemployment more acceptable to society. Ideas on this subject can be located somewhere between two extreme models. Model A would require every member of society to contribute to society by way of paid work, through which he acquires an income. Next to the 'duty' to work everybody would also have the 'right' to work, in order to develop his or her abilities (with the exception of traditionally fixed groups such as the aged and the very young). That model would be more or less applicable to the present situation. The other extreme would be model B in which there would be neither a right nor a duty to work. To work or not to work would be a matter of choice rather than obligation. Everybody would have a guaranteed minimum income. In this approach a reevaluation of household work would fit. Individual development and self-realization would take place outside the working place.

Public Administration

Two aspects of public administration are covered: functional decentralization and the role of planning in public administration. The following aspects of functional decentralization are the subject of study:

(a) experiences with functional decentralization at the national level in view of the assumed overburdening of the political top; a decrease in the number of matters covered by ministerial accountability; an increase of governmental efficiency and effectiveness;

(b) possible tasks, power, roles, shapes, etc. of functional organs;

(c) aspects relating to the democratic form of government: involvement of individual citizens in functional government, on the one hand, problems of political accountability, participation, judicial remedies and equality, on the other. This study has a mainly empirical character and will draw on experiences in the Netherlands, but also in other countries such as Sweden, the United Kingdom and the United States.

The study of the role of planning in government covers the following aspects:

(a) the relationship between governmental planning and the principles of the constitutional state with regard to law-making participation, judicial remedies and equality;

(b) effectiveness of planning in public administration; the distribution of responsibilities, the problem of coordination;

(c) the character of various plans, possibly including: the development of a typology of plans; an inventory of plans; the exploration of bottlenecks; the development of mechanisms of coordination.

International Affairs, especially the Relationship between the Netherlands and the Federal Republic of Germany

The Council is aware of the fact that developments in the Netherlands are very much subject to influences from abroad. Following initiatives taken during the first term of office, the Council is pursuing the study of these foreign influences. Within the original study of the 'international economic process' the Council selected the relationship with the Federal Republic of Germany, the main trading partner of the Netherlands, as its main subject of study. The following aspects are covered in the study:

(a) bilateral relations, mainly in the economic field, with attention also being paid to other forms of interdependence, such as security, the European context and cultural contacts;

(b) an analysis of policy matters which may arise in the relationship between the two countries, seen in the context of internal developments in the social and economic field;

(c) a study of the way in which similar problems are being tackled in the two countries.

PROBLEMS IN THE FULFILMENT OF THE TASKS OF THE COUNCIL

This section deals with a number of problems the Council has encountered in the process of carrying out its tasks. The following problems are considered: (a) identification of issues, (b) depth of the studies, (c) the development of an integrated approach,

(d) contacts with other organizations, (e) the development of a multi-disciplinary approach, (f) the effectiveness of the Council's work and its follow-up.

Identification of Issues

The tasks of the Council, as set out in law, are far- and wide-ranging. It would be hard to think of aspects of government policy that are not at least in principle covered by the establishing law. That makes it even more important to pay due attention to the way in which the Council develops its programme. The establishing law is often consulted, interpreted and re-interpreted, in order to determine what the lawmakers had in mind when they originated the Council and what sorts of consequences this must have for its programme of work. As the law gives no guidelines to solve the problem, it is left to the Council as to how it wants to reach a decision about its programme of work. The Council rejected an approach by which each member would name his or her areas of greatest interest and would pursue these during their term of office. It reasoned that better ways should be found to identify society's most pressing problems now and in the future. Incidentally, there is a grave problem here in that it is not certain that whatever are now considered to be society's most pressing future problems, will be the ones that are considered most pressing in the near or distant future.

When the first term of office drew to an end, lengthy discussions developed among the members of the permanent staff regarding the question as to which problems should be carried over from the first to the second term and which new problems should be taken on. A large number of ideas, suggestions and proposals was floated, some of a rather elaborate nature, others more primitive or by way of trial balloon. The executive secretary paid visits to the secretaries-general of some of the key ministerial departments, such as Economic Affairs, Social Affairs and the Department of the Interior to elicit further suggestions.

Thus, when the Council met for the first time in its second term of office, it was faced by a host of proposals and suggestions, some of which were being further developed in outside contracts in the form of so-called 'feasibility studies'. To these, the newly appointed members of the Council added some of their own ideas. It took several months of internal debate and discussion before the programme emerged.

In the introduction to the programme a number of criteria is mentioned which the Council applied in arriving at the themes, as set out in the programme:

(a) issues dealt with by the Council should be considered as problem areas by at least part of the population. It would be wrong if the Council, whose composition may be considered, to say the least, somewhat arbitrary, were to identify problems all by itself. It should use existing mechanisms in the political process for that purpose. Therefore, the Council's studies should stress analyses and approaches using various, alternative conceptions: it should be noted, incidentally, that one person's problem may turn out to be another person's solution to a problem;

(b) the approach to problems should in principle be open to influence from the government; the government should bear a certain degree of co-responsibility for that approach. Problems with too little policy relevance should stay outside the working sphere of the Council;

(c) the selected themes should cover more than one sector of government and therefore more than one ministerial department. In this respect the Council can develop material and capacities which the ministerial departments lack;

(d) finally, the Council should have a certain expertise in the fields selected.

The themes selected for study, as mentioned in the previous section of this paper, are considered to be among the most important, though not necessarily the most important, faced by society in the future.

The work programme was sent for comment to the Cabinet, the ministerial departments, the two chambers of parliament, and various selected experts. It was also made publicly available. The response of the various consultants, including the Cabinet, has on the whole been positive. Although the overall problem of identification of issues has not been solved in principle, the Council feels that it has at least done as much as it could, under prevailing circumstances, to ensure that its admittedly subjective selection of issues has met with a positive response in the present phase of its operations.

Depth of the Studies

The Council's terms of reference encompass a rather wide range of subjects, comprising in principle all matters covered by government policy. It is obviously impossible for the Council, with its limited number of members and staff, to do full justice to so many fields of activity. This means that one may opt for a broad approach, involving a wide variety of long-term policy aspects, which carries the risk of remaining at too superficial a level. Moreover, aiming at all aspects of government policy will make the task of achieving an integrated approach — difficult enough as it is — an even harder proposition. The alternative is to choose an in-depth approach, involving an intensive analysis of only a few fundamental aspects of government policy and assessment of their relevance to long-term problems. The advantage of the latter approach would be that it would be more 'scientific' in the sense that it would be possible to investigate all possible consequences of various policy developments.

During the first term of office no explicit choice was made between the two approaches. In practice, however, emphasis came to be placed on the broader approach. It was, moreover, the considered view of the Council that it would be wise not to wait too long in presenting itself to the public. It was considered important to make clear to government officials as soon as possible what the Council was supposed to do and what kind of use they could make of the Council's work. This kind of presentation could best take place by way of publication. This explains why the Council was rather quick in presenting some of its first findings. (The first publication in the series 'reports to the government' was sent to the Prime Minister on 16 January 1974, i.e. only a little over a year after the Council had been established on a provisional basis.)

It seems that during the second term of office emphasis is also being placed on the broader approach. Should the second, more profound approach be preferred in the future — and it is up to the Council so to decide — this would mean that the selection, and

more specifically the method of selection, of projects would require
even more systematic attention. It might then become as interesting
to find out which topics the Council decided *not* to study as the
ones it did select for study.

The Development of an Integrated Approach

It follows from the Council's statutory terms of reference that it
should seek to embody its activities in an integrated framework.
One of the Council's major tasks is to consider the extent to which
long-term developments in one policy area affect other areas. The
'anomalies' and 'bottlenecks' which the Council is expected to an-
ticipate are partly the result of this interaction. This, however, is no
simple matter, as the Council discovered during its first term of office. The approach it chose was to deal with separate projects
distributed among its members and among the research staff. An
advantage of this approach was that it was possible to concentrate
on a number of different topics, different lines of approach to each
topic, and different formulations of each problem. This facilitated
the production of reports while at the same time helping the Council to establish contacts with other institutions. A disadvantage of
this approach was, however, that projects tended to lead a separate
existence, to be insufficiently attuned to one another. That did not
make it any easier for the Council to evolve a more or less integrated framework for long-term policy. During the first term
there was a certain measure of segmentation, which was partly the
result of the separate projects approach.

During the second term, a certain degree of segmentation has
also taken place, though the chairman, the executive secretary and
the deputy executive secretary are making an effort to keep this
segmentation at a minimum.

Contacts with Other Organizations

From the beginning it has been considered of fundamental importance that the Council should maintain close contacts with other
relevant bodies, both private and public, in the Netherlands as well
as abroad. It should be obvious that the Council needs these con-

tacts in order to receive the necessary information on which to base its reports. Another important reason is that contacts with other institutions should help to prevent the Council from developing too much into an 'ivory tower' organization. Outside contacts may help an organization to reflect from time to time on its own manner of operations, on its own procedures.

The law deals with at least two forms of outside contacts. In the first place there is the group of advisory members of the Council, who are expected to support the Council with their advice (see above, p. 95). Secondly, the research budget offers the Council the opportunity to contract out part of its work. Usually, these contracts are made with university institutes or other public bodies, private research firms or private persons. By now, the work of the Council has become almost unthinkable without the aid of these contributions from outside. Furthermore, the Council has organized different kinds of advisory or sounding board groups, which are used to elicit commentaries and criticism with regard to activities that the Council has undertaken or intends to undertake.

For example, the project which resulted in the study *Do We Make Work Our Business*? was aided during the first term by an advisory group of ten individuals: some top civil servants, a few members of parliament, university professors and others. From time to time, ad hoc meetings take place with representatives of the research divisions of the political parties, the trade unions, the employers' organizations or selected individual experts to discuss specific aspects of the Council's work.

Special attention is paid to contacts with the various ministerial departments. These contacts take place both at the ministerial level and at the working level. It is of vital importance to the Council to remain assured of the cooperation and support of these departments in order to be supplied with the information it requires. Good personal and institutional relationships are important in order to receive information about activities and intended activities of the government, as prescribed by the law, in time. On the other hand, care must be taken to prevent the activities of the Council from being too heavily influenced by the ministries. Obviously, there is a *Scylla* of too little information and a *Charybdis* of too much influence between which a wise course must be steered. So far, the ministerial departments have refrained from trying to influence the activities of the Council unduly. A top civil servant once tried to change the contents of a report that had been formally adopted by the Council by offering to 'help' bring the conclusions of the report more in line with its contents, as he put it. (Representatives of the Council listened politely to his views and then kept the text of the report as it was before.)

In future, more of this type of influence may take place, as the reports of the Council become more involved with activities of the departments and become potentially more damaging to vested interests in the departments. Formal requests for advice constitute a special type of contact with the ministries. Such requests must be discussed in advance with the chairman of the Council, in order to make sure that they do not interfere unduly with the Council's programme of work. After such initial contact has taken place, the request must pass the Cabinet before formally being put before the Council. The Council is free to reject the request even then, but will of course do so only under very special circumstances. So far, four such requests have reached the Council (see above, p. 96). Should the number of such formal government requests vastly increase, the Council might be confronted with a problem. Though it would certainly be a sign of the government's confidence in the Council's judgement and would illustrate the importance it attaches to the Council's role in the preparation of long-term policy, it would at the same time make heavy demands on the Council's programme of work.

Regular contacts with organizations of the same kind in other countries are also considered of great importance. The purpose of these contacts is to discuss the ways in which similar problems as they arise in the respective work programmes are being solved and to compare results. Institutions working on policy-relevant, long-term research activities have been set up in various ways in different countries. They are all in some ways unique. The closest contacts of the Council have so far been developed with the Swedish Secretariat for Futures Studies in Stockholm.

Ad hoc visits abroad take place within the framework of the programme of the Council. At times it is considered necessary to collect information abroad on ways in which similar policy problems, e.g. in the area of industrial innovation, labour, etc., are solved abroad. From time to time, similar groups from abroad come to visit the Council.

The Development of a Multi-Disciplinary Approach

The Council decided at an early stage in favour of a multi-disciplinary approach. In the explanatory memorandum accompanying the bill providing for the establishment of the Council it was explicitly stated that the major disciplines were to be represented in the Council. A multi-disciplinary approach was also chosen for the composition of the staff. Here too, there are advantages and disadvantages. An advantage is that a given policy can be approached from various angles, which can yield useful results; the combination of different disciplines on one and the same project has been highly stimulating in many respects. On the other hand care must be taken to prevent 'multi-disciplinary' meaning working solely outside one's original professional field.

A special problem would seem to concern the cooperation between social scientists and natural scientists. The background and way of approaching problems are vastly different. Agreements on how to proceed in a scientific manner which are taken for granted by social scientists are unknown to natural scientists and vice-versa. A great deal of openness and understanding on the part of both groups of scholars is called for in order to achieve results.

The advantages of a multi-disciplinary approach should be constantly weighed against its disadvantages. This process yields a solution whereby the advantages of both the multi-disciplinary and the uni-disciplinary approach can be fully utilized.

The Effects of the Council's Work and its Follow-Up

It is a debatable question whether the Council should pay attention to the effects and results of its work, after publication of a study. It may be argued that with the publication of a study the Council has completed its activities in that specific area and that the follow-up should be left to the government, to the public discussions within and outside parliament. Another view would be that it is the Council's responsibility to see to it that its reports receive a maximum of public attention and that, where possible, its recommendations should be put into effect.

So far, the Council has taken a position somewhat in between these two views. It takes care that its publications get the necessary publicity, by way of holding press conferences, the appearance of Council members on radio and television and through press interviews. It is also willing to give the government a reminder, if this has not reacted to its recommendations within the agreed period of three months. From time to time it also organizes conferences or public meetings at which its studies are discussed.

It has, however, been reluctant to participate in the implementation of its recommendations within the governmental machinery. It is the view of the Council that it is up to the government and the organs which control the government to decide how and to what extent its recommendations should be implemented. The task of the Council is to offer information and policy alternatives. It is the government's task to use (or not to use) that information and to choose (or not to choose) between those alternatives.

CONCLUDING OBSERVATIONS

A time period of only seven years is far too short to draw any valid, lasting conclusions. If only for that reason the following concluding observations are of a rather tentative kind. They may very soon have to be revised. Nevertheless, it may be useful to try to draw some conclusions based on this limited experience, in order to establish a foundation for comparison with similar activities, of either a theoretical or practical nature, elsewhere.

First of all, it is important to note that the idea of being active in the field of policy-relevant futures studies has been seriously challenged, from both the left and the right. During the debates in parliament on the bill of establishment in 1976, serious opponents of the proposal were to be found only on the extremes of left and right: communists and orthodox calvinists respectively, who both argued that there is little of relevance to be said about the future that is not inherently of a normative and therefore political nature. This task, they argued, should be left to the research divisions of the political parties. Their opposition constituted a minority then and has remained so ever since.

It is, incidentally, interesting to note that the political composition of the Cabinet has changed twice during the existence of the Council: the bill of establishment was introduced in parliament under the right-of-centre Cabinet of Biesheuvel; during its first term of office the council operated under the left-of-centre Cabinet of Den Uyl; since 1977 it has worked under the right-of-centre Cabinet of Van Agt. So far, these changes of Cabinet have not negatively affected the work of the Council. It has also been possible, on the whole, to persuade highly qualified individuals of different political persuasion to become members of the Council. All of this serves to illustrate how the idea of futures studies in itself, and as interpreted by the Council, has received and still receives general support in the Netherlands.

The Council has so far directed the bulk of its activities to the production of reports on substantive policy issues of a long-term nature. The reports on public administration, social inequality, the general survey of the future and the relationship between economically active and non-active persons (see pp. 97-99), earlier received most attention. Implicitly or explicitly the analysis and recommendations contained in those reports have played a role in talks with employers' organizations, trade unions, the Social-Economic Council, etc.

The Council has not yet served as a forum or meeting place for activities in the field of futures studies and forecasting. It is the intention of the Council during its second term of office to pay more attention to this function, which is at least implicitly mentioned in the bill of establishment ('...to make recommendations with respect to studies on future developments and long-term planning in both the public and the private sector...'). No decision has yet been reached on how this will be implemented. One way would be to function as a meeting place, to hold regular conferences in which the results of futures studies would be discussed. Another way would be to relate this activity much more strongly to the working programme of the Council and let it act as a permanent source of critical comment.

There can be little doubt that the existence of the Council and the publication of its reports has helped to direct attention to future problems in the political area of people who in the absence of these reports would probably not have bothered about the future. This is even more the case with individuals who have become actively involved in the work of the Council. In this respect the observations which Björn Wittrock has made for the Swedish scene are true for the Netherlands as well:

Furthermore, in connection with the Swedish Secretariat's futures studies some
ministerial observers have emphasized that for them the actual experience of participation in forecasting and futures studies activities has been more important
than reading final results and forecasts. (Björn Wittrock, 'Long-Range
Forecasting and Policy-Making — Options and Limits in Choosing a Future', in:
T. G. Whiston (ed.), *The Uses and Abuses of Forecasting* (London: Macmillans,
1979), 277.

This is certainly one of the positive aspects of a decision which
the Council took in regard to the general survey of the future during the first term of office, that has met with considerable criticism:
the decision to appoint a committee, chaired by a member of the
Council but mainly consisting of outside experts, to conduct the actual work. It is true that the Council thus transferred one of its
prime responsibilities to a group of outsiders. It formally retained
the right to adopt or reject the findings of this group, but when the
final report of the committee was completed in 1977, the Council
had little option but to adopt and publish the report (which it did,
with a brief four-page introduction). The Council has decided that
it will not follow this procedure again, but keep much tighter control over any activities in the field of futures studies and
forecasting. Outside experts will be consulted to provide specific
material and comments. What will be gained in emphasizing the
full responsibility of the Council will probably be lost in the involvement of outsiders in futures studies.

Of crucial importance for the work of the Council is its relationship with the government. The Council has succeeded in building
and maintaining a position of *independence* vis-à-vis the government. This independence manifests itself in the organization of the
working programme and in the content of its reports, which are
published free of governmental interference. Theoretically, the
government has at least three ways in which it can influence the activities of the Council:

(1) It can appoint only those members to the Council who are
sympathetic to its views; (2) it can decrease or even cut out the
Council's financial possibilities through its control of the budget;
(3) it can refuse or delay taking cognizance of the Council's
reports, which may postpone their publication indefinitely. So far,
the government has not made use of these possibilities, and it is
rather unlikely that it will do so in the future for the good reason
that both the government and the Council can only gain by stress-

ing the independence of the latter. Once it became known that the Council could do no more than express views sympathetic to those of the government in power, the impact of its reports and suggestions would soon decline. As nobody knows what the political composition of future Dutch governments will be, the ideas put forward by the Council on future developments can only be of practical use if they are not unduly influenced by present day political considerations. The government itself is fully qualified to express its political view as to what it thinks the future should look like. It should be noted in passing that this is also one of the reasons why the Council is as a rule hesitant to express itself on 'hot' political issues of the day. That would endanger it of becoming involved in day-to-day politics, which might call into question its independent position.

Fear of becoming involved in political disputes certainly contributed to the caution expressed by the Council when it concentrated the general survey of the future on 'expected' rather than 'desired' developments. This approach has been criticized by some commentators as being overcautious. For instance, it has been suggested that it may be very worth while to investigate possible future developments which are not in line with present expectations and to consider problems these developments may pose for future policymakers. In its second term of office the Council has responded to these and similar comments by taking desired developments, as projected by political parties and other social groups, as one point of departure for a second, more policy-relevant survey of the future. This should make it possible for the Council to take a more explicit position with regard to its views on the development of values and norms in society than it did during its first term of office. It may also entail the risk that the Council will not always be able to operate on the basis of consensus among its members as it did during the first term. Members may find it necessary to express dissenting views in minority reports — something that has been studiously avoided during the first term. There seems to be no reason why this should necessarily be a bad development. As nothing would seem to be certain about the future, society might well benefit if various possibly conflicting views were expressed in the Council's reports.

If the Council were to take more explicit stands on matters of values and norms, the interest of parliament in the work of the

Council might become even greater than it is today. So far, the Council has been in the position, unique among governmental advisory bodies, that it can directly consult with parliament (usually, in the presence of a representative of the Prime Minister). These consultations could become more productive if the Council were to use parliament as a sounding board to find out which desired future alternative, among many existing ones, it should further develop and investigate for its consequences. Parliament, for its part, might find it desirable to suggest problem areas for the Council to investigate. This might complicate the Council's work, but might at the same time make its activities more effective.

It is hard to judge the effects of the Council's work so far. Many of the effects of its reports may be invisible in that they indirectly influence views and options held by public officials, members of parliament, journalists, etc. Its effectiveness lies more in the drawing of attention to certain problems, in putting problems in a certain perspective, than in the solutions which are suggested to these problems. The Council might in the future pay more attention to the effects of its work, but this should never become a major activity. Nevertheless, within the context of a permanent evaluation of its own work an effort could be made to gauge the effects this work has had.

In view of the fact that the Council was explicitly not designed as a council for planning, the question has been raised at various times whether or not the Council should make explicit recommendations to the government. In the beginning of the first term of office the Council was more reluctant to do so than toward the end, when it had more clearly established its position. It has been argued by some commentators that the Council should limit itself to providing information about possible alternative developments. This is, however, a somewhat moot question. In the selection of alternatives one may well implicitly put recommendations to the government. If this is the case, an argument might also be made for making these recommendations explicit to begin with. This is indeed the position the Council has taken toward the end of the first term of office and in its second term.

Finally, this brings us again to the difficult problem of the selection of issues which remains (or ought to remain) a major bone of contention. In the end it will always remain a subjective judgement on the part of the Council as to which subjects it considers of sufficient importance to include in its programme of work. It would, however, be worthwhile to investigate to what extent objective criteria could be developed to guide the Council in this judgement. So far, little progress seems to have been in this respect.

Based on its short experience to date, it would seem that the Scientific Council on Government Policy is an interesting experiment (to say the least) for the investigation of future problems that are relevant to governmental policy. To compare this experiment with similar efforts in other countries would seem to be most useful. A more definite proof of this particular pudding would lie (where else?)... in the future.

NOTES

1. The author thanks Rien van Gendt, Theo Quené, Frank Veeneklaas, Kees Vijlbrief and Jan Volger for their critical comments on an earlier version of this article.

2. This section is based on participant observation, part of which has been published in: Netherlands Scientific Council for Government Policy, *Report on the First Term of Office, 1972-1977*. An earlier survey of activities is found in: Rien van Gendt, 'The Scientific Council for Government Policy: Indirect Advising on the Central Level', *Planning and Development in the Netherlands* VIII: 1 (1976), 34-43.

3. *Facing the Future: Mastering the Probable and Managing the Unpredictable*, Paris: Organization for Economic Co-operation and Development, 1979.

6 Futures Studies Without a Planning Subject: The Swedish Secretariat for Futures Studies

Björn Wittrock
University of Stockholm

POLICY ANALYSIS, FUTURES STUDIES AND PLANNING

In the 1960s and 70s policy-makers in Western Europe and North America increasingly emphasized the need to bring systematic knowledge and analysis to bear upon the formulation, planning and implementation of programmes and policies in all fields of policy-making. At an organizational level this was seen in the creation of bodies specializing in analysis, evaluation and forecasting attached to governmental offices and agencies. This development was tangible in most OECD (Organization for Economic Cooperation and Development) member countries. Thus, in the United States such bodies were established in all major departments and agencies in the 1960s (Allison 1980: 237-42). In Western Germany a special planning department was set up within the Federal Chancellor's Office. In the UK a Central Policy Review Staff was established in 1971 under the supervision of the Prime Minister to

Author's note: The study presented in this chapter has been supported financially by the Bank of Sweden Tercentenary Fund. The final text was written during my time as a Research Associate of the Center for Studies in Higher Education, University of California, Berkeley in the Fall Quarter of 1979. For comments on an earlier draft of the test I am particularly indebted to Professors Peter R. Baehr and Andries Hoogerwerf, and to Dr. Robert Hoppe.

render advice, independently of government departments, to ministers and to analyse basic implications of policy alternatives and decisions (Berrill 1977: 121-26; Rothschild 1977: 111-19). In the Netherlands the so-called De Wolff Commission worked out a proposal for the organization of a scientific basis for a more integrated long-term government policy, eventually in 1972 resulting in the creation of the Scientific Council for Government Policy (Gendt 1976: 34-43; Baehr 1981). In Sweden new bodies for policy analysis, advice and forecasting were gradually introduced into the government offices from the mid-1960s, initially in the fields of national physical planning, regional development, defence planning and economic forecasting. In the early and mid 1970s delegations and expert groups came to be attached to most ministries to help achieve a closer connection between, on the one hand, current research and policy analysis and, on the other, actual policy-making in the given fields of responsibility.

This development is related to a redefinition of the role of science policy within the OECD area leading to an increased stress on mechanisms to ensure the utilization and direction of scientific activities towards the fulfilment of social and in a wide sense political objectives. However, it is also related to the emergence of special, more or less formalized, techniques of analysis and planning. One such important technique was, of course, PPBS (Planning-Programming-Budgeting System), introduced first in the US Department of Defense in the early 1960s and from 1965 and onwards also in other parts of the executive. PPBS shares with other techniques such as cost-benefit analysis, systems analysis and econometric modelling a basic reliance on the validity and applicability of elements of economic theory to the whole range of policy-making (Allison 1980: 237-60).

A systematic analysis of policies is part of the process of preparing and planning policies to be carried out. But what kind of measures policy-makers undertake will vary considerably between different sectors of society even in a given country, e.g. between the planning objects of major weapons systems in defence planning and composition and pricing of products of various branches of industry respectively. Thus, the degree of control exercised over planning objects by policy-makers will vary. But then an increased emphasis on the importance of systematic analysis and preparation of policies will entail a shift away from any narrow conception of planning as merely the specification of a detailed planning document and towards a generic concept of planning. Such a generic interpretation of the concept of planning is clearly brought out in a number of official Swedish reports and documents during the 1970s. The primary function of long-range planning emphasized in these documents is not the listing of a long sequence of decisions to be carried out at a definite point in time. Long-range planning is rather seen to involve the systematic preparation of decisions that may have long-term consequences, and the aim of this activity is not the specification of future commitments but to guarantee that policy-makers will in the future have as wide a range of options open as possible (Ministry of Defence 1969; Ministry of Finance 1974: 42-45; SAFAD 1974: 7; Government Commission 1975: 274-75; SAFAD 1977: 12-13; Government Commission 1977: 123-24). This latter concept of planning seems furthermore to be well in line with the delimitations proposed in theoretical planning literature by authors such as Yehezkel Dror and Erich Jantsch (Jantsch 1969: 471-91; Dror 1971: 69).

The late 1960s witnessed the posing of fairly fundamental questions concerning the long-range prospects of highly industrialized and technology-dependent societies. An interest of this sort was, for example, manifested in concern about the human environment, in OECD's reassessment of relationships among science, economic growth and society and demand for an orientation towards so-called qualitative aspects of growth, and in efforts to undertake systematic studies of sequences of events stretching far into the future.

The growing interest in long-range forecasting and futures studies during the late 1960s was a consequence both of the emergence of new techniques of policy analysis and planning — in most countries originally mainly in connection with defence and military planning — and of a widely felt concern about long-term human prospects. Futures studies can be characterized by the general ambition to aid decision-making by yielding information of relevance in a long-range perspective (Boucher 1977: 6-9). Thus, futures studies cannot be narrowly associated with some specific technique of analysis but should rather be considered a generic concept encompassing a series of activities within a broad approach. Even so futures studies present a number of distinguishing features and problems. Generally speaking, the task of futures studies to provide information relevant in a very long-range perspective makes many problems familiar from various forms of policy analysis and planning more pronounced and demanding.

In the following, Swedish experiences of futures studies in government will be examined. The empirical material for this study is derived from an analysis of official documents, internal memoranda, interviews with members of the Swedish Secretariat for Futures Studies, its project groups, and interministerial reference groups as well as with politicians, and from experiences of participation in seminars and meetings of the Secretariat in the years 1974-79. Results from this empirical study will then be related to dilemmas of comprehensive planning. First, however, important characteristics and problems of futures studies will be discerned along the following dimensions (see Schwarz 1977a: 115-27; Schwarz 1977b: 25-35; Schwarz, Svedin and Wittrock 1981; Wittrock 1977: 351-57; Wittrock 1979: 267-88).

1. *Time horizon*. The time horizon of futures studies is sometimes indicated with reference to some time span such as 'from five to fifty years and sometimes even longer' or the time period 'beyond the next two or three decades'. However, it is not the time horizon as such which is the distinguishing feature of futures studies, it is more the emphasis which is put on how things vary in time. The time horizon chosen is often so distant that a number of different 'futures' are possible, the alternative that emerges being dependent on the decisions made today. In connection with Swedish futures studies it has been stated that the studies should be oriented towards a time horizon defined by 'the relative lack of major commitments so that consideration can be given to qualitative changes'. This latter notion obviously implies a policy-making and action orientation.

2. *The problems* which the futurists treat tend to have an open-ended character in at least three respects: (i) the problems often do not fall directly within the area of responsibility of any existing administrative or policy-making unit but cut across sectoral boundaries, and this in a more fuzzy way the more distant the time horizon. (ii) An interdisciplinary approach is often recommended in connection with complex real-world problems. For emerging problems of the future the need to draw upon competence from a number of different disciplines, or in fact to utilize any kind of knowledge which can be brought to bear on the problem becomes

more pronounced. (iii) The problem formulation itself may constitute a major part of the analysis and definite solutions often cannot be expected, i.e. futures problems are wicked problems if we use the Rittel-Webber distinction between tame and wicked problems (Rittel and Webber 1973). Otherwise expressed, in the case of several important fields of interest to futures studies well-established scientific theories are simply lacking. Our knowledge is partial and will have to remain partial although improvements can be made.

3. *Uncertainties and discontinuities*. Uncertainties are common both in everyday life and in many problems and processes empirically studied. However, most often we know what variable we are interested in, i.e. the dimension, and we may also know something of the probability distribution if it can be considered as a statistical phenomenon. Usually the term 'risk' is used when we know the probability distribution but not the outcome. The situation when the dimension but not the probability distribution is known is sometimes termed 'pure uncertainty' (Dror 1971: 64; Strangert 1977: 147-65). In a long-term perspective several of the assumptions underlying short- and medium-term forecasting may be drastically different and new variables may gain importance. We are thus sometimes faced with 'primary uncertainty', that is the condition of uncertainty when the dimensions of possible results are unknown. Pure uncertainty and primary uncertainty seem to pose the challenge of proceeding 'with the identification of discontinuous changes and innovations' (Shani 1974: 643). Some authors claim this kind of identification to be a main element of futures studies. In this context it may be illuminating to recall that one of the origins of what nowadays is termed 'futures studies' was the development of the Delphi technique for interviewing experts about possible future technological breakthroughs and their probable occurrence in time.

4. *Criterion of adequacy*. The future is uncertain both because of our limited knowledge of the world in general and because the future will emerge as a result of decisions not yet made. Futures studies, therefore, do not aim primarily at producing predictions of future events but at giving an overall picture which is relevant for the problem at hand. Hence, futures studies often deal with the design of alternative futures. The given picture of the future has to be adequate in the sense that it permits the identification of

'thresholds which would dictate that qualitatively different allocation of resources should be made' (Cole 1976: 310).

5. *The role of theory*. It has already been noted that futures
studies often cannot rely on established theories defining relevant
sets of causal relations. This, however, should not be taken to imply that futures studies are inherently atheoretical using some sort of
'naive' forecasting methodology (Edman 1976). But the
hypothetical nature of many of the relationships and sequences
dealt with in futures studies seems to make futurists feel more free
in the choice of theoretical assumptions than traditionally appears
to be the case among most social scientists. Futures studies may
then encompass an effort not only to use but also to reconstruct
theories and theoretical assumptions. In this way futures studies
may have an effect on the development of theories within various
disciplines.

6. *Techniques of analysis*. It is sometimes suggested that futures
studies involve the use of so-called intuitive forecasting techniques
in contradistinction to more formal and rigorous ones. Examples of
such intuitive techniques are scenario construction, Delphi techniques, brainstorming and morphology. However, the utilization of
intuitive techniques does not necessarily exclude the use of formal
or quantitative techniques within the context of the same study. On
the contrary, some of the more interesting experiences, at least
from Swedish futures studies, relate to the combination of, e.g.
formal econometric modelling and scenario writing. Moreover,
general approaches such as systems analysis and policy analysis
often associated with futures studies incorporate or are consistent
with a series of both intuitive and more rigorous techniques of
analysis.

7. *Proximity to application of results*. The proximity to application of the results of futures studies may vary considerably. In
Sweden the Alva Myrdal commission on futures studies made a
distinction between three categories which can be defined as
follows: (i) studies that may serve fairly directly as inputs into existing public planning and decision-making; (ii) oriented basic
research actually or potentially having an indirect importance for
the amelioration of existing planning and decision-making processes; and (iii) so-called autonomous futures studies that should
neither directly nor indirectly be guided by the requirements of existing governmental bodies.

8. *Linkage to planning processes.* Hence, futures studies may be oriented more or less closely to planning and decision-making processes. Planning is sometimes described as a process involving the preparation of a set of decisions such that a 'system' or 'planning object' can be adapted to its 'environment' in a way that is consistent with prevalent goals and values (see e.g. Ingelstam 1977: 127-45). From this description it follows that planning needs to be based on information about the future development of the environment of the planning object. Studies of such developments of a long-range nature can be considered as a form of futures studies. In this case the role of futures studies is to yield direct inputs into the planning process.

However, long-range planning sometimes involves the design of alternative futures of the planning object itself. When this is the case planning itself can be considered as a form of futures studies. There is thus no clear borderline between planning and futures studies. However, Shani (1974) has developed a conceptual framework aimed at sufficiently distinguishing between planning and futures studies to make an exploration of their interrelationship worthwhile (Shani 1974). As far as organizational matters are concerned, Shani argues that futures studies 'should be liberated from ways of thinking conditioned by existing organizational patterns. Thus while in planning reference to the future world would inevitably have to be from the organization outwards, in futures studies the orientation would be from the environment to the organization'. Needless to say, these orientations refer primarily to shifts in emphasis; any realistic process of planning or futures studies will have to consider the interplay between environment and organization from both perspectives.

9. *Values, goals and norms.* It is often said that in futures studies values and norms should be explicitly stated. One aspect of this is related to the idea that futures studies directly or indirectly should influence planning and policy-making. However, given the complexity of planning processes and the changeability of values and goals over time, the role of values in futures studies cannot be an unambiguous one. It is sometimes argued that the generation of alternative futures from widely different value-premises may lead to insights into the range of real uncertainty (Cole 1976: 314; Clark and Cole 1975: 114). Experiences from the Swedish studies treated below indicate, however, that the nature of more precise relation-

ships between value dimensions and actual activities of futures studies is far from clear. This is so even if attention is restricted to some specific version of, say, scenario writing. Hence, some set of values and norms may have to be considered in each scenario. There may also be a condition to the effect that certain values will have to be satisfied in each scenario presented. Furthermore, the changing nature of values and norms can be included as an element of scenarios. Finally, an important function of ambiguous values and norms can be to initiate a discussion process in a group of forecasters or futurists (see Wittrock 1979: 271).

FUTURES STUDIES AND POLICY PLANNING IN SWEDEN

Origins and Objectives of Swedish Futures Studies

Against the background of the establishment in several countries of bodies within the central government with the task of performing cross-sectoral and long-range oriented policy analysis and futures studies the emerging interest in futures studies in Sweden should not be surprising. Already in the early and mid-1960s professional competence in the field of futures studies was being created within the Swedish National Defence Research Institute. This development was partly stimulated through contacts with American institutes and think tanks specializing in systems analysis, e.g. Rand Corporation. In the late 1960s the Academy of Engineering Sciences, an institution with close links to Swedish industry, worked out a proposal for the setting-up of an independent institute for futures research to be supported jointly by the state and a foundation of private industry. This proposal was favourably treated in initiatives by some liberal members of parliament. However, it also met with considerable opposition from spokesmen of the trade unions and the Social Democratic Party and it did not lead to government action. But it served as one input into the discussions on futures studies within the Government Research Advisory Board from 1969 onwards. These discussions focussed on the potentials of futures studies as an instrument to promote a more coherent and long-range oriented research policy and research planning. Futures studies were also seen as desirable as a means for the creation of an improved basis for a more coordinated policy planning, particularly by outlining long-term developments of the environment of planning objects and by tracing interactions between different policy areas. Another promiment element in these discussions was concern for the human environment and for environmental research and policy, a theme of many deliberations of the Board and its chairman, Prime Minister Erlander, in the 1960s. Pending the 1972 Stockholm UN conference on the human environment and the results of the global modelling projects of the Club of Rome the need to strengthen domestic competence to interpret these developments was felt.

As a result of these discussions a governmental commission was set up in June 1971, at the initiative of Olof Palme, the then Prime Minister, to review the field of futures studies. A salient motive was a perceived need to elaborate a conception of futures studies that was opposed to the one underlying 'most futures studies produced so far... sponsored by military establishments and by the world's major multinational corporations' — to quote Alva Myrdal, chairman of the commission and then a member of the Cabinet. It was feared that such 'studies may be based on scales of values that are not democratically acceptable. We must avoid any "colonizing of the future" by powerful interest groups, national or international'.

Originally, the tasks of the Alva Myrdal commission were supposed to be confined mainly to problems of research and methodology in futures studies and to a survey of potential fields of study for Swedish contributions against the background of national needs and the international state of the art of futures studies. Aspects of immediate relevance to government policy and to the coordination of public long-range planning had earlier been assigned to an informal governmental working party directed by the Prime Minister's Office. However, one year after its inception in June 1970 this working party was, for all practical purposes, defunct, and the mandate of the Alva Mydral commission widened correspondingly. In August 1972 the Alva Mydral commission submitted the results of its work in the form of a report, 'To Choose a Future'. Some main value dimensions to be discerned in this report are:

— the opposition to any form of technological determinism and the focus on degrees of freedom of conscious action and choice in the long run;

— the idea of a need for public participation and involvement in the work of futures studies;

— a sense of international obligation or solidarity; futures studies should not be oriented in such a way that they 'are liable to come into conflict with legitimate aspirations among the majority of people in a developing country'.

The Secretariat for Futures Studies: Organization and Operation

In the report of the Alva Myrdal commission, *To Choose a Future*, a typology of futures studies was elaborated under two main headings.

A. Proximity to application of the results of studies, where a distinction was made between the following three categories: (1) studies that may serve directly as planning inputs and as a basis for long-term planning; (2) oriented basic research having at least a potential effect for the amelioration of planning and decision-making; and (3) so-called autonomous futures studies that should neither directly nor indirectly be guided by the requirements of existing governmental planning and decision-making bodies.

B. A hierarchy of the levels of aggregation at which society is being studied, ranging from a global to an individual level, and where the levels can be used in the classification both of bodies utilizing results of futures studies and of social phenomena being studied.

Studies of the category (A1) were considered futures studies proper, and the commission recommended the establishment of a Secretariat for Futures Studies to consider the initiation and organization of such studies. This proposal was accepted and early in 1973 a Secretariat was set up, attached to the Prime Minister's Office. Given the Secretariat's orientation towards comprehensive issues not neatly falling within well-defined ministerial boundaries, this meant that in a sense it was situated at the crossroads of different organizational units within the central executive.

In June 1974 a parliamentary reference group, composed of members of all parties in parliament, was set up establishing a direct relationship between the Secretariat and parliament. In May

1975 parliament decided, following proposals from the conservative, liberal and center parties, that this reference group should be given the status of an Executive Committee and that the Secretariat should be separated from the Prime Minister's Office. In October 1975 this change was brought into effect and the Secretariat was, in administrative and budgetary terms, transferred to the Ministry of Education.

The importance of this change for the actual ongoing work of the Secretariat should not be exaggerated. However, it restricted the potentials of the Secretariat serving as an effective agent improving the basis for cross-ministerial and long-range planning in the government offices. The Secretariat nevertheless remained a body within the central government system, working in a highly open fashion and having current and close contacts in both ministerial and parliamentary quarters. Recently, a governmental commission, stressing the importance of the Secretariat's having relationships both with the government offices and governmental commissions and with parliament, has proposed that the current organization of official Swedish futures studies should be retained.

However, in a Bill submitted by the liberal government in February 1979 and passed by a parliamentary majority in May, it was suggested that gradually — within one year — studies of type (A1) and (A2) should be performed within the same organizational framework: the Swedish Council for Coordination and Planning of Research. It was argued that such a change would provide a further guarantee of the autonomous position of the Secretariat. Furthermore, scholarly competence in the fields of futures studies, long-range oriented basic research and applied systems analysis would then be kept within a common administrative framework.

A main task of the Secretariat for Futures Studies has been to initiate, coordinate and support project groups reviewing long-range trends and tendencies in central areas of policy-making and planning and outlining alternative courses of development and action. The Secretariat has, of course, also an important role to play in work relating to the presentation and utilization of project results. In addition to this, the Secretariat was intended to be a source of knowledge and service to the government offices and to governmental commissions in the fields of futures studies and technology assessment. The Secretariat, furthermore, maintains an extensive system of contacts outside governmental bodies in an effort to stimulate a general public debate on future oriented issues, and most reports from the Secretariat are characterized by an ambition to present results that are both reliably documented and intelligible to non-specialists. This has probably contributed to the amount of attention devoted to many of the reports in the press and other mass media.

Four project groups, composed of both academic scholars and administrative professionals, were set up in 1974-75. The themes of the projects — Energy and Society, Resources and Raw Materials, Sweden in World Society and Working Life in the Future — were selected through a process that involved both discussions with representatives of different ministries and an analysis of the comments from some 130 governmental agencies and non-governmental organizations on the report *To Choose a Future.*

This first generation of project groups finished their work in late 1977 or early 1978. New projects are now underway, dealing with the following themes: Care in Society, Sweden in a New International Economic Order, The Vulnerable Society — focussing on the interaction of complex technical systems and problems of social and individual trust — and Forecasting and Political Futures Planning.

A project group normally consists of four-six full-time members but well over twenty persons may contribute to reports in an expert capacity and on a part-time basis. The groups enjoy an independent status from the government, but each of them has an inter-ministerial reference group, headed by an Under-Secretary of State, continuously following and commenting upon its work. Although both plans and reports can be discussed at the meetings of reference and project groups, it is not the task of the inter-ministerial group to approve project reports for publication. So far, project groups and the Secretariat have issued more than 60 reports and half a dozen full-scale books, a number of which are also available in English. The Secretariat's futures studies activities are financed over the government budget, the sum for the year 1979/80 being 4.0 million Swedish crowns.

From the outset discussions on futures studies in Sweden were characterized by a certain ambiguity. Futures studies were perceived as a set of activities performed in a fuzzy region comprising processes linked directly to public policy planning but also stretching well into the domains of university research. The Alva Myrdal commission had proposed a conceptual and organizational distinction between the research oriented and the political and planning oriented functions. This proposal was, as mentioned, accepted and implied that futures studies proper were seen as providing inputs into planning processes in the public sector. The responsibility for initiating such studies was entrusted to the Secretariat for Futures Studies. Undoubtedly, this conception was influenced by experiences from Swedish defence planning where an elaborate system linking futures studies and long- and medium-range planning had been established in the late 1960s and early 1970s.

In this sector the activities being planned — the planning object — were delimited, and a set of decision-makers — a planning subject — was clearly defined, at least in formal terms. In many other sectors the situation was certainly different. And in contrast to, e.g. France or the Netherlands, there was no strong domestic tradition in terms of existing policy-planning bodies entrusted with the handling of problems of cross-sectoral long-range forecasting. Hence, the planning functions of futures studies did not emerge as an extension of the activities of established units for cross-sectoral planning. Rather it was seen, at least by the Alva Myrdal commission, as a method of facilitating some form of coordination of sectoral planning. But what planning subject was there to utilize the results of futures studies as inputs into comprehensive and long-range planning?

The administrative apparatus of the Prime Minister — the Prime Minister's Office — was small in numbers and although its coordinating functions were graudally strengthened during the last years of the social democratic government, it could not be regarded as a body performing a long-term, cross-ministerial planning function (Larsson 1978).

Although powers of decision are constitutionally vested in the government collectively, the authority and position of a Cabinet member heading some ministry are undoubtedly strong. The ministries, constituting the government offices, are fairly small bodies; the total number of ministries now being fourteen, each with a staff in the region of 50-200 people, all categories included. This small size facilitates close contacts and efficient cooperation in the handling of the large number of issues and policy matters that have to be dealt with in the ministries. It also, however, necessitates an orientation towards the processing of policy matters of a mainly short- or medium-term nature on which action has to be taken. The outlook of the Swedish central civil service in the early 1970s can best be described in terms of attitudes of pragmatism and piecemeal social engineeirng, with some exceptions among younger civil servants with an educational background in social science (Mellbourn 1979).

True enough, ideas of planning began by the mid-1960s to permeate the Swedish central administration. Thus, the concepts of planning and coordination were focal to the 1965 reform of the government offices. New forms of cross-sectoral or 'facet' planning were also emerging in those years, e.g. in the fields of regional development (from 1964) and national physical planning (from 1966/67 onwards). The capabilities of economic planning were also strengthened. An Economic Planning Council, with representatives of the government, the labour market organizations, private industry and university scholars, was set up in 1962. It had purely advisory functions. In the following year work on mid-term economic surveys was entrusted to a permanent unit within the Ministry of Finance (today within the Ministry for Economic Affairs), that was also to serve as a secretariat to the Economic Planning Council.

But despite this development budgetary procedures of a short- and, to a certain extent, medium-range nature have remained the main instruments of planning and coordination. The introduction of futures studies directly related to the Prime Minister's Office and with a potential impact on long-range planning were viewed with mixed feelings in some quarters of the Ministry of Finance. However, except for a few members of the Cabinet this potential was not appreciated in the Cabinet or the Prime Minister's Office. Rather the older conception of futures studies as an element of research and research policy lingered on. Some of the main problems and characteristics of the operation of Swedish futures studies in the central executive will be illustrated in the following section by examining a futures study project on energy and society.

It is interesting to note that significant features of the new enthusiasm for planning in the 1960s and 1970s were distinct from those of the international — and Swedish — debate of the 1940s about a 'planned or free economy' (Friedmann and Hudson 1974: 2-16). Both roots and implications differed. The new ideas of long-range planning had grown out of the traditions of military and corporate systems analysis. Long-range planning in this new sense did not necessarily entail central control of a set of decisions to be taken and implemented in a linear sequential fashion over a long period of time. In the new conception of long-range planning, however, the key phrase was freedom of action; long-range planning was seen as a matter of preparing future decisions in such a way as to avoid an unnecessary narrowing of the range of available options.

A Futures Studies Project in a Turbulent Environment

The long lead times in the introduction of new technical systems make energy policy a natural area for the evolution of a forecasting tradition, primarily in connection with electrical energy. In the Swedish administrative and planning system energy forecasting has been performed by several public bodies; the Energy Forecasting Commission sketching out alternatives for the periods 1975-85 and 1985-2000, the Delegation for Energy Research up to the year 2000, the State Industry Board and the Central Dispatching Board, an organization for cooperation between major electricity producers, private and public. At the ministerial level the main responsibility for the translation of these forecasts into policy planning has been with the Ministry of Industry. By and large, contacts between energy forecasters and planners in different bodies and commissions were well developed.

The oil crisis of 1973-74 dramatically illustrated the fact that the present energy supply of most industrialized countries is mainly based on fossil fuels. In Sweden oil accounts for some 70 percent of total energy consumption. Expectations that within the foreseeable future a stagnation and decline in the production of oil and natural gas will occur inevitably brings forth considerations of possible substitutes. In the Swedish case it has generally been argued that such substitutes should involve the use of domestic energy sources as far as is feasible. Thus, it was not surprising when in the spring of 1974 the then newly set up Energy Policy Delegation (a coordinating body of Under-Secretaries of State that was later dissolved) and the Secretariat for Futures Studies jointly launched a project on future options in energy policy. The idea was that the futures study project on Energy and Society should trace longer-term consequences than was customary in the forecasts produced by bodies such as the Energy Forecasting Commission, the State Industry Board or the Central Dispatching Board. It should be noted that the initiation of this futures study coincided in time with the erosion of the non-partisan character of energy policy in political terms. Up to 1973 parliamentary decisions on, e.g. nuclear power had not been preceded by divergent opinions between political parties. From 1973 onwards energy policy in general, and the safety and environmental problems of nuclear power in particular, became a major issue on the political agenda. It was of crucial importance for the outcome of the 1976 general election and for the break-up of the ensuing three-party coalition in October 1978 (Petersson 1977; Holmberg, Westerståhl and Branzén 1977; Petersson 1979; Vedung 1979). Following the Three Mile Island accident, the Swedish parliament decided that — contrary both to earlier plans and to a government Bill already submitted — no major decision on the future of nuclear power in Sweden should be taken in 1979. Instead the issue should be made the object of a formally advisory referendum in the spring of 1980, this being the fourth occasion for a Swedish referendum this century.

A starting point for much of the discussion on energy policy and also for the work of the project group on Energy and Society was the assumption, already mentioned, that it is not possible to combine a continued growth in energy consumption with a continued basic reliance on fossil fuels. It might then seem natural to start out with an investigation of the determining factors and characteristics of various levels of energy consumption. This was essentially the strategy chosen by the energy policy project of the Ford Foundation. In 'A Time to Choose' three main development alternatives were discerned; historical growth, technical fix and zero-energy growth involving respectively 3.5 percent, 2 percent, and (from 1990) 0 percent annual growth in energy consumption. Within each of the these alternatives it was possible to examine effects on economic development, employment, capital needs, environmental problems, and on the orientation of production (different types of goods and services).

Originally the Swedish study adopted a similar approach, although with a slightly different set of characteristics to be analysed, e.g. effects on working environment, income distribution and the developing countries. However, the group gradually came to look upon energy problems in terms of the transition over time of combinations of energy technologies, based on different energy sources, rather than in terms of physical scarcity of energy resources or distinct levels of energy consumption. Discussions within the group that were instrumental in bringing about this conceptual change were related to the widening of the project group so as to include a nuclear physicist, a systems analyst and an economist. But the general conception that the basic problem of energy policy is how to manage a transition from dependence on oil and natural gas towards less scarce — but perhaps more costly — resources is open to many analytically different interpretations.

The economist William D. Nordhaus's article 'The Allocation of Energy Resources' might serve as one exemplar (Nordhaus 1973). Nordhaus has sketched out a schema for the allocation of energy resources for a series of phases starting with five ten-year periods, followed by two 25-year periods and two 50-year periods. The final stage involves the transition to breeder technology, gradually introduced from 2020 and by 2120 having completely replaced fossil fuels and other energy sources. Transitions over time in the utilization of energy technologies are estimated where the discounted costs of meeting a set of demands are minimized; the main driving forces in this analysis are the costs of production.

The formulation of the transition conception of the Energy and Society project was a different one. The group argues that there are essentially three kinds of long-term energy sources, viz. coal, uranium and renewable energy sources. Coal, like oil, fails to fulfil the requirement of being a domestic Swedish source. Furthermore, it shares with oil a number of negative consequences as far as environmental aspects are concerned. The introduction of energy technologies based upon different energy sources is in the conception of the Energy and Society group not so much a matter of adaptation to changing costs of production. These are seen as highly dependent upon technical and organizational systems that are open to change through acts of political will. These different interpretations of the problem of transition indicate that fairly fundamental ideas of the nature of society and of man's place in society — e.g. concerning the potentials of consciously bringing about changes in given states of affairs — are relevant for the theoretical assumptions that underlie forecasting activities.

To clarify the range of options open in a long-term perspective the group outlined two extreme alternatives (Lönnroth, Johansson and Steen 1980; Johansson and Steen 1978). In one of these fossil and nuclear fuels had in a future been entirely replaced by renewable solar energy sources. In the other one nuclear energy, involving the introduction of fast breeder reactors, accounted for more than 80 percent of total energy supply. (The remaining share came from hydro power and bark and lye in the same proportion as today.)

It was then necessary to examine whether these two scenarios were at all feasible: A starting point for the sketching out of the two extreme alternatives, is the specification of a set of conditions that are common to both, viz. the following: *time perspective* (2015), *population* of Sweden (same as today), *number of dwellings* (increase by 40 percent from 1975, with a slightly larger increase in space per dwelling), *production of goods and services* (increase by 100 percent from 1975 till 2015), *specific energy consumption* (a decrease from 1975 till 2015 by 20 percent in industry, 50 percent in the services and transport sector, and by 30 percent in dwellings).

The feasibility of the two extreme alternatives in the face of these conditions is then examined with respect to the following dimensions: technology, economy, siting and land-use planning, branch structure in the energy sector, capital market for the energy sector and professional groups in the energy sector. The overall conclusion is that even with fairly conservative assumptions about costs and available technologies it is not possible to state now that either of the extreme options is an infeasible one. Both seem able to satisfy the set of conditions specified at the outset. This, however, certainly does not preclude that they may later appear to be undesirable or impracticable.

To retain freedom of action the problem is then to formulate short- and medium-term policies of such a nature that none of the extreme alternatives, or any mixed alternative, is foreclosed. To achieve this it seems necessary to clarify those mechanisms that determine the choice of energy system. Without such an idea there is obviously a risk that future options are being foreclosed unintentionally.

A major conclusion of the study is that the set of feasible options is largely decided by (1) the amount and quality of energy used, (2) the existence of large, complex systems of energy production (e.g. the nuclear fuel cycle) and energy distribution, and

(3) organizational inertia; the orientation of research and of the given administrative apparatus, rules and policies that are adapted to already operating technologies and that have an effect on the competitiveness of different technologies, e.g. via rules of the capital market. According to the group active measures are necessary in a short- and medium-term perspective if there is to be a balance between the uranium (involving the introduction of fast breeder reactors) and the renewable option. Such measures pertain not only to research and development work but also to amounts and qualities of energy being used and to characteristics of energy transmission and distribution systems (e.g. the degree of centralization of the distribution system, the choice of heating systems based on electricity or water).

Thus, the generating mechanisms that have been singled out are technological and organizational rather than, say, economic or political. International economic dependencies and domestic economic constraints are not seen as factors that preclude any of the options. The energy system in a wide sense — including not only energy production, but also distribution systems and consumption patterns — is in the last instance seen as a system that is manageable by public measures.

In a turbulent environment where energy policy and nuclear power policy in particular, as previously mentioned, has been a major political conflict issue the group has advocated a short- and medium-term policy of non-commitment and non-foreclosing in relation to all major long-range energy policy options. This has permitted the project leader to be intimately allied to the chairman of the project's reference group, an energy policy advisor to the former social democratic government, and another member of the project group to serve as policy advisor to the energy minister of the ensuing three-party coalition. The professional role conception can perhaps be expressed as follows: Advocacy for non-commitment, where non-commitment was interpreted as entailing an active state policy to ensure a balance between the nuclear and the solar alternatives. In a situation where political actors at large either did not share the passion for non-commitment or — if they did — did not see this as entailing the consequences for short-term policy advocated by the group, there is little doubt that the platform of advocacy for non-commitment could not but be a problematic one.

The analysis of the project group had obvious policy implications of a short- and medium-range nature that were heterodox
from the point of view of policy planners and administrators in the
government offices and in the State Power Board. In spite of this
the views of the project group have received widespread attention
in the public debate. The group also succeeded in transferring some
key elements of its analysis to bodies performing a review of the
field of long-term options and limits in the choice of energy
systems, mainly the Energy Commission. This politically broadly
composed commission was set up in December 1976 to review the
entire field of energy policy and to lay the foundations for a major
parliamentary decision on a medium-term energy policy. The
publication of its main report late in the spring of 1978 coincided
with that of the final report of the Energy and Society project.

However, both in the case of this commission — where individual members of the futures study project were active in an expert capacity — and in the case of positions taken by various politicians and groupings, the utilization of results from the futures
study has been selective and scattered. Certain findings, illustrations and key concepts have been taken over. The insistence of the
project group on the necessity of having a firm grasp of the driving
forces and basic generating mechanisms behind the emergence of
energy systems has, with a few exceptions, not been appreciated.
The change in the policy-making environment of energy policy
from one of closure to one of redefinition and turbulence —
though with current signs of efforts to produce a re-closure of the
field — was probably a condition for any impact at all of an un-
conventional analysis of the type performed by the Energy and
Society project. Indeed, in a different situation the study might not
even have got off the ground in the first place. Actually, there was
some initial resistance in the Ministry of Industry to the idea of
having a futures study project dealing with the energy issue.

The important point is that policy innovation might be seen as
akin to dispositional concepts. Potentials must be present in the
form of an innovating body such as the Swedish Secretariat or its
project groups. Heterodox proposals produced by such a unit will,
however, have no real impact unless certain external conditions
release these potentials. Situations characterized by redefinition,
erosion of closure and of turbulence might well constitute such external conditions.

DILEMMAS OF COMPREHENSIVE PLANNING

The role of futures studies and policy analysis in central executives is intimately linked to that of integrated or comprehensive planning. In the Netherlands the De Wolff commission discerned the need for planning that aimed at some form of synthesis of different forms of sectoral and cross-sectoral so-called facet planning. This formed one of the motives for the establishment of the Scientific Council for Government Policy (Gendt 1976; Baehr 1980). In Sweden the Alva Myrdal commission perceived the want of futures studies as a basis for long-range planning intended to coordinate sectoral planning activities. However, both Swedish experiences and others reported in the literature indicate that any effort at comprehensive planning will come up against a formidable array of difficulties. Some of these can be briefly outlined (cf. Gideonse 1972: 64-70; Gideonse 1976: 21-33; Gray 1977-78: 177-94; Mayntz and Scharpf 1975: Chap. VII; Wenk 1979; Whiston 1979).

The Problem of Psychological Time Frames

The constant stream of policy matters requiring more or less immediate action is a powerful incentive to the formation of a short-range time horizon among policy-makers in central executives. To this normal time-urgency, concerns about the demands of electoral cycles should be added. Under these conditions, the risk is only too obvious that comprehensive reviews of a long-range nature appear as an esoteric and superfluous luxury. These limitations of time horizons will contribute to a further problem:

The Problem of Utilization

Comprehensive planning will, like futures studies, involve participants from different quarters in activities of cross-sectoral overviews. Possibly, the main outcomes of such activities are not well-formulated policy documents and final reports but rather experience gained of actual participation in these activities. The primary effects of the activities should then be interpreted in terms of success in reshaping deeply rooted sectoral paradigms of problem-definition and problem-solving. Undoubtedly, such a process will require participants to see themselves as more than mere guardians of the interests of their respective ministries and departments. This might put a strain on loyalties and would be time-consuming. In the case of Swedish futures studies there were initially a number of unrealistic expectations on the part of members of inter-ministerial reference groups as to the capability of project groups to supply them with the answers to specific and short-range policy problems dealt with by individual ministries.

The Problem of Immunization

Any effort at truly comprehensive policy preparation of a long-range nature will depend upon some degree of cooperation and information supply from regular ministerial and agency personnel charged with the handling of some policy area. However, comprehensive planning must not be allowed to be unduly influenced by any one department or viewpoint (cf. Mayntz and Scharp 1975: 118-19). How can this be achieved? Some authors argue that the problem cannot be solved unless strong top-level support for comprehensive planning activities is forthcoming (cf. Mayntz and Scharpf 1975: 118-19; Scharpf 1973: 87). If this is so, then it seems to justify locating such activities in the immediate neighbourhood of the Prime Minister. Needless to say, location itself is no sufficient condition for a viable combination of immunization and cooperation.

Futures studies intended to produce inputs into processes of comprehensive planning pose similar problems. In the case of the Swedish Secretariat's futures studies the effects of a pattern of regular cooperation with a formal advisory group of civil servants and policy-makers seem to be twofold. First, it tends to create favourable conditions for a gradually increasing appreciation, trust and acceptance of the given forecasting activities. It is clear that the Swedish group studying resources and raw materials, e.g., came to be very generally accepted by the interests represented in the inter-ministerial reference group. Second, the existence of a formal group regularly commenting upon the work of forecasters cannot but indirectly influence the general perspective of forecasters. The number and precise composition of advisory bodies in terms of, e.g. policy, time, and, possibly, research orientation, will then be a significant matter, not least in the handling of relations between short-, medium- and long-term forecasting.

One of the Swedish project groups, that on Energy and Society, tried to impose a partial immunization upon themselves by consciously avoiding some outspoken producer oriented perspectives prevalent among parts of the regular energy policy administration. The problem of immunization was recognized in one of the very first memoranda on futures studies drawn up by the staff of the Government Research Advisory Board. It was claimed that futures studies should be performed under full intellectual integrity and be protected from any undue influence that could be exerted by different interest groups. This was essentially the original model introduced in Sweden in 1973. The following years have witnessed a series of demands for representation in the direction of the Secretariat by, e.g. the opposition parties and by interest groups such as trade unions. Paradoxically, the success of the 1975 opposition Bills to transform the parliamentary reference group of the Secretariat into an executive committee implied increased protection of project groups against outside demands. Related to the problem of immunization is a phenomenon that can be termed:

Strategic Screening

Strategic screening is a generic concept denoting stratagems by which someone responsible for a policy area, e.g. the head of a ministry or a unit within a ministry, can keep an issue within his or her own realm and shield it from outside intervention. One way of achieving this in the Swedish governmental system is by formulating the terms of reference for a governmental commission in such a narrow way that their contents do not appear to significantly affect other ministries (Larsson 1978).

Information Overload

Should comprehensive planning succeed in unlocking the gates closed by stratagems of strategic screening, it will face the problem of handling an information flow that will increase with the new and

significantly larger number of interactions between different policy
areas and subareas that have to be considered (see Scharpf 1973:
90-93).

Consensus and Blocking

This is the other side of the coin of the problem of immunization.
Comprehensive planning requires at least some minimal
cooperation from individual ministries, agencies and units. In this
sense it cannot work unless supported by some weak form of consensus among sectoral interests. If planning processes go on for a
long time, then the possibility of blocking and vetoing them increases
accordingly (cf. Scharpf 1973: 88-89, 93-94).

The Fallacy of Reproduction

It might be tempting for comprehensive planners to try to avoid
blocking and excessive demands on consensus by getting direct access to information on developments in all policy areas. This,
however, only presents a new problem. The very build-up of
capacities of overview and monitoring will necessitate some division of labour within the central planning organization. Gradually,
it will come to resemble a miniature replica of those sectoral bodies
it is trying to coordinate (cf. Wildavsky 1972: 514; Scharpf 1973:
84). If this development continues we will end up with two
organizational frameworks with similar features. So the process
will have to start all over again. But then, in the face of series of
difficulties of considerable magnitude, why bother? Why not just
discard the idea of comprehensive planning as impracticable?
There appear to be at least five major arguments for the necessity
of comprehensive planning.

The Epistemic Argument

Real-world problems do not respect administrative boundaries.
The preparation of sets of decisions with long-range effects must
include an assessment of their interaction irrespective of whether

these happen to fall within the domain of one or several ministries or agencies. Perceptual screening of such interactions will effectively limit the capacity of a government to solve the given problems; counterproductive and unintended effects are likely to occur.

The External Costs Argument

If policy preparation is limited to sectoral concerns, then public planning will not be concerned with the negative side-effects of policies as long as they are efficient in one given sector. Governmental bodies in other sectors will then probably incur external costs in the form of additional difficulties in implementing their own policies. Or possibly, externalities will be shifted to fuzzy regions between the areas of responsibility of different governmental units. In this case external costs might just fall upon individual citizens and go largely unnoticed by policy-makers and administrators.

The Mortgaging Argument

If there is no comprehensive planning to supplement sectoral planning, then there will be an unforeseen mortgaging of the future. Plans and decisions of one sectoral body will narrow the range of options available to other bodies. The temporal sequence of planning and decision-making between different governmental units will then determine how alternatives are being foreclosed in different policy areas (cf. Scharpf 1973: 97-98). Actually, this was seen by members of the Alva Myrdal commission as one of the chief motives for coordination of sectoral planning. Agencies such as the National Board of Health and Welfare and the National Board of Education were found to be elaborating large-scale sectoral plans that might effectively mortgage the future and restrict the set of feasible policy alternatives.

The Normative Argument

If sectoral planning restricts or even determines what courses of action are open, then the role of parliamentarians and politicians might be reduced to one of recording or legitimizing antecedently prepared policies that can no longer realistically be derailed. From the perspective of normative theories of parliamentary democracy the supposed implementors would be making the policies and the elected decision-makers ratifying these; the political process would then be running backwards, to use D. Tarschys's expression. In this case there seems to be an apparent need for comprehensive planning to ensure that overall priorities are established by decision-makers publicly responsible to all citizens rather than by professional planners with undefined sectoral allegiances.

The Uncertainty Argument

Planning is basically the art of handling uncertainties surrounding distant effects of our present actions (Ingelstam 1977: 131). Planning aims at managing and reducing uncertainties that are impediments to the realization of our objectives and goals. Paradoxically, however, the very building-up of sectoral planning competence gives rise to new forms of uncertainty. Apart from normal more or less predictable events within their area of responsibility — their planning object — planning bodies must now face increased uncertainty about their environment. Different units might vitiate each others' plans, and the probability that this will occur will increase with the growing number of planning bodies in various sectors. Hence, uncoordinated planning to some extent engenders its own demand.

The least costly and most obvious remedy would then be to create some form of common informational basis for planners and decision-makers. This is actually the main function of the medium-term economic surveys in Sweden. They serve as an important reference document, predominantly within the public sector, which is utilized in several types of non-economic forecasting and planning, e.g. in connection with the energy forecasts of the State Industry Board. It should be noted that this coordinating role is an important one irrespective of whether the specific economic forecasts outlined in the medium-term surveys happen to be confirmed or not. Hence, while alleviating uncertainty stemming from uncoordinated organizational behaviour, this remedy contains no guarantee against intellectual myopia and parochialism. Actually, the authoritative nature of a central reference document might well foster such traits.

This latter view was implicit in the comments of the Alva Myrdal commission on the role of the Swedish medium-term economic surveys. The commission argued that this form of informational coordination was unduly limited to a medium-term perspective and to one analytic perspective — that of economic theory. An extension of both the temporal and the analytic framework was advocated. It was hoped that futures studies might contribute towards this end. With some interesting exceptions — e.g. in the form of cross-sectoral national physical planning — the overall Swedish situation today is still characterized by the relative weakness of cross-sectoral planning and by the absence of comprehensive or integrated planning as a supplement.

Comprehensive planning might, therefore, appear to be both necessary and impossible. Is there no way out of the dilemmas of comprehensive planning? At least four different types of strategies present themselves.

Strategies of Reduction and Simplification

These involve the reduction of alternatives of action to be considered in comprehensive planning (see Scharpf 1973: 94-99). Problems of consensus, blocking and information overload could perhaps be handled if integrated planning focussed on a strictly limited number of crucial cases and relied upon simple trend extrapolations and the natural course of events for the rest. This would presumably also contribute to more favourable conditions in general for the solution of problems of time frames, utilization, immunization and strategic screening. Futhermore, there appears to be no reason to assume that the fallacy of reproduction would constitute a major difficulty in the case of this strategy.

Strategies of Metadecisions

These strategies presuppose that decisions on general objectives and procedures for policy-making — including rules specifying how the set of feasible policy options is to be delimited — could somehow be distinguished from the actual making and processing of decisions on specific policy matters (cf. Dror 1971: 63-79; Gershuny 1978: 295-316). By way of appropriate metadecisions some comprehensiveness could conceivably be achieved without detailed policy regulation. This might directly alleviate the problems of consensus and blocking and, indirectly, those of information overload, strategic screening and immunization. The basic rationale of the strategy is to affect the rules governing the activities of various bodies of policy-makers. The strategy of metadecisions is attractive. However, it suffers from one obvious weakness: it assumes that crucial policy-makers have a clear awareness of the problems of immunization, strategic screening and blocking and are able to relate these problems to the political feasibility of specific policy proposals. Should a policy-maker's application of this strategy be abortive, she or he is likely to have rallied considerable opposition among entrenched interests and will run a corresponding risk of being ousted from office. Some analysts claim that the fate of the anti-nuclear power oriented energy minister of the Swedish three-party coalition government of 1976-78 bears some resemblance to this case.

Strategies of Deregulation

These strategies could start out from the stance that most of the alleged arguments for the necessity of comprehensive planning depend crucially upon the fact that a large amount of sectoral planning is already going on and is taken for granted; comprehensive planning is then necessary not for its own sake but as a remedy for negative effects of sectoral planning. One way out of the dilemma would be to limit all kinds of planning severely. Obviously, this would reduce information overload, whereas the consequences in terms of other problems appear to be open-ended. Still, such a strategy would, of course, require arguments for the alternatives to sectoral and comprehensive planning.

Strategies of By-passing and Dispositional Policy Innovation

Problems of information overload, strategic screening, consensus and reproduction may be entirely avoided if the problem areas of several sectoral units could be analysed in terms of cross-cutting problems that could be understood and affected in terms of generating mechanisms hitherto neglected by the administrative apparatus (cf. Scharpf 1973: 104; Majone and Wildavsky 1978: 108-109). This possibility may sound unrealistic but is, surely, not altogether unlikely. On the contrary, given the often arbitrary administrative lines that demarcate different fields of responsibility it might well be that an effort at by-passing traditional interpretations could pay off well. An effort in this direction was undoubtedly made by the Swedish futures studies project group on Energy and Society. However, even the most successful application of a strategy of by-passing will really just shift the problem from the stage of policy-preparation to that of decision-making and implementation. The potentials of by-passing cannot be realized unless dispositional policy innovation occurs; the ideas of innovation and comprehensive policy preparation must in each situation be supported by external political and social conditions favouring redefinitions and involving changes in rules of closure.

Nevertheless, this strategy, although often neglected, appears to be promising, especially in combination with either of the first two strategies. The experiences of the Swedish Secretariat for Futures Studies, and in particular its project group on energy, seem to bear this out. A small cross-sectoral analytical unit can achieve considerable leverage even in an administrative and political environment characterized by an emphasis upon sectoral administrative responsibility and upon corresponding, officially sanctioned channels for generating policy innovation. Cross-sectoral and long-range oriented policy analysis will inevitably meet with some initial suspicion in administrative and ministerial quarters. However, despite such problems as well as those of ambiguous top-level political support, Swedish futures studies in government indicate the potentials of an approach to policy innovation based upon selective by-passing and dispositional policy innovation. The fate of innovative policy proposals under this scheme is crucially dependent upon the existence of favourable political and social conditions external to government offices proper.

REFERENCES

Allison, G. T. (1980) 'Implementation Analysis', pp. 237-60 in L. Lewin and E. Vedung (eds.) *Politics as Rational Action*. Dordrecht and Boston: D. Reidel Publishing Company.

Baehr, P. R. (1981) 'Futures Studies and Policy Analysis in the Netherlands: The Netherlands Scientific Council for Government Policy', pp. 93-117 in this volume.

Berrill, K. (1977) 'The Role of the Central Policy Review Staff in Whitehall', *Management Services in Government*, Vol. 32: 121-26.

Boucher, W. I. (1977) 'Introduction', pp. 3-13 in W. I. Boucher (ed.), *The Study of the Future: An Agenda for Research*. Washington, DC: National Science Foundation.

Clark, J. and S. Cole (1975) *Global Simulation Models: A Comparative Study*. London: John Wiley Interscience.

Cole, S. (1976) 'Long-term Forecasting Methods: Emphasis and Institutions', *Futures*, Vol. 8: 305-19.

Dror, Y. (1971) *Design for Policy Sciences*. New York: Elsevier.

Edman, M. (1976) 'There is no Naive Way of Making Forecasts', pp. 1-27 in S. Schwarz (ed.) *Knowledge and Concepts in Futures Studies*. Boulder, Colorado: Westview Press.

Friedmann, J. and B. Hudson (1974) 'Knowledge and Action: A Guide to Planning Theory', *Journal of the American Institute of Planners*, Vol. 40: 2-16.

Gershuny, J. I. (1978) 'Policymaking Rationality: A Reformulation', *Policy Sciences*, Vol. 9: 295-316.

Gendt, R. van (1976) 'The Scientific Council for Government Policy: Indirect Advising on the Central Level', *Planning and Development in the Netherlands*, Vol. VIII: 34-43.

Gideonse, H. D. (1972) 'Can the Federal Government Use the Futures Perspective?', pp. 64-70 in M. Marien and W. L. Ziegler (eds.) *The Potential of Educational Futures*. Worthington, Ohio: Charles A. Jones Publishing Company.

—— (1976) 'The Contribution of the Futures Perspective to Management: A Case Study', *Educational Planning*, Vol. 2: 21-33.

Government Commission (1975) *Forskningsråd*, SOU 1975:26. Stockholm: Liber.

—— (1977) *Forskningspolitik*, SOU 1977: 52. Stockholm: Liber.

Gray, C. S. (1977-78) ' "Think Tanks" and Public Policy', *International Journal*, Vol. 33: 177-94.

Holmberg, S., J. Westerståhl and K. Branzén (1977) *Väljarna och kärnkraften*. Stockholm: Liber.

Ingelstam, L. (1977) 'Basic Problems of Planning', pp. 127-45 in C. G. Jennergren, S. Schwarz and O. Alvfeldt (eds.) *Trends in Planning*. Stockholm: Försvaretsforskningsanstalt.

Jantsch, E. (1969) 'Adaptive Institutions for Shaping the Future', pp. 471-91 in E. Jantsch (ed.) *Perspectives of Planning*. Paris: OECD.

Johansson, T. B. and P. Steen (1978) *Solar Sweden — an Outline for a Renewable Energy System*. Stockholm: Secretariat for Futures Studies.

Larsson, T. (1978) *Regeringskansliets arbetssätt och funktioner*. Stockholm: Department of Political Science, University of Stockholm (mimeo).

Lönnroth, M., T. B. Johansson, and P. Steen (1980) *Sweden Beyond Oil: Nuclear Commitments and Solar Options*. Oxford: Pergamon Press.

Majone, G. and A. Widlavsky (1978) 'Implementation as Evolution', pp. 103-17 in H. E. Freeman (ed.), *Policy Studies Review Annual, Volume 2*. Beverly Hills, Ca: Sage Publications.

Mayntz, R. and F. W. Scharpf (1975) *Policy-Making in the German Federal Bureaucracy*. Amsterdam: Elsevier.

Mellbourn, A. (1979) *Byråkratins ansikten*. Stockholm: Liber.

Ministry of Defence (1969) *Planering och programbudgetering inom försvaret*, SOU 1969:25. Stockholm: Försvarsdepartementet.

Ministry of Finance (1974) *Proposal for a Reform of the Swedish Budget System*. Stockholm: Ministry of Finance.

Nordhaus, W. D. (1973) 'The Allocation of Energy Resources', *Brookings Papers on Economic Activity*, Vol. 4: 529-76.

Petersson, O. (1977) *Väljarna och valet 1976*. Stockholm: Statistiska centralbyrån.

—— (1979) *Regeringsbildningen 1978*. Stockholm: Raben & Sjögren.

Rittel, H. W. J. and M. W. Webber (1973) 'Dilemmas in a General Theory of Planning', *Policy Sciences*, Vol. 4: 155-69.

Rothschild, N. M. V., Baron (1977) *Meditations of a Broomstick*. London: Collins.

SAFAD (1974) *Statsförvaltningen planerar: aktörer, rollfördelning, samverkansformer*. Stockholm: Statskontoret.

—— (1977) *Om planering vid statliga myndigheter*.Stockholm: Statskontoret.

Scharpf, F. W. (1973) *Planung als politischer Prozess: Aufsätze zur Theorie der planenden Demokratie*. Frankfurt am Main: Suhrkamp Verlag.

Schwarz, B. (1977a) 'Long-range Planning in the Public Sector', *Futures*, Vol. 9: 115-27.

—— (1977b) 'Programme Budgeting and/or Long-range Planning', pp. 25-53 in C. G. Jennergren, S. Schwarz and O. Alvfeldt (eds.) *Trends in Planning*. Stockholm: Försvarets forskningsanstalt.

Schwarz, B., U. Svedin and B. Wittrock (1981) *Methods in Futures Studies*. Stockholm: EFI/SP Report.

Shani, M. (1974) 'Futures Studies Versus Planning', *Omega*, Vol. 2: 635-49.

Strangert, P. (1977) 'Adaptive Planning and the Resolution of Uncertainty', pp. 147-65 in C. G. Jennergren, S. Schwarz and O. Alvfeldt (eds.) *Trends in Planning*. Stockholm: Försvarets forskningsanstalt.

Vedung, E. (1979) *Kärnkraften och regeringen Fälldins fall*. Stockholm: Raben & Sjögren.

Wenk, E., Jr. (1979) 'The Political Limits to Forecasting', pp. 289-322 in T. Whiston (ed.) *The Uses and Abuses of Forecasting*. London: Macmillan.

Whiston, T. G. (1979) 'The Uses of Forecasting', pp. 344-50 in T. Whiston (ed.) *The Uses and Abuses of Forecasting*. London: Macmillan.

Wildavsky, A. (1972) 'The Self-Evaluating Organization', *Public Administration Review*, Vol. 32: 509-20.

Wittrock, B. (1977) 'Sweden's Secretariat: Programmes and Policies', *Futures*, Vol. 9: 351-57.

—— (1979) 'Long-range Forecasting and Policy-Making: Options and Limits in Choosing a Future', pp. 267-88 in T. Whiston (ed.) *The Uses and Abuses of Forecasting*. London: Macmillan.

7 Futures Studies and Cross-Sectoral Policy Analysis: The Canadian Scene

Simon Miles

INTRODUCTION

What follows is an assessment of the contribution of futures studies and cross-sectoral policy analysis to the political process at the federal level in Canada.

Considerable importance is attached to conveying something of the context within which those studies-analyses have been pursued in the firm belief that we are, in Ingelstam's words, very much 'prisoners of our own culture' and that the spirit of the age has a profound effect on attitudes and approaches toward the longer term. Canada is beginning to recognize that it has to be more concerned with 'holes avoidance' than with 'goals achievement' but it is still using conventional 'old style' forecasting techniques that are ill-equipped for providing guidance on either the minimum activity of 'keeping the show on the road' or, more importantly, of going beyond this and offering alternatives.

The concern with the production of alternatives then becomes the major theme of the chapter. A number of suggestions are made as to what is likely to be required if such alternatives are to be generated. Against this backdrop, the structure, studies and working procedures of a number of bodies are reviewed: first on an institution by institution basis and then through a summary assessment of the outstanding characteristics of the studies and the machinery. This review is seen as substantiating the case for a paradigm shift and the chapter concludes by elaborating on what this involves in terms of a new concept of development (focussed more on human development), how it might become operational, and the role of futures studies in such a development planning context.

OVERVIEW

The Change in Attitude and Approaches toward the Longer Term

In Canada, as in other countries, there has been a marked shift in attitude toward the future in recent years. *Fascination* with the future in the 1960s gave way to an *interest* in problems in the early 1970s which in turn was replaced by an *uncertainty* about the future in the late 1970s. The distinction is significant since it helps to explain the approaches taken toward understanding the future, presenting it and dealing with it.

The first of these phases was dominated by the 'we know' trends extrapolators working in an environment dominated by economic and technological considerations. The fascination with the future arose from what was shown to be possible technologically. The climate of economic growth suggested the probability of these technological developments and that conditions would likely continue to improve. Focussing on economic conditions alone made forecasting even easier and thus expectations of forecasting and planning ran high. Economic development ruled the day and technology was its handmaiden: in the southern part of the country the big cities of Toronto, Montreal and Vancouver became vast building sites, while for the northern part there was much talk of a grand scheme of service settlements in a country-wide corridor for natural resources development.

As the 1960s ended so a second phase set in, characterized more by the 'unanticipated side effects' on the social and environmental side, and later by external disturbances, such as the OPEC-initiated oil crisis. The problems were, however, seen as quite manageable — an intellectual challenge in terms of presentation and appreciation, but certainly soluble through rational, comprehensive and longer-term planning. Marshall McLuhan had the ear of the Prime Minister and in the Privy Council Office (PCO) a highly imaginative Mr C. R. Nixon was using multi-media techniques to brief the cabinet. Illustrative of the cabinet's response to the major problems of the day was the establishment of the Ministry of State for Urban Affairs (MSUA) to deal with those burgeoning cities. Its initial staffing was very pro-intellectual and multi-disciplinary in support of a clearly cross-sectoral approach to policy formulation. It was expected to produce policy directives for the central executive to reflect in the delivery of programmes by other departments. But the lack of political clout accorded the new small policy ministry (without programme delivery responsibilities) effectively denied it the ability to put its policies into action. This, coupled with (among other things) poor demographic forecasts at the time, began to give highly visible physical planning and associated economic and technological forecasting a bad name. OPEC's jolt to the world in 1973 further tarnished the image of planners and forecasters, even though Canada, with its more plentiful domestic oil supplies, was assumed to be in a far less vulnerable position than most other industrialized nations.

By 1975 a third phase had taken hold, characterized by a marked uncertainty about the future and a lack of confidence in forecasting and longer-term planning to take Canadians to where they would like to go. Indeed, the future began to be marked out not so much in terms of the goals to be achieved but the holes to be avoided. Keeping one's options open and maintaining manoeuvrability became all-important. Monitoring of current developments along with what might be called futures studies (as described by Wittrock), as distinct from forecasting and long-term planning, began to acquire greater interest. But still, for futures studies at least, not all that great.

What Next...and Why

Canadians are still in this third phase and are likely to remain so for some time. Part of the problem may be that insufficient distinction has been made between, on the one hand, futures studies of the type described by Wittrock, and forecasting and long-term planning on the other. But it is useful to make such a distinction and in so doing one may refer first to that used by the Lamontagne Survey of Futures Studies.[1] The Survey was undertaken in Canada in October 1975, reported on in November 1976, and published in June 1977. The Introduction to the summary of the Survey opens as follows:

> Projections to anticipate patterns of future change and complex interactions of new policies, must of necessity be based on judgement, with its varying degrees of certainty and confidence. Such projections may sometimes benefit from techniques which contain the ability to elicit and process judgemental data for use in on-going decision-making processes. Applied economic analysis, operations research, systems analysis, cybernetics, morphology, all help to meet this need. In recent years, there has grown out of these approaches a new discipline known as futures studies which are defined as follows:
>
> > They are studies that focus specifically on identifying and clarifying possible social, economic and technological trends, changes and needs, thereby strengthening the ability of decision-makers to recognize and choose among complex alternatives those which have a long-term beneficial impact on society.
>
> One can differentiate between forecasting, long-range planning and Futures Studies. In practice they may be woven together but they have certain independent characteristics.
>
> > Forecasting tends to assume some set of definable causal relations between events through which one can predict their future states — with varying levels of probability of occurrence. Many forecasting activities are also restricted within some given set of value premises.
> > This particularly applies in much economic and technological forecasting. This latter 'value free' aspect is undergoing a subtle transformation as activities such as technology assessment grow in importance.
> > Long-range planning is generally concerned with the organization of events within the next five to ten years. Its horizons are usually limited by its functional relationship to some specific sector of the society. Such planning is also characterized by implied value assumptions. The concern is with how some activity may be planned rather than with why it should be planned. As longer-range planning begins to move to the international level, differences in value preferences have moved to the fore. In national planning, the need for better social indicators to aid planning has led to more explicit value measures.

However, it would appear that, to the extent that such a distinction has been made in the process of defining futures studies, the emphasis in Canada until now has been placed more on the identification of trends and the holes to be avoided than on the identification of genuine alternatives. Futures studies have therefore tended to be seen very much as part of long-term planning as Wittrock[2] has described it (see page 121) — i.e. concerned with keeping options open. And hence in Canada they have also tended to suffer the same ignominy as forecasting and long-term planning.

The identification of clear alternatives will not likely come about through futures studies until there emerges a clearer understanding, on the part of those conducting them, of the characteristics of such studies. There should be more attention given to studies oriented towards a time horizon defined by 'the relative lack of major commitments so that consideration can be given to qualitative changes'. These studies should, however, attempt to clarify the implications for decisions to be made in the immediate term and the nature of any value change. Indeed, the identification of clear alternatives may well require the ability to make a paradigm shift from economically and technologically led development to socially led development. The exploration of any such alternatives would, for example, have to make clear not only the improved global viability and human fulfillment to be derived from those alternatives but also demonstrate why any one of those alternatives will not simply come about in time and that there are indeed opportunities that are being lost in not actively inducing the changes implied.

In short, futures studies have to be able to demonstrate *why* we should be concerned with the future. When this has been clarified it will be easier to examine further *how* we are to examine the future. To obtain the attention of any cabinet there has to be a problem. The problem with the future is that it is not very apparently with us now.

A clearer concept of human and societal development and how major activities of the public sector contribute to that development is obviously a prerequisite. Without this, the societal implications of future developments cannot easily be spelled out. I do not see this in Canada or in most other countries. There are, however, signs of awareness of the need for it in some countries — as in Norway, France and the Netherlands, and perhaps even in Japan if one is to be optimistic about Prime Minister Ohira's first major policy address[3] made in January 1979. There are indeed some such signs in Canada. But even in these countries it is difficult to find sufficient actual exploration of clear alternatives.

Whether these alternatives can be fully explored by existing institutional structures is debatable. Certainly, frustration with any

existing order sparks new initiative occasionally, and in Ottawa
there has always been some scope for initiative by enterprising and
imaginative public servants. But the exceptions that stand out are
limited almost to the efforts of individuals or small groups, as will
be seen below. More important than structure, however, are attitudes, perceptions and preparedness to take initiatives in exploring new ways (on which structure does, of course, have considerable influence). Thus it is likely that far greater progress in
identifying alternatives can be made by groups outside of the
public service. This has been recognized in part by federal government and considerable financial support is made available to outside groups. There does, however, appear to be a real reluctance
to finance genuine alternatives in terms of a paradigm shift.

Again there are exceptions as, for example, with the support that
has been given by the Federal Department of Environment to the
'Ark' project (an experiment in self-reliant community living) in
Prince Edward Island. Whether public money should be spent for
or withheld from such activities has been raised by Gustavsson.[4]
This point seems critical.

Against this overview, it is possible to comment briefly on what
certain bodies have been doing in Canada.

SELECTED BODIES ABLE TO INFLUENCE THE USE
OF FUTURES STUDIES AND CROSS-SECTORAL
POLICY ANALYSIS IN THE POLITICAL PROCESS

There is no single central planning agency in the Canadian Federal
Government. There is no plan, either adopted or unadopted. Nor
are there targets set on any regular basis. There are, however,
numerous vehicles for consultations between the federal government (elected and appointed) officials and the private sector and
labour. These range from permanent representation of each group
on councils like the Economic Council of Canada and participation
in 'ad hoc' committees. However, although management seems
very prepared to participate, labour is quite frequently withdrawing
from active involvement. In some instances, as with a survey of 23
sectors of industry produced in early 1979, the private sector may
play a leading role in this partnership.

There are, however, fewer consultations on broad and integrated social and economic questions. These tend to be confined to discussions with the provincial governments, especially through 'First Ministers Conferences'. Specialized councils, such as the Science Council, may support policy options for governmental consideration but very often these never reach cabinet.

Although there is no central planning agency in Canada, the following are some of the more significant bodies relative to the coordination of government activities and/or the shaping of thinking on national development policy. These tend to have, or could have, a significant influence on the use of futures studies and cross-sectoral policy analysis in the Canadian political process.

The Privy Council Office

PCO's function is to provide staff support to the Prime Minister, to cabinet and to its committees. There are about 100 professional staff with a very high percentage of very senior ranking officials. Turn-over is, by design, frequent. The two major divisions are Plans and Operations, each headed by a Deputy Secretary. There are eight cabinet committees, two of which have their own separate staffs (the Treasury Board and also, as of 1979, the Board of Economic Development Ministers) and a third (the Committee on Priorities and Planning and Federal-Provincial Relations) which is partly served by the Federal-Provincial Relations Office. The other committees are Economic Policy, Social Policy and Cultural Policy, Government Operations, Legislation and House Planning, External Policy and Defence. Some of these committees meet weekly, others every other week. There are numerous 'ad hoc' committees (e.g. labour relations) that meet very infrequently (some as infrequently as every five years). The pressure on the cabinet ministers being what it is, the time horizons tend to be limited to most immediate concerns. The current policy within PCO is to avoid doing anything more than necessary in house. If something can be done by one of the departments, it should be.

Thus in keeping track of developments in the futures studies field, there have been, as of mid-1979, only two persons in PCO specifically identified with such a responsibility. Their task is to keep the rest of the PCO staff informed of futures studies that appear significant for their work in relating to cabinet. Running files are kept on issues that in the eyes of these staff appear worthy of monitoring and intermittent newsletters are issued on various topics. A second activity is the organization of visits by outside experts of global stature (e.g. Peccei, Dubos) to meet with the PCO staff and under the previous Liberal Government thought was being given to extending this to meetings with cabinet members. Another initiative launched in 1979 was a Futures Fair. The first one was on 'communications and information' to enable the PCO staff to become more familiar with currently available technology (e.g. the home computer and inter-active television). This was well received and consideration has been given to follow it with a Futures Fair for the Parliament. A third initiative has been to offer PCO staff training on data bank access and other skills useful for their work.

The extent to which issues coming before PCO staff obtain exposure to long-term cross-sectoral analysis probably depends largely on the time available for examination. Each individual is expected to make use of the resources of the Office and each has a relatively broad background. At one time, in the late 1960s, the innovative use of multiple screens for visual presentations on the inter-relations of dimensions of critical and complex questions facing cabinet appeared to be making some headway. However, with the promotion of Mr C. R. Nixon (the man responsible for initiating this Briefing Team approach) to more senior positions in the PCO and then to Deputy Minister for National Defence, the approach lapsed in use.

The PCO has a contract with the Institute for Research on Public Policy (IRPP), a non-governmental body, heavily supported by governments, to provide futures studies (see below).

The Ministry of State for Science and Technology (MOSST)

MOSST, like MSUA, was established as a policy ministry. Unlike MSUA, which was disbanded in March 1979, it has not suffered at the hands of the provinces in the federal-provincial debates over jurisdictional responsibilities. Like MSUA, although not to the same extent, it has suffered from interdepartmental disputes over 'turf'. Following the Lamontagne Survey of Futures Studies, a Secretariat for Futures Studies (SFS) was established, in 1976, in the Technology Assessment Division (TAD) of MOSST. Its functions are to keep track of federal government and non-governmental futures studies, provide assistance and advice and identify the scope of futures programmes of activities within the federal government, and service an Interdepartmental Committee on Technological Forecasting. It started with two professionals. Later, a Futures Planning Group (FPG), under one of these two, was set up to provide the PCO with information on the long-range needs of the government and the extent to which they are being met. This involved an initial survey of fifteen departments and a more detailed look at Defence, Transportation and Communications plus an examination of such items as world models, long-term models, Canada's CANDIDE econometric model, environmental prospects for Canada, the Science Council's 'Conserver Society' study and IRPP's Futures Programme. The FPG has also become involved in developing a programme on research necessary to identify futures priorities. Thus the FPG has tended to assume some of the functions originally given the SFS. In reality, as of mid-1979, they are both being run by one lone professional.

With such limited staff and resources there has been little scope to launch a concerted futures programme in the federal government. The limitations of MOSST's jurisdiction, and more specifically that of the TAD, are obvious further constraints on what should be a more extensive cross-sectoral effort with a more global outlook.

Beyond PCO and MOSST, with their most direct responsibilities for keeping the central executive apprised of futures developments, a number of other bodies within the federal machinery have responsibilities for a longer-term view of developments. Two of these are councils, bringing together persons from outside of government.

The Economic Council of Canada (ECC)[5]

The ECC is an economic research and policy advisory agency bringing together leaders from business, industry, agriculture, the professions, labour unions and universities. It is chaired by a senior civil servant and reports to the Prime Minister. Its prime functions are: to develop a body of research and analysis for 'some sort of "economic blueprint" for the future'; to try to influence public policy on important national issues; and, to pursue a public education role.

The research programme is initiated through debate between staff and council members and is organized around a number of project areas, each served by a number of staff, generally a mix of in-house personnel and consultants, but with a strong emphasis on training in economics. Time horizons are generally from two to ten years but studies tend to relate more to known conditions and constraints. The CANDIDE econometric model, which has recently been improved, has been used to make projections of up to ten years of economic activity, and to examine alternative scenarios involving the impact of future policies. More recently, long-run growth projections to the year 2000 have been made to provide information on the stability of the system and its long-run properties.

Another recently-completed project of particular significance to the role of futures studies and cross-sectoral policy analysis is that on international development and Canada's long-term options in its relations with the developing countries. Some of the major topics covered were: political and economic trends; distribution of income and poverty in developing countries; characteristics of Canada's trade with these countries: immigration from these countries; and, the adequacy of Canada's organizational structures and processes to respond to the new realities of international development. The significance of the report may well lie with its extension of the ECC's interest to a truly global dimension — something that may receive further treatment in future reports.

Other issues typical of the ECC's recent concerns are: pensions; technological change; regional studies; labour markets and socio-economic research; and growth and productivity. But in each case it is difficult to discern whether sufficient attention is being given to the societal implications. The ECC can argue that as an economic policy advisory body it should concentrate its efforts on economic matters. The question then is: 'who is responsible for providing the other points of view?' Is it for PCO to resolve? To some extent the ECC has begun to move on this front by encouraging increased public debate on some of its reports (as with that on the implications of Quebec's separation from the rest of Canada). Also of significance may be the emergence of a social policy secretariat of the Conservative Government which came to power in May 1979.

The Science Council of Canada (SCC)[6]

The SCC, like the ECC, brings together a body of persons from outside of government and again with a broad range of backgrounds, but again from institutions that one would expect on such a body. It reports to the Minister of State for Science and Technology through its chairman who happens to be from outside of government. It has the responsibility to report to and advise the Minister on virtually all matters relating to the development and use of scientific and technological resources, and the research, planning, manpower and institutional relations relative to furthering this. A major problem it faces, however, is that the cabinet portfolio for Science and Technology has always been held by a minister who has had additional responsibilities and when this is something as significant as Energy, as is the case with the new Conservative Government, very little time is given by the Minister to the Council's concerns.

Most of its work is futures oriented with a three to five year time horizon although there has only ever been one futures group as such and all three members have since left the staff. That group, operating with a modified delphi approach, did not gain any significant exposure to the public. However, the SCC staff, in contradistinction to that of the project oriented teams of the ECC, tend to operate as small groups or as individuals with a great deal of freedom to use their time to explore their topics through their informal networks inside and outside the public service.

The SCC has also tended to put considerable effort into promoting public debates of its reports. There are generally funds set aside for this type of follow-up for a three to six month period. In some instances, as with the much-publicized 'Conserver Society' report, the frequent appearance of the staff and those Council members acting as a committee for the project have been interpreted by other policy advisors as an overly proactive rather than advisory role. Whether this is so or not is debatable. But the appearances themselves are certainly most justifiable in that they contribute to creating a more informed electorate and thus a more politically sensitive cabinet. In the case of the Conserver Society report it can fairly be said that every type of group, of every political stripe, extended invitations to the Council members of staff to talk on the findings of the report. Clearly normative, the report incited the ire of only the 'advertising' community. In addition to these many invitations, the report was also the subject of a series of conferences (organized by MOSST) designed to reach a broad mix of interest groups across the country. Unfortunately, insufficient or inappropriate resources given to this activity, and frequent changes to plans, produced little from the enormous potential of this exercise.

The Canadian International Development Agency (CIDA) Department of Environment (DOE) Joint Programme on Environment and Development

This programme, launched by CIDA/DOE several years ago, has always been a very low budget effort to explore, through papers and conferences for senior federal officials of most departments, alternative and more ecologically sound approaches to development in Canada and in developing countries. It has utilized international expertise (e.g. Sachs, Mende, Galtung) to work with Canadians on developing alternative frameworks for development. It is part of a gathering movement in Canada but it is difficult to say how much impact this programme has had on efforts by the public in Canada. However, by 1978 it had responded to the request by one developing country with an aid programme devoted to ecodevelopment. It would appear, however, that the programme lacks the 'minimum critical mass' of support necessary to continue as a joint programme. As the few individuals involved moved on so the commitment to a joint programme was eroded. Although this does not mean that work will not continue separately, this is regrettable.

The Institute for Research on Public Policy Analysis (IRPP)

The IRPP was established as an independent body with major financial support from the federal and most provincial governments. After an initially slow start it is now working quite successfully under the direction of a former aide to Prime Minister Trudeau towards establishing an endowment fund (from federal, provincial and private sources) to give it the independence that a body of this nature should have. In terms of Gustavsson's typology the shift in leadership has been to a power-based system.

Currently, the IRPP is very dependent on contract work. One such contract is with the PCO to launch a Futures Studies Programme over a three-year period (1977-79). This programme has employed twelve full-time researchers and these are supplemented by an equally large or larger body of part-time consultants. The reports cover a wide range of topics though judging by the titles there is a lack of attention to the societal implications of the matters examined. Sample topics are: issues in Canadian/US transborder computer data flows; sea-bed mining; the electronic briefcase; Canada in the new monetary order; economic relations with Japan; home computers; health status; trends in life satisfaction; energy R & D decision-making; communications; microelectronics; pensions; attitude trends (1960-78). The emerging foci are, on the economic side, the computer, microprocessors and communications.

Social trends are to be covered in a Social Trends Report expected in late 1979 that is expected to integrate trends in a variety of areas to advance the task of identifying some fundamental structural components of social change in Canada. To introduce the public to the issues in advance a series of *socioscope* documents, utilizing questionnaires for feedback, is being introduced. It is too early yet to see how these will work.

Conferences are likely to be held on more of the reports as they are published. Experience with methodological concerns is just beginning.

Just as Daniel Tarschys observes of Sweden's central public finance agencies,[7] so in Canada there are two federal bodies that could give greater attention to futures studies and cross-sectoral analysis and have a beneficial effect on other departments. These are the Treasury Board and the Department of Finance.

The Treasury Board is responsible for integrating spending in programme areas (e.g. energy) through approval or otherwise of projects above a certain level of funding. This level varies from one programme area to another. There is, however, little long-term perspective or evaluation of what has gone before. The introduction of a 'foresight' assessment procedure, along with the oversight for management and budgetary control, would be valuable here.

The Department of Finance produces budgets that are clearly designed to maintain a healthy economy over the next year. Some measures are introduced with an eye to longer-term developments but the overriding characteristic is that of an operating budget rather than the financial underpinning of a longer-term development programme. The budget in November 1978 did, however, reflect a shift toward medium and longer-term thinking at a time when it had become patently clear that the continued pursuit of short-term measures would no longer suffice. But at the same time it did not address itself sufficiently to the need for structural change. There is a Long-Range Planning Division in the Department which could be used to do some long-range planning. The Norwegian model, utilizing a multi-disciplinary team, a four-year development plan and budget with the current budget reviewed every year by the legislature, would be worthy of examination by Canada.

A SUMMARY ASSESSMENT OF THE PATTERNS, PROBLEMS AND POTENTIALS

The Studies

At the time of the Lamontagne Survey (1975) the futures field was still dominated by those using more conventional techniques such as trend extrapolation, scenario writing and econometric techniques, even though numerous other methodologies were also being employed. The centre of gravity, or focus, of these studies was certainly Canada, with very little attention being given to global development and Canada's relations with other countries. The favoured subjects were, in terms of funds expended, resource conservation, human environment and the economy. Low on the list came social structure and science.

Since 1975 there has probably been some increased use of certain techniques such as gaming and delphi techniques although trend extrapolation is still very popular. The centre of gravity is still very much Canada, and although a greater concern for the global scene may emerge as agencies become more aware of its existence and significance, all the signs suggest that by the time this is reflected in serious futures studies much of the potential contribution that such studies could make to policy-making will have been foregone. With regard to the shift in sectoral concern, the increased attention to the economy and to energy resources studies — on the supply side — has probably put these subjects well ahead of the human environment.

There continues to be a lack of attention to the societal implications of possible future developments and even less to possible societal response — something which a significant number of key civil servants are aware of but which they seem unable or unprepared to do much about. This is tied in with the public sector's marked lack of free searching and exploration of alternatives and attention to desirable *processes* for development as opposed to *end states*. One exception to this is the CIDA/DOE work referred to above. Likewise, there has been little work on concepts of societal development to provide the underpinnings for an understanding of the 'environment' for such development, a check list of criteria to be observed in the process of the improvement of that environment, and thus a frame of reference for decision-makers in making trade-offs in the shaping of development policy and programmes.

The Machinery

Certainly it is difficult to conclude that it is a shortage of resources available for futures studies that accounts for these shortcomings. Some $8 million was spent for 1971-75, and in FY 1975/76 a total of 187 man years was so used. Further, with some 70 bodies (public and private) involved in futures studies in 1975 there was no lack of interest.

The more immediate problem seems to be with the deployment of those resources, as exhibited by the lack of interest of most departments in going beyond their 'turf', the lack of a truly comprehensive body with programme responsibility for assessing societal (not just social) development, and a lack of attention on the part of cabinet members to fostering this overview in terms of both time and sectoral integration.

Supposedly these situations could be rectified if the cabinet were to act. It is not as though the cabinet members are completely unaware of the implications of not heeding possible future developments, it is more that their time budgets are dictated by the immediate pressures upon them. To bring pressure to bear by creating greater awareness upon the part of the more junior members of the legislature is something that Senator Lamontagne, who has continued to take a keen interest in this field, has been exploring. The 'Question Period' in Parliament could then be used to raise with cabinet ministers issues that do require this more comprehensive treatment. Experiences of other countries in obtaining the attention of cabinet are much needed.

Beyond cabinet action, it is not as though there is no room for manoeuvre by civil servants. A limited number have demonstrated considerable ingenuity in developing interdepartmental support for multi-disciplinary/multi-sectoral studies. However, unless there is political support for their activities they will never become truly legitimized and an accepted way of formulating policy options.

Naturally, one cannot omit reference to the need for a more aware and politicized public when discussing cabinet priorities. This should be part of the strategy of anyone concerned about rectifying the shortcomings of the existing machinery. Conferencing, use of the media and the educational system are all part of the standard tool kit.

A Paradigm Shift?

There will doubtless continue to be reviews in Canada and elsewhere, by academics and by governments, of the machinery of government and how it should be reorganized to permit the cooperation of different professionals and departments in the political process. There is a danger, however, in assuming that this reorganization will result in improved futures studies and in a future that is more globally viable and humanly fulfilling. Certainly, the machinery has to permit the cooperation and for this reason the analysis of institutional roles is useful. But we should not assume that the rest will necessarily follow.

For what the above assessment of the patterns exhibited by the studies of the functioning of the machinery suggests is that there are two levels of explanation of the problems identified. The more immediate and more superficial explanation of the dominance of the economically led development process and the blinkered sectoral structuring of the machinery lies with the greater political appeal of the concrete and tangible. Hence the attraction of 'end states' and of having a product to show for one's efforts and thus of channelling one's efforts towards a clearly definable goal. A more fundamental explanation is, however, doubtless rooted in the cartesian or linear thinking that pervades all Western industrial societies and especially that in North America.

This has very much affected the patterns of public sector organization and operation and within this prison of our own culture development has tended to be perceived as a linear process of accretion and the use of resources in the sense of their absorption. Thus, until now the various sectoral bodies have been looking at their separate futures and finding that they can, generally speaking, find some way of resolving their needs within that sector. A blind eye is turned to the externalities. And this has been especially so with regard to social implications, whether it be for energy, where the emphasis has been on the supply side, or communications where the emphasis has been utilizing available technology, or. . .and the list is a long one.

Thus if one is looking to improve the political process through the improved use of futures studies and cross-sectoral policy analysis one has first to give more attention to bringing about a paradigm shift that puts more emphasis on 'know why' than 'know how'. And what we have to ask is: 'What do we mean by development?' Only by obtaining a rethinking of the answer to this question can the relevance of the future for those who are now living and acting in the present be made clear.

What would hopefully emerge from such an exercise would be a new concept of development and thus a different framework which, while not rejecting economic growth, would be grounded in a different perception of how Man's individual and group development can be enhanced on a sustainable basis.

NOTES

1. *The Lamontagne Survey of Futures Studies: An Analysis and Summary* was published in June 1977 as a brief received by the Special Committee of the Senate on Science Policy (Ottawa: Supply and Services Canada, Ottawa KIA OS9).
2. Björn Wittrock, 'Futures Studies Without a Planning Subject', this volume, 119-50.
3. Address given by Prime Minister Ohira before both Houses of the National Diet on 25 January 1979.
4. S. Gustavsson, 'Where Research Policy Erred', this volume, 45-58.
5. This section draws heavily on the *1977 Annual Report* of the ECC (Ottawa: Supply and Services Canada, Ottawa KIA 0S9) and David Slater, *Planning Notes, The Annual Review and Research*, December 1978, unpublished.
6. This section draws heavily upon the *1977-78 Annual Report* of the SCC (Ottawa: Supply and Services Canada, Ottawa KIA 0S9).
7. See Daniel Tarschys 'Public Policy Innovation in a Zero Growth Economy: A Scandinavian Perspective', this volume, 9-25.

8 The New Zealand Commission for the Future: Origins, Objectives and Development

Juliet Lodge
University of Hull

In April 1976, the New Zealand Minister of National Development announced the establishment of a Task Force on Economic and Social Development to study planning and the main issues affecting the country's economic and social development (*New Zealand Yearbook 1977*, 945). The Task Force worked to a six-month deadline and issued a report, *New Zealand at the Turning Point*, in December following extensive consultations with government departments, interested organizations, groups, individuals and the sector councils established as a result of the National Development Conferences in 1968-69. The Task Force's major conclusions were that planning would be ineffective unless there was regular appraisal of the extent to which planning objectives were being achieved to enable governments to identify when goals were not been fulfilled and to adapt them or policies accordingly; that adequate mechanisms for coordinated planning did not exist; and that shortcomings could be attributed to governmental preoccupations with short-term policy options which were not integrated into longer-term strategies. The Task Force, therefore, advocated the strengthening of planning machinery and the creation of a body concerned with future planning; improving data processing and information gathering; widespread participation in planning and greater publicity and debate about future options related to internal and external factors. After the Task Force's disbanding, the government acted upon its recommendations and an Act was passed designed to improve planning in New Zealand.

Under the New Zealand Planning Act of 1 December 1977, statutory recognition was afforded the New Zealand Planning Council[1] and the Commission for the Future (CFF). The purpose of the New Zealand Planning Act was 'to make better provision for national planning in New Zealand' (New Zealand Planning Act 1977, 1). The Act also provides for regular consultation between the chairmen of both the New Zealand Planning Council and the CFF, and the coordination of their activities in order to avoid duplication of effort (*New Zealand Official Yearbook 1978*, 291). We shall concentrate on the work of the CFF. However, it is important to bear in mind that the CFF does have formal links with the New Zealand Planning Council, and that the latter is a body largely responsible to the Treasury (see Appendix I). The CFF does not have such close links with the New Zealand Productivity Centre which was established as an aid to planning and national production within the Department of Trade and Industry in January 1973. While the CFF is responsible to the Minister of National Development, and like the New Zealand Planning Council submits not later than the last day of February each year its proposed work programme for the period of twelve months commencing on the first day of April of that year, it also submits simultaneously a copy of its programme to the Minister of Science and Technology. By virtue of its composition and membership, the CFF has ready access to and links with a number of government departments.

The CFF, although given statutory recognition by the New Zealand Planning Act of 1977 and funded by the government, had in fact been established in September 1976 upon the initiative of the Minister of National Development. This initiative itself grew out of public debate during the 1974-76 period — much of it conducted via talk-back radio programmes, and within government and academic circles — over the question of New Zealand's future in an international political and economic world generally regarded as hostile to New Zealand's aspirations. This perception of the international environment, coupled with a desire to manage New Zealand's future at a time when New Zealand appeared to be subject to vacillations in international politics and trade over which it had no control, was instrumental in the establishment of a CFF. An appreciation of the socio-economic and political environment of the 1970s is, therefore, crucial to an understanding of the motives behind the CFF's establishment. This will be outlined briefly prior to an examination of the composition and functions of the CFF.

BACKGROUND

Following Britain's accession to the European Economic Community (EEC), the international oil crisis and domestic questioning of New Zealand's traditional international status as an ally of the USA and as a former colony of Britain's, close attention was afforded the question of New Zealand's future. Such attention coincided with domestic political changes in the guise of a Labour Government led by the late Norman Kirk, and subsequently by Mr Wallace Rowling. The New Zealand Labour Party's success at the 1972 General Election was significant since there had been a National Party Government in office continuously since 1960. The Labour Party's success was significant also in terms of international politics because the Labour Government adopted an avowedly anti-Western European stance.

Thus, it was asserted that New Zealand was a small, weak state in the South Pacific: an identity of interest with the developing islands of the South Pacific was proclaimed, and the hankering after a European identity resting on Anglo-Dutch immigrant roots repudiated. Coinciding with this was a rejection of continuing membership of military alliances — notably ANZUS with the USA — which were seen as of little practical value to an isolated island of, hitherto, little strategic importance in the South Pacific. Whereas the projection of a different international (qua Pacific) image was official policy (Lodge 1975b, 101-12; Lodge 1977, 75-91), the latter was not. However, the effect of this was a reappraisal of traditionally accepted norms and values.

The self-scrutiny to which New Zealanders submitted themselves was stimulated by New Zealand's (and the world's) changing economic circumstances. In particular, Britain's accession to the EEC had happened. As a consequence, New Zealand could no longer look forward to continuing unrestricted access to its traditional (British) market for increasing butter, cheese and lamb exports. That New Zealand would face some restrictions on its trade in these commodities with Britain had been apparent since the first British EEC entry bid. However, it was a fact that New Zealand was loathe — and remains loathe — to accept (Lodge 1975c, 287-99; Lodge 1978, 303-10; Lodge 1980). Indeed, New Zealand's attempts at diversifying its markets and commodities did not really take off until British entry to the EEC was imminent. Even then, New Zealand government ministers did not disguise their hopes for British secession, and New Zealand continues to claim that no alternative markets for its butter and lamb exports exist save in Britain.

However, the importance of Britain's accession to the EEC for New Zealand extended beyond the question of export markets and stimulated a reappraisal psychologically of New Zealand's international identity and a questioning of what an appropriate role might be for a relatively developed, militarily weak state dependent for export earnings on the exportation of a very limited range of primary, agricultural products. In order to give such speculation some form, and so that any conclusions reached would be useful to the policy-making processes of government and export agencies, the establishment of a committee or organization to promote 'socially relevant research' (Lodge 1975a, 9-10) and collate information and views about New Zealand's prospects was deemed desirable.

Prior to the creation of the CFF, academic discussions on New Zealand's future prospects crystallized into a plan to create some formal channel for exchanging information. These were indubitably stimulated by government agencies. In 1976, experts in their own right were issued with questionnaires asking what their specialist interests were and whether they would be interested in participating in discussions on the future. Shortly thereafter, the CFF was launched.

COMPOSITION AND ORGANIZATION OF THE CFF

The CFF comprises a commission and a secretariat. It is linked specifically with the Ministry of National Development. The composition of the CFF shows that its members are drawn from a range of professions, and include two MPs (one, the Minister of Broadcasting), two professors, a Vice-Chancellor, a lawyer, a businessman, the head of programme services (Radio New Zealand), the director-general of the Department of Scientific and Industrial Research, and the director of planning for the Auckland Regional Authority (Auckland being a city of 1.5 million people — New Zealand's population is 3.5 million). The commission is served by a permanent six-person secretariat which includes science and social science investigators.

MEMBERSHIP OF THE CFF COMMISSION

The commission of the CFF consists of not more than seven members appointed by the Governor-General of New Zealand on the recommendation of the Minister of National Development. One of these is appointed chairperson. The other members include:

— a Minister of the Crown appointed by the Minister of National Development (any Minister of the Crown designated for the time being by the Minister of National Development as an alternative member of the commission may act as a member of the commission in the place of the Minister for the time being holding office as a member of the commission). The fact that any Minister of the Crown acts as a member of the commission in the place of the member for the time being holding office under sub-section (1) (b) (New Zealand Planning Act, Part II, Section 10 [4]) shall be conclusive evidence of his authority to do so;

— an MP appointed by the Minister of National Development on the nomination of the Leader of the Official Opposition;

— a member of the New Zealand Planning Council appointed by the Minister on the nomination of the Council's Chairman;

— and the director-general of the Department of Scientific and Industrial Research.

In choosing the members of the CFF, the Minister has regard to their personal attributes, and the need for a diversity of knowledge and qualifications in fields relevant to the functions of the CFF. Members of the CFF hold office for such term as the Governor-General, on the recommendation of the Minister of National Development, specifies. The term may not exceed three years but the Act does provide for a person's re-appointment, and also for her or his 'retirement' by the Minister (New Zealand Planning Act 1977, 5-6).

FUNCTIONS OF THE CFF COMMISSION

The general functions of the commission are:
— to study the possibilities for the long-term economic and social development of New Zealand;
— to make information on those possibilities available to all MPs, and to publish such information for wider dissemination;
— to promote discussion on those possibilities and information relating to them;
— to report to the Minister on those possibilities.

In carrying out its general functions, the commission gives special attention to the long-term implications for New Zealand of new or prospective developments in science and technology; and has regard to prospective trends, policies, and events in New Zealand and overseas which could have important consequences for the country's future.

The commission has such other functions, powers and duties as are conferred or imposed upon it by or under the New Zealand Planning Act of 1977 or any other enactment. It is not, however, charged with making policy recommendations to government, being involved instead in examining possibilities and informing the public. Additionally, the commission has such other powers as may be reasonably necessary to enable it to carry out its functions.

WORKING PARTIES OF THE CFF COMMISSION

Four main working parties report to the CFF commission:
1. A *Technological working party* entrusted with identifying those areas of technology likely to have a significant impact on New Zealand and with reporting on them to the CFF. The working party has prepared a report on telecommunications/computers, plant and animal breeding (genetics in the widest sense), new energy technologies, resources satellites, the production of local raw materials, processing industry

technologies, non-processing manufacturing and service technologies, and transport. It has also highlighted major issues affecting health, education and welfare which require investigation but which are outside the working party's terms of reference;

2. *Systems and Modelling working party* charged with providing advice and consistency checks to world modelling and with explaining their relevance to New Zealand. It has prepared a futures matrix to provide a framework for the general study;

3. *Individuals in the Future working party* is charged with 'advising on the effects of possible new developments on the individual, and to look at the crucial issues for both the individual and corporate entities, including governmental, professional, voluntary and community groups (Commission for the Future *Newsletter* 1978, 3);

4. *Public Participation committee* involves individuals drawn from government departments, statutory bodies, universities, professional associations and private enterprise.

Additional committees may be established from time to time, and the CFF may appoint competent people, whether CFF members or not, to form a committee or committees to assist the CFF on matters within the scope of the CFF or as they are referred to it.

The CFF is also empowered to commission any person having expertise it needs to conduct research to assist the CFF. Neither CFF members nor CFF committee members are personally liable for either any act done or default made by the CFF or committee in good faith in pursuance of the powers and authorities of the CFF or CFF committee (New Zealand Planning Act 1977, 12).

CFF ACTIVITIES

The CFF has established a clear programme of work and activities for itself. In September 1977, it published a *Report on the First Year of Work* which was formally submitted to the Minister of National Development. Copies were sent to all MPs, respondents with whom the CFF was working already and other interested parties.

It is clear from Table 1 that a precise programme of activities was

TABLE 1
Work Schedule....
New Zealand in the Future World

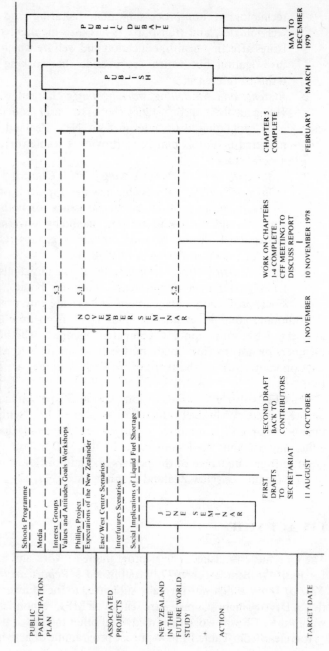

formulated and target audiences isolated. Apart from the programmes outlined below, colourful kitsets and leaflets were circulated informing the public about the creation of the CFF, and inviting them to write to the director about their ideas; to discuss New Zealand's future at home and at work; to join in workshops locally; to read futures books; to watch television programmes about the future; and to organize groups on the above. The CFF felt that one of its tasks was to encourage New Zealanders to think more positively about the future:

> If we see ourselves as insignificant, ignored by the larger and stronger nations, with little to contribute to the world, our choices will diminish along with our waning confidence. If we can correctly analyse the growing commodity dependencies that are bringing nations into new alliances then we may realistically set New Zealand's course and carve a new role for ourselves (*Report of the Commission for the Future* 1978, 4).

In keeping with the focus on New Zealand's international geopolitical position, dependence on exports and international status, the CFF decided that one of the first major studies that it undertook should concentrate on New Zealand's 'place in the world'.

It was decided that choices open to New Zealand would be determined by international factors. Consequently, the CFF decided that the programme for future studies should commence with an examination of New Zealand's place in the world. This study was *scheduled* for publication in March 1979 (See Table 1). Its aims were:

1 . to show New Zealand what its international image was and to isolate opportunities for developing international links;
2 . to identify what needed to be done in order to restructure developing needs;
3 . to educate the public about the inter-relationship between New Zealand's international, economic, social and ideological links and the country's capacity for national development;
4 . to promote understanding of New Zealand's responsibilities towards the world, especially as custodians of the social, physical and economic environment.

Having established a work programme for the study of *New Zealand in the Future World*, position papers were commissioned on: New Zealand and World Society: Towards the year 2000; New Zealand: Alternative Futures; and Attitudes and New Zealand's Future.

The findings of the CFF concerning New Zealand's international position were collated and abstracted from numerous reports submitted by government officials and outside experts (drawn mainly from New Zealand). They were then prepared for publication in booklet form.

The first booklet, *Resources and Technology: Sustainability*, set for publication in August 1979, posed a number of social and economic questions likely to influence resource use: to what extent should new Zealand trade with the rest of the world to obtain material goods? to what extent should New Zealand aim to become more self-sufficient, even if it means dependence on overseas capital and expertise to develop new industries? to what extent should New Zealand decentralize power, economic activity and welfare services? how should New Zealand adapt to new technologies, particularly the microprocessor? how should land be allocated among competing users? in what direction should New Zealand diversify? how can New Zealand make better use of imported and indigenous minerals? how can New Zealand plan a sustainable transport strategy based on renewable resources (the sun, hydro-electricity and wood)? should New Zealanders restructure their way of life so that much less commuting is necessary? and do New Zealanders prefer energy technologies which are large in scale and capital intensive, or smaller in scale and employing the skills of New Zealanders?

The second booklet, *Societies in Change: A Question of Scale*, scheduled for publication in September 1979, asks: what should be the scale of New Zealand's post industrial society? how can encouragement of diversity be achieved? to what extent can an informal economy contribute towards national growth? what should be the role of education and experts in New Zealand? to what degree can New Zealand afford to give equal opportunities to citizens in the future? what kind of welfare system should New Zealand adopt? how important is the survival of the family for the future? and what policies can New Zealand adopt to ensure a population structure which will be adequate for future economic and social needs?

The third booklet, *International Relations: Opportunities*, to be published in October 1979, confronts some key questions affecting foreign relations, economics and trade: would any modification of New Zealand's defence and trading stance improve its ability to weather the effects of any major world conflict? should New Zealand offer support for the development of a new international order? what action can New Zealand take to protect itself from the worst effects of a world depression? should New Zealand aim to create a Pacific Trade and Defence area? in which commodities should New Zealand try to become self-sufficient? to what extent should foreign investment and know-how be accepted in New Zealand? which commodities can most easily give a high return in markets which are easily penetrated without large transport costs? which multinationals either in New Zealand or overseas could be invited to develop a special relationship with New Zealand as a means of developing new industries? and should tourism be developed as a major industry?

The aim of the discussion booklets is to promote consideration of alternatives open to New Zealand. Indeed, in its paper (*Where Does This Country's Future Lie?*) promoting the booklets, the CFF asks New Zealanders which of the choices appeal to them and suggests that they should list the essential policies which need to be followed in order to realize their 'vision of the future', and then send them to the CFF in Wellington.

Associated with the study of *New Zealand in the Future World* are seven projects concerning the following:

1. significant qualitative futures studies forecasts for the period from the end of the 1970s to 2000;
2. an investigation of development alternatives for New Zealand (undertaken at the East-West Centre, Hawaii) to formulate and investigate scenarios for the Pacific region using the Mesarovic-Pestel computer model;
3. evaluation of futures literature;
4. social implications of the liquid fuel shortage in the long term (a highly topical question in view of the contentiousness of developing nuclear power stations for New Zealand);
5. the possible place for New Zealand in the prospective world food market around the year 2000 (a study born out of speculation that New Zealand could become one of the world's farms);

6 . international relations: New Zealand in the future world study;

7 . OECD interfutures study on development/developing country relationships using the SARU model.

The OECD's Interfutures project (more formally entitled 'a study of the future development of advanced industrial societies in harmony with that of developing countries'), designed to help governments place their day-to-day actions in a long-term and worldwide context, was launched in 1976. The project was initiated by Japan and seventeen other countries, including New Zealand, are taking part. Recognizing that many exercises in exploring the future fail to analyse sufficiently the existing data, Interfutures began its work with a systematic review of a large number of world problems (energy, population, food, armaments, raw materials, technology, trade, aid etc.), examining what has been done already throughout the world, highlighting the main trends, and asking key questions before moving on to examine likely future trends. After the preliminary phase, the team was organized into three working groups: (1) to examine the outlook for international trade; (2) to consider changes in values and resulting new demands in advanced societies and analyse the structural and sectoral changes likely to affect economic activity, both in these societies and the developing world; and (3) to focus on the long-term outlook for developing countries and construct scenarios of world development. The scenarios obtained, via macro-economic analyses and models and micro-economic or structural analyses of the main industrial sectors, are designed to facilitate understanding of the interaction between economic, social and political factors and to explore consequences of various possible strategies that might be adopted by OECD governments.

Apart from the activities of the experts, the CFF has made special efforts to involve the public in discussions about New Zealand's future and to persuade the public that the CFF was sensitive and receptive to the views of the community.

THE CFF AND PUBLIC PARTICIPATION

The interest in involving the public stemmed from the notion that New Zealand was an egalitarian society eschewing esoteric notions advanced by distant elites and favouring instead evaluation by the interested public. Accordingly, five public participation projects were launched:

1 . a project to ascertain the expectations of New Zealanders;
2 . a workshop programme to discover values and attitudes of New Zealanders;
3 . a schools participation project;
4 . a project in association with the Commission for the Environment to instigate community involvement in both regional and wider national interests;
5 . a public debate on responses, options and choices for New Zealand. This was to consist of a major study report and monitoring of the media.

The aim was to ensure the involvement of all sectors of New Zealand society in the debate on the future. The CFF saw its role as being to assemble and disseminate information about the future in such a way that New Zealanders would be drawn into the process of exercising choices as to the development of New Zealand society. A sporadic 'Newsletter' was produced to keep people informed about the progress of work undertaken by the CFF.

In addition, kitsets were produced and sent to more than 100 organizations, and all community groups have been encouraged to participate. Anxious to educate the public about futures concepts, the CFF secretariat is working closely with the Education Department to prepare educational aids for schools. A simulation game for high school students was designed and the first Mark 1 version has been tested in the schools. Links are maintained with teacher organizations and a resource list of current futures material is being prepared. Over and above this, the CFF has published several reports — including a report on the CFF's seminar on forecasting techniques, a submission to the Royal Commission on Nuclear Power Generation, and yearly reports on its work. It has despatched to its respondents a number of reports prepared for it by government departments, professional groups and individuals.

EVALUATING THE CFF

The CFF has embarked upon an ambitious and impressive programme of work which countries in Western Europe that have yet to try and confront futures dilemmas in an organized manner may learn something from. To some extent, any evaluation of the CFF's activities and accomplishments must be premature and tentative. This qualification aside, some evaluation can be attempted with a view to indicating possible problems inherent in the process of bureaucratizing and institutionalizing studies of the future. While not wishing to detract from the CFF's endeavours, it is important to recognize that New Zealand's political culture generally has a stultifying effect upon efforts at innovation. The emphasis upon preserving a conservative consensus of opinion may inhibit the acceptance of any recommendations made by the CFF. It also accounts for the CFF's accent on publicizing its work and stimulating public involvement in it.

From our brief survey of the activities of the CFF, it is apparent that its achievements to date have been restricted to two things: (i) stimulating informal public debate about changing socio-economic and international political realities; and (ii) re-educating public expectations as to the kind of standard of living that can reasonably be expected during the next 30 years in view of New Zealand's changing economic fortunes.

It is equally apparent that the CFF has attempted to make use of social science methods and models on which to base its forecasts for the future. However, it remains unclear as to whether they will have operational use and translate themselves into specific recommendations which politicians and governments may adopt. Moreover, some of the contributors to the projects have clearly been influenced — in their approach — by models and views propagated and developed outside New Zealand, and it is possible to discern a desire on their part to keep up with international developments. But it remains unclear as to how, or whether, those are relevant to New Zealand.

One of the problems that the CFF must face concerns the extent to which any of its prognostications become relevant or operational. Useful as it is to re-educate the public into expecting less in material terms, it is insufficient simply to stimulate public debate — and with it, public expectations of government action to change (and improve) New Zealand's international position, especially if government is either unwilling or unable to respond accordingly.

Moreover, it is difficult to determine how valuable the futures reports are or will be. Obviously, their utility to New Zealand would be improved if the CFF were to take a bolder stance and to make specific policy recommendations instead of publicizing a series of conjectural notions in a form best described as dry bureaucratic language. Furthermore, it would no doubt be useful to both New Zealand government officials and the CFF if feedback could be obtained not only from New Zealand sources but also from bodies in other countries which, though not having a New Zealand-centric approach and perceptual framework, share a liberal-democratic outlook and have futures studies of their own. Their perceptions of both their own, and New Zealand's, future options could be usefully compared. Obviously, great disparity in expectations between any studies produced by commissions for the future and committees examining the future would be interesting to scrutinize and explore, as would the coordination of simultaneously conducted programmes in different countries.

In the interim, it is necessary to assess the effectiveness of the CFF as a policy planning body. To what extent does it perform the function of futures planning? As yet, hardly at all. So far it has been little more than a forum for debate. This is useful in itself. But presumably it is hoped that its conclusions will have some practical applicability. The involvement of government officials drawn from the Ministries of Foreign Affairs, Defence and the Department of Scientific and Industrial Research, together with agricultural and economic experts, attests to this. Yet, it is difficult to discern how the CFF's views will translate themselves into specific policy recommendations or policy advice. The existing publications of the CFF offer no guidelines. This could well have been deliberate and justifiable in terms of the notion of it being an 'independent' body and one unwilling to adopt a paternalistic/elitist directing and advisory role vis-à-vis government or — as yet — more especially vis-à-vis New Zealand society which is strongly enamoured of the ideals of egalitarianism, of everyone having an opportunity to 'have a say', and which resents and distrusts 'experts'.

The CFF's non-involvement in making clear-cut policy recommendations may also be partly attributable to its youth, and to desires to ensure that it is apolitical and does not become associated with an ideological stance perpetuated by any one political party or government. (New Zealand's system of government, though based on a unicameral parliament, is founded on British principles and in practice results in alternating one party governments. Every three years a General Election is held.)

This is a particularly important consideration in view of New Zealand's political culture and the widely-held view that government officials (referred to as 'public' rather than 'civil' servants) are both politicized (that is sensitive to the political climate in which decisions are announced) and partisan (that is, self-identify with and advance certain political ideals). Indeed, after the 1960-72 period of unbroken National Party rule (the National Party is a right of centre party), it was argued that difficulties encountered by the Labour Government (replaced at the 1975 General Election by a National Government which was again returned to office in 1978) in implementing policy stemmed from obstructionism on the part of bureaucrats partisan to National Party ideals. There has been little rigorous testing of the proposition. This has been attributed to New Zealand government restrictions on access to information (Smith 1975, 410). However, such studies as have been done conclude that there is evidence of partisanship and evidence of bureaucratic frustration with rational and administratively sound policies formulated by government officials being overturned for reasons of political expediency by government ministers (Smith 1975, 406-10). The implications of this for the CFF's non-partisanship require some appraisal since government officials *are* associated with its work.

The involvement of government officials and the association of government ministers with the activities of the CFF means that keen government attention is paid to the work done by the CFF. Moreover, they have access to the detailed reports commissioned by the CFF from independent outside experts, and issue 'advice' to the CFF's own secretariat and committee responsible for drafting booklets to be published and made available to the public.

The implications of this are twofold. First, that the CFF does make a greater input in terms of the quantity of information disseminated into a few official-level government channels. Second, that irrespective of whether they do so or not, government officials are in a position to advise against the publication for public debate of any views submitted to the CFF which may be deemed to be too innovative, or not in keeping with dominant views about future developments. This means that rather conservative and consensus-based views will come to be distributed by the

CFF and that it will — possibly inadvertently — foreclose the discussion and consideration of futures scenarios not enjoying group support. This could prove dysfunctional to effective, critical evaluation of policy alternatives.

Finally, it is worth considering why — apart from the reasons given in the introduction to this paper — it was considered desirable to have a CFF. On the one hand, it can be suggested that its establishment represented both a positive attitude on the part of the government towards the question of planning for the future, and a desire to promote independent (party politically speaking) analysis of contemporary and future problems. In this respect, it may have been hoped that 'group-think' could be avoided. On the other hand, the establishment of an independent body to examine futures problems also represented tacit acknowledgement of the fact that such futures analysis and planning could not be accomplished effectively within the echelons of existing government departments and bureaucracies.

Indeed, if such futures research and planning requires the pooling of specialist skills and expertise, then no single interdepartmental working group coordinated perhaps by the Prime Minister's Office, or by the Minister of National Development, would have the necessary skills at its disposal. The reliance, too, on 'generalists' rather than 'specialists' within government departments, and the preference for 'generalist' MPs unable for the most part to contribute specialist knowledge to the debate (Jackson 1973, 138; Goldstein 1975, 190-96), also militated against entrusting futures research simply to government officials. Any interdepartmental working group comprising representatives from all departments would not only be unmanageable but even then would lack the requisite expertise. It would, therefore, still call on submissions from outside bodies and experts. The administration of such an interdepartmental working group would also prove so cumbersome that both logistic and political reasons would favour the establishment of a separate organization to which key government departments would have ready access.

Whether or not it was felt that the nature of bureaucracies and bureaucratic politics, or that the limited extent to which short-term forward planning was engaged in by different government departments militated against medium and long-term forecasting and conjecture is difficult to ascertain. However, it may be surmised that the comparatively small size, limited skills and resources (Vital 1967; Rothstein 1968; Schou and Bruntland 1971; Spiegel 1972) of the hard-pressed government officials and bureaucrats in New Zealand, coupled with the tendency for there to be little formal forward planning, meant that there was little time, finance and scope for them to undertake the longer-term projections entrusted to the CFF. To remedy deficiencies in the capacity for government officials to engage in such long-term planning, it was deemed expedient to draw upon the resources of outside experts, thereby supplementing the pool of ideas and capabilities at the disposal of the policy-makers. This would be perfectly rational and logical. Yet, it must be recognized that it means in effect that the CFF is performing tasks that individual government departments either would like to fulfil but are unable to, or which they feel New Zealand society would not wish to be restricted to, or which they might not consider an appropriate sphere for exclusive government activity. Indeed, were such futures study to be confined within the ranks of the New Zealand bureaucracy, there can be little doubt that there would be a public outcry at government officials 'wasting time on science fiction' at the expense of dealing with problems of the day.

Whatever the reasons for the CFF, it is clear that its utility must depend ultimately upon the extent to which its outputs are realistic, become usable inputs into government policy-making processes, and isolate appropriate series of policy alternatives and choices for the future. Moreover, if the CFF's views become inputs into committees within government departments charged with short-term policy-making, then they must go beyond mere statement of conjecture and translate projections to the year 2000 into short-term operational policy recommendations. However, this assumes that fundamental decisions as to an appropriate policy to attain them can be made, and that consensus on policy can be created. It may be that the CFF is indirectly fulfilling a publicity and educative function in trying to shape such a consensus among the public.

Yet, at some point, political and governmental thinking and choices must be made manifest. If the intention is for government to 'follow' public opinion, then several years will elapse before any futures studies have operational relevance. Too great a delay between the publication of the first futures research booklets and their translations into policy-relevant recommendations (by either the CFF itself, the government, or MPs) will negate the usefulness of the CFF's work. However, against this, it must be recognized that the very nature of the CFF's links with the New Zealand Planning Council may mean that this body capitalizes on its findings and seeks expeditious action on them.

The short period of time since the establishment of the two bodies makes it impossible to assess whether the two organizations' work has become mutually reinforcing and complementary, and whether their outputs are being heeded and adopted by MPs and government members. At most, one can hazard a guess that debate will be stimulated as intended, and that some MPs and political parties may adapt recommendations for their own political purposes. This is unlikely to occur before mid-1980, following several months of public debate about the trends and options for New Zealand published by the CFF in late 1979.

NOTES

1. The New Zealand Planning Council, having been set up in March 1977, issued a document in August 1977 entitled *A Moment of Truth* . This was designed to secure a response from a wide cross-section of the community to assist it in the preparation of its first major report. In February 1978, the Monetary and Economic Council was disbanded and its role in monitoring economic trends and policies was assigned to the Planning Council. The formation of a new independent group (the Economic Monitoring Group) charged with monitoring current economic trends and policies was announced by the Chairman of the Planning Council in April 1978.

REFERENCES

Commission for the Future (1978) *Newsletter*.
—— (1978) *Report for the year ending 31 March*.
Goldstein, R. (1975) *Labour in Power: Promise and Performance*, Wellington: Price Milburn for New Zealand University Press.
Jackson, K. (1973) *New Zealand: Politics of Change*. Wellington: Reed.
Lodge, J. (1975a) 'Socially Relevant Research', *New Zealand Monthly Review*, Vol. 16, No. 167: 9-10.
—— (1975b) 'In Pursuit of Regionalism: New Zealand Foreign Policy Under Mr Kirk', *Cooperation and Conflict*, Vol. 10: 101-12.
—— (1975c) 'New Zealand, Britain and the EEC in the 1970s', *Australian Outlook*, Vol. 29: 287-99.
—— (1977) 'New Zealand Foreign Policy in 1976', *Australian Outlook*, Vol. 31: 75-91.
—— (1978) 'New Zealand and the Community', *The World Today*, Vol. 34: 303-10.
—— (1980) 'New Zealand and the EEC in 1979', *New Zealand International Review,* Vol. 5, No. 2: 27-28 and No. 3: 24-25.
New Zealand Official Yearbook (1978) Wellington: Government Printer.
New Zealand Yearbook (1977) Wellington: Department of Statistics.
New Zealand Planning Act (1977) Wellington: Government Printer.
Rothstein, R. L. (1968) *Alliances and Small Powers*, New York: Columbia University Press.
Schou, A. and Bruntland, A. (1971) *Small States in International Relations*, Stockholm: Almquist.
Smith, T. B. (1975) 'Politics and the Bureaucrat', in S. Levine (ed.), *New Zealand Politics: A Reader*, Melbourne: Cheshire.
Spiegel, S. L. (1972) *Dominance and Diversity*, Boston: Little Brown & Co.
Vital, D. (1967) *The Inequality of States*, Oxford: Oxford University Press.

APPENDIX

New Zealand Planning Council

Functions and powers of the Council

The general functions of the Council shall be:

  (a) to advise the Government on planning for social, economic and cultural development in New Zealand;
  (b) to assist the Government to coordinate such planning;
  (c) to comment to the Government on programmes for social, economic and cultural development in New Zealand, and to recommend the priorities that should be accorded to them;
  (d) to act as focal point for a process of consultative planning about New Zealand's medium-term development;
  (e) to foster discussion among those agencies (Government and private) concerned with planning, particularly in the economic, environmental, social and cultural fields;
  (f) to submit advice to the Government on links between planning at the national and regional levels;
  (g) to prepare reports on any matter affecting the economic, social, or cultural development of New Zealand;
  (h) to submit any report prepared by it to the Minister if it thinks fit;
  (i) to recommend that any report submitted to the Minister under paragraph (h) of this subsection be laid before Parliament;
  (j) to publish documents on planning topics which in the view of the Council merit wide consideration and public debate;
  (k) to consider any other matter which is referred to the Council by the Minister or which is relevant to the proper performance of the functions mentioned in paragraphs (a) to (j) of this subsection.

The Council shall have such other functions, powers, and duties as are concerned or imposed on it by or under this Act or any other enactment.

The Council shall have such other powers as may be reasonably necessary to enable it to carry out its functions.

Membership of the Council

The Council shall consist of:

  (a) not more than 12 members to be appointed by the Governor-General on the recommendation of the Minister, of whom one shall be appointed as Chairman;

(b)   the Minister;

(c)   the Secretary to the Treasury;

In recommending persons for appointment as members of the Council the Ministers shall have regard to

(a)   their personal attributes;

(b)   the need for a diversity of knowledge and experience in fields relevant to the functions of the Council to be present among its members;

(c)   the capacity of the Council as a whole to promote a sense of common purpose among different sections of the community in planning New Zealand's future.

Terms of office of members of the Council

Except as otherwise provided by this Act, every appointed member of the Council shall hold office for such term as the Governor-General on the recommendation of the Minister shall specify in his appointment, being, in the case of the Chairman, a term not exceeding 5 years and, in the case of any other appointed member, a term not exceeding 4 years.

Every appointed member of the Council shall be eligible for reappointment from time to time.

Every appointed member of the Council, unless he sooner vacates his office under section 18 of this Act, shall continue in office until his successor comes into office, notwithstanding that the term for which he was appointed may have expired.

Source: New Zealand Planning Act 1977.

III Policy Innovation, Policy Analysis and Futures Studies: Barriers and Bridges

9 What Should Forecasters Do? A Pessimistic View

Jonathan I. Gershuny
University of Sussex

I. INTRODUCTION

What role should forecasters play in the process of public policy-making? The various answers to this question form the major part of normative policy analysis. Very broadly, there are two alternative views. The first, held by proponents of 'rationality', suggests that forecasters should act as the *technical instruments* of political authorities, comprehensively reviewing the alternative feasible options, and assessing the consequences of their adoption. The second, held by the proponents of 'incrementalism' in public policy-making, is that technical debate about the range of alternatives and their consequences can safely be left to the concerned political interests, so that the role of the forecaster is seen as *partisan participation* in the political debate over policy choice. In this paper I shall try to demonstrate that rationality and incrementalism are not, in fact, alternative normative prescriptions, but, respectively, the unachievable ideal and the regrettable reality.

There is a strange personal relationship between these two views; incrementalists are frequently rationalists who have got older. Rationality, or rather its adoption as a norm for the making of public policy, is certainly an ideal of youth, and may be all too easily dismissed as the product of high aspirations and inexperience. Incrementalism, on the other hand, is seen as an attribute of the wise and the experienced, who know how things work. A prize example of this aging process is to be found in the person of the American political scientist Lindblom who, in the years following the publication of his *Politics, Economics and Welfare* (written in collaboration with R. Dahl), in which the rationalist case is quite moderately but clearly expressed, so fundamentally changed his views on the matter that he wrote (with Braybrooke) the classic text on incrementalism, *A Strategy of Decision* (1963). Other examples of policy analysts who have changed sides in this direction are not infrequent:[1] I know of none who have moved from an incrementalist to a rationalist position. It appears that experience of the real world of public policy-making turns the young, optimistic and radically inclined social engineer into a pessimistic reactionary in spite of himself. The present writer has, unhappily, experienced some part of this process of disillusion.

The impossibility of rational policy-making — and hence, the lack of a real role for forecasters — is, it will emerge, a worrying symptom of a deep malaise in Western political systems. The ultimate theoretical justification for our systems of government is that the collective political institutions can, with reasonable regularity and reliability, improve people's welfare. If governments cannot calculate and compare the effects of alternative courses of action — if they cannot act rationally — then they cannot guarantee to improve or even protect individual interests. In this context, our ability to prescribe a role for forecasters in public policy-making provides a fundamentally important challenge. In this paper I shall spell out the theoretical issues that underlie this rather unhappy view.

2. THE INCREMENTALISTS' CRITIQUE
OF NAIVE RATIONALITY

The simplest view of rational policy-making runs approximately as follows. We assume the existence of a politically responsible executive, which in some manner embodies, or represents, the values of the community as a whole. Answering to this group of politicians is a group of technical experts, whose business is to *identify* the full range of alternative policy options available to the politicians, *forecast* the likely consequences — the costs and the benefits — of each of the feasible policies, and *report* the results of their investigations to the political authorities. The politicians are then in a position to choose that policy which best fits the values that they embody. This straightforward view, as expressed by such writers as Herbert Simon, may be referred to as 'comprehensive' or 'holistic' rationality.[2]

Incrementalists have two fundamental criticisms of holistic rationality.[3] The first objection centres on the impossibility of a 'Social Welfare Function'. Kenneth Arrow demonstrated that, under a very general set of assumptions, we cannot expect to find agreement within a society over the values to be embodied in policy-making; there is no general procedure for identifying a 'best' policy for a society. So how do the politically responsible authorities choose among alternatives? If there can be no Social Welfare Function, argue the incrementalists, the political authorities can have no moral sanction for their choice. If there is no agreed set of values against which to assess the consequences of alternative courses of action, then there is no need for impartial technical analysis; all that is necessary is that the various political interests decide on their own preferred policies, and press them through the partisan political processes.[4]

This first objection is a theoretical one, undermining the philosophical foundations of rationality. The second objection is a practical one: that the comprehensive rational programme of action is not feasible. Experts have a strictly finite ability to comprehend reality, and yet the holistic rational programme calls for a complete survey of policy options. In most cases the available range of policies is very large, and the range of effects of each is limitless. And worse, these effects are not evenly distributed across the population, so numbers of sub-populations for which the effects must be separately evaluated is in principle only limited by the number of individuals in the population. Clearly, a truly comprehensive policy assessment exercise must be infinitely costly — and yet any less than comprehensive policy review cannot meet the rationalists' ideal. And even if, somehow, such a comprehensive analysis were achieved, how could the political authorities use it? The quantity of information that would be generated would overwhelm even the most zealously hard-working politician. The comprehensive rational ideal is impractical because the quantity of analysis it requires is without limit.[5]

In fact, both the theoretical and the practical objections are beside the point, since rationalists have a rather more subtle argument in mind. It is, however, important to follow the objections through to their conclusion, since on these two objections is founded the incrementalists' own prescription for public policy-making.

The incrementalists' prescription has three parts. First is a limitation on the scale of innovation in policy choice. Changes in public policy-making are to be only marginal, so that the consequences of the innovation may be seen by comparison of the present performance of the system with its previous behaviour. In this way prior technical analysis becomes unnecessary; the affects of the policy can be monitored and assessed as they happen. The second element of the prescription concerns this process of assessment: rather than expert evaluation of consequences of policies, assessment is to take place entirely within the partisan process. Where a new policy is found to have a deleterious effect on some section of the population, so the incrementalists argue, a political interest group will emerge and participate in the process of 'partisan mutual adjustment' with the purpose of contesting the policy. Which brings us to the third element; if the policy innovation has been suitably cautious and marginal, and if the political interests which oppose it are sufficiently powerful, it can be abandoned, thus (the incrementalists hope) returning the system to its state prior to the innovation. These three elements in combination — incremental changes, partisan mutual adjustment and reversibility — combine to form a policy-making system in which forecasters have no substantial role whatsoever.

Now, of course, the only real merit of this system (as a normative *prescription* — we will return to its status as a *description* in a moment) — is that it does not fall foul of the incrementalists' criticisms of rationality. And since, as we shall see in section 4 of this paper, these criticisms are aimed at a man of straw, and do not threaten the rationalist aspiration to any considerable extent, the argument in favour of incrementalism is not all that strong. But before turning to the more subtle and substantial arguments in favour of rationality, and hence undermining the justification of incrementalism, it will be helpful to examine some of the internal problems with the incrementalists' prescription.

3. INTERNAL OBJECTIONS TO INCREMENTALISM

The question we have to ask is not whether incrementalism can work; we know from the examples provided by its proponents that it does. Rather, we need to know whether incrementalism can be *justified*. In the next section I will outline an argument which provides a theoretical basis for assessing alternative policy-making systems from first principles; but for a moment it may be helpful to consider some rather less fundamental issues — particular circumstances in which incrementalist policy-making must operate in a clearly pathological manner.

Consider a political system experiencing a change in its external environment — a change in the nature of its foreign markets, perhaps, or in the technical organization of production of its staple export. If the change takes place sufficiently slowly, then clearly marginal policies may be able to cope with the problem. New markets, new products, may be explored on an experimental, small-scale basis, to be further encouraged if successful, and abandoned if not. But the larger or faster the change, the more difficult it becomes to find policies which are both effective and also small scale and easily reversible. The first and most substantial internal problem with incrementalism is simply that it provides no protection for political systems against radical changes in their environment.[6]

The next pair of problems concern the time scale of policy-making. Consider a policy designed to meet a particular problem, which would in fact be successful in the long run, but which would initially show no results, or even negative results. We can easily envisage circumstances in which such a policy would be reversed before it could prove its effectiveness. We can even imagine circumstances in which the consistent adoption of *any one* course of action might cope with an intrinsically resolvable issue, but the frequent reversals in policy to be expected from incrementalism would prevent any resolution. And just as policies with a long time scale may present problems for incrementalism, so may quick-acting policies. Any policy innovation, however marginal, may affect new interests; but interest groups take time to form, gain legitimacy, political knowledge and experience. There is no way to ensure that incremental policy innovations and the articulation of new political interests remain in phase.

Are small changes necessarily reversible? The incrementalist model assumes that they are, but this is not necessarily so. How often do we obliterate a motorway, however small? And even if we did, could the damaged community revert to its previous status? Can we in fact reverse a nuclear energy programme, however slowly implemented? For the model to work, politicians would have to impose on themselves a self-denying ordinance — not to adopt irreversible policies. A mechanism through which this might be achieved is difficult to imagine. And the proponents of incrementalism do not state clearly that as part of their preferred strategy they abjure a particular wide range of public policies. Certainly this objection might be taken to unreasonable lengths — after all, every policy is irreversible in the ultimate sense that it is impossible to blot out the memories of those who have experienced its effects. But nevertheless the central point here is quite fundamental; it will always be risky to adopt a course of action without a substantial analysis of its consequences — except in cases where its effects can be reversed.

And finally we must face up to the problem of those who do not have, and cannot reasonably be expected to have, an audible voice in the partisan political process. The participation in interest groups and the lobbying of party politicians are predominantly middle-class activities. Other sorts of interest — children, for example — may be actively excluded from the political process. If we could be certain that existent interest groups would necessarily assume moral responsibility to protect the interests of those not actively involved in the political process, then we might be content. But how is such moral responsibility to be promoted? This problem becomes particularly difficult in circumstances of rapid social change, where traditional moral responsibilities (e.g. care of the aged) are removed from individuals, while new dependencies (e.g. of the Third World on rich states) emerge. It would seem that in general the only way that such interests may be included in the political process would be through the deployment of experts, relatively free of partisan concerns, in the assessment of alternative policies.

Each of these objections to incrementalism consists of cases where the behaviour of the system might not conform to our intuitive ideas of how political systems ought to behave. From where do we derive these intuitions? In the next section I shall try to outline in a very general manner the theoretical basis of our notion of 'good government', and show how norms for the design of a policy-making process may be derived from this.

4. A NORMATIVE BASIS FOR THE PRESCRIPTION OF POLICY-MAKING STRATEGIES

There is a traditional form of political argument, in which individuals are placed in some artificially abstracted circumstances, and set to discussing the appropriateness of alternative systems of government. We may sometimes be in doubt as to the relevance of conclusions arrived at, under such artificial circumstances, to everyday conduct. But nevertheless, *to the extent that we can agree on the specification of these artificial circumstances as an appropriate simplification or reduction of everyday life*, we are bound to accept the conclusions reached within them as morally binding. Where such political authors find agreement within their hypothetical debates, we can only reject their conclusions by rejecting the procedures they use for simplifying the context under which the debate takes place. And, trivially, if some political writer were able to identify political values which every conceivable participant in the debate would accept, and could do this without at all simplifying the context of the debate, then we would have no grounds for rejecting his arguments, and would have to accept his conclusions as fundamental political truths.

Of course, no one has been able to identify such truths concerning those issues — social justice and liberty for example — to which political philosophers traditionally address themselves; we may perhaps suspect that these issues are quite intractable because of the conflicts stemming from economic scarcity. This form of argument is not typically adopted in normative policy analysis; the 'oughts' in this field of endeavour are usually obscurely derived, and seldom explicitly justified. It may, however, prove to be a fruitful activity for our purpose; in particular, it does appear that the requirement for rationality in public policy-making may be a consensual value. In spite of conflict over which policies should be chosen, we can still expect every member of a society to agree on the requirements for a rational policy-making *process*.

The argument proceeds as follows.[7]

1. Without assuming any particular process of optimization, individuals may be expected to seek to improve the circumstances of their lives whenever possible, and to avoid any decline in their style or standard of life.

2. They may be expected to recognize the existence of a diffuse set of specific and non-specific benefits which accrue to them as a result of the existence of a system of making decisions collectively for the society as a whole.

3. The knowledge of these may outweigh the specific costs accruing to particular groups as a result of adverse decisions on particular issues; these groups, though resenting the outcome may still accept it. (The specific costs may on the other hand *not* be justified by the diffuse benefits — see 9 below.)

These three assumptions are very loose, and it is difficult to imagine any objections to them; and yet we can develop some strong conclusions from them. Let us, for the purposes of the argument, divide the society into two parts, consisting of one group which does not suffer any adverse decisions ('winners'), and another which does suffer such decisions ('losers'). What principles will guide peoples' evaluation of alternative policy-making procedures? We can only say that:

4. The losers will want reassurance that the costs they bear are necessary in the sense of resulting from irreconcilable political conflict. In particular they will wish to know that there is no unconsidered policy that would produce a 'Pareto Improvement' for the society (i.e. leave the losers better off without worsening the position of the winners).

5. The winners will wish to be reassured that they are doing as well as they can do from the policy-making process.

Implication 5 follows trivially from assumption 1, and forms an almost tautological justification for rationality. Implication 4 is, however, much more interesting, and, in combination with 5, produces a rather powerful criterion for assessing policy-making strategies. Let us consider first the incrementalists' strategy.

6. It is clear that the process of partisan mutual adjustment does not provide for Pareto Optimization as required by 4 except in the case where a Pareto Improvement is sought in order to construct a winning coalition. In general, the partisan political process tends exclusively to the interest of the winners.

7. It is also clear that the winners can only be reassured that they are doing as well as they can do if they have carried out some sort of survey of the options available to them — if, in fact, they have undergone a rational analysis!

In points 6 and 7 we have in substance the set of objections to incrementalism outlined in the previous section — but derived from some rather primitive and unobjectionable principles. Similarly, with regard to the rationalists' prescription, we can say:

8. Points 4 and 5 require some process of comprehensive review and evaluation of the full range of feasible policy options.

— we have in effect a normative justification of policy-making rationality.

This may seem a rather involved procedure, but it does enable us to do two things which carry the argument considerably further. The first is to dispose of one of the incrementalists' objections to rationality outlined in section 2: the lack of a Social Welfare Function. Our argument here suggests that even in the absence of any one 'best' policy for the society as a whole, we can still choose policies as a result of a comprehensive rational survey; we choose that policy which is preferred by the winners, and is also Pareto Optimal for the losers.

The second is, unhappily, to derive conclusions on which this whole system founders:

9. There may, however, exist issues such that the losers feel that their costs outweigh the benefits in 2 above, and therefore wish to secede from the system — the political consensus breaks down. (We will refer to this situation as 'issue dissensus').

10. This dissensus may stem not from the content of the issues, but from the manner in which they are treated — from failures in terms of 4 and 5 above. (We will refer to this as 'process dissensus'.)

Where consensus breaks down, either the political system itself breaks down — or else the level of coercion within the system rises.

The purpose of the last sections of this paper is to consider these last two conclusions in the context of the question of the role of forecasters in the policy-making process. But before coming to this point, we must briefly consider the other objection to rationality outlined in section 2 — its impracticability.

The answer to this second objection is simply that the incrementalists have oversimplified the rationalists' prescription. In fact, none of the principal rationalist authors believe that comprehensive or holistic analysis is feasible; they each propose procedures for limiting the scope of rationality. Thus, Simon (1957) prescribes 'satisficing', Etzioni (1968), 'mixed scanning', while Dror (1968) advances a complex procedure under the rubric of an 'optimal model'. These procedures differ in their details, but they have in common that they are *iterative* processes requiring;

— a preliminary, comprehensive if superficial, scan through the full range of feasible options and effects;

— a consideration of the implications of choosing alternative bounds for detailed study;

— the selection of a limited range of options and effects for detailed consideration, bearing in mind the relationship between the marginal costs of the analysis and the marginal benefits likely to accrue from it.[8]

Comprehensive rationality is certainly impracticable because of its open-endedness — but the ends of rationality may in principle be approximately approached by some procedure of bounded rationality. But unfortunately there are a number of practical problems which are not identified by the incrementalists — and not so easy to evade.

5. THE CRITIQUE OF BOUNDED RATIONALITY

So far we have been concerned with incrementalism in its normative guise; we have been able to show quite clearly that there are no good grounds for *prescribing* its adoption. Nevertheless, some aspects of the model still stand as an adequate *description* of how policy-making actually proceeds; in the patterns of behaviour of political systems lie the real problems of implementing rational policy-making. In this section we will consider a number of these problems.

The first problem is simply that policy-making bureaucracies are naturally resistant to rationality. This results from the processes of bureaucratic development; in order to achieve efficiency, administrative institutions specialize. Typically they develop into a series of independent offices, each of which bears complete responsibility for one area of administration, and no competency whatsoever outside that area. Initially this pattern of organization may well be the result of a rational analysis which identifies the economies of scale which may be expected to accrue from specialization. But once in existence these individual 'offices' acquire their own interests, which are limited to the performance of the specific tasks allotted to them and which exclude consideration of issues outside their competency. Individuals within these institutions acquire functions whose fulfilment gives them satisfaction. The institutions develop procedures which relate to their own internal requirements rather than to those of the society as a whole; the society's purpose are *displaced* by those of the institution. Rationality requires some broad consideration of issues facing the society; bureaucratic offices are by their nature unable to take this broad view, and, because of the process of goal displacement, are inclined to resist it. Furthermore, since wide authority over limited areas has been vested in the offices, and since they necessarily develop considerable resources in the form of expertise and information, they acquire the power to resist the broad view. So the natural behaviour of bureaucracies is to countenance only incremental change and to oppose (successfully) the implementation of any comprehensive view which threatens the interests of individual 'offices' by crossing the boundaries between separate 'competencies'.

The second problem compounds this; politicians also have personal interests which develop independently of the public purpose. They have constituencies on which their effectiveness depends; if they are to remain effective political actors, these must be protected before the public interest. Initially these constituencies may be geographical regions, but as the politicians' effectiveness grows they may become, first national interest groups or demographic categories, and finally perhaps some particular section of the public bureaucracy. Again we see pressure on the political actor to *behave* in the way the incrementalists *prescribe*; to maintain his effectiveness he must act in a partisan manner and pursue the narrow interests of his constituents rather than taking the broad view required by the norm of rationality.

And if we are honest, we have to admit that a third problem is constituted by the weakness of comprehensive analysis. Social science is quite as departmentalized as the most fragmented bureaucracies, social scientists are just as prone to defend the borders of their disciplinary specialisms. Accordingly the forecasts we are able to produce are typically partial and unconvincing. Why should politicians take one 'expert' seriously when they can always find some other 'expert' to disagree with him? We cannot expect social scientists to be adopted in the instrumental role required by rationality while the instruments of social science are so unreliable.

And from here we get into really deep water. As the role of the state extends itself, the moral foundations of collective decision-making — the promotion of the general welfare — are threatened. As it becomes more apparent that politicians and politicial institutions are incapable of using rational analysis, and that social scientists are in any case incapable of producing it, we can expect the growth of what we called in the previous section 'process dissensus' — the wish to secede from the political institutions of the state because of failures in the functioning of the political process. And as the state becomes more intrusive and the scale of intervention grows, we get an increasing number of issues where diffuse though undeniably large benefits are bought by inflicting very heavy specific costs on some small part of the population — so we may expect growing 'issue dissensus', desire to secede because specific costs seem to outweigh general benefits. In terms of Hirschman's (1970) three strategies, 'loyalty' is forfeited, 'voice' is ineffective, so 'exit' is inevitable.

What this whole argument reduces to is the proposition that the choice between rationality and incrementalism is not a choice between alternative normative principles. The incremental model presents what policy-making systems *do*. The rational model puts forward what they *ought to do*. Forecasters, to the extent to which they play a role in incrementalist policy-making, act, intentionally or unintentionally, as partisans in the political process. And, insofar as the policy-making process becomes more dissensual, their role is an increasingly coercive one, buttressing and legitimizing decisions for which the moral authority is ebbing away. We need only consider the role of expert witnesses in public enquiries, into new roads perhaps, or into nuclear power stations, to get a sense of the reality of this role; they, we, stand, for or against the proposal, giving our partial arguments, knowing full well that the issue will be decided, has been decided, arbitrarily and elsewhere.

6. CONCLUSION

So what *should* forecasters do? It appears that normative political theory cannot help us answer this question; rather, it enables us to demonstrate that the question is unanswerable. We have explored two lines of prescription. The first, the rational model, we find to be a counsel of perfection, unattainable, because of the nature of policy-making bueaucracies, the nature of partisan politics, and the infant status of social science. The second, the incrementalist model, is a description of what actually happens in policy-making, masquerading as a normative prescription, which seeks to provide a moral sanction for the partisan role that experts actually play. The only normative conclusion to be drawn is perhaps that we should take care that we do not allow ourselves to be mistaken as 'neutral instruments' in politicians' hands, that we make our partisan role in policy-making as clear as we can.

But, more speculatively, we might make a second observation. Underlying this whole argument is a techno-economic assumption. The 'diffuse benefits' accruing from collective decision-making (point 2 in section 4) reflect economies of scale in the production of goods and services. If these economies were not present, then there would be no need for collective decision-making, and hence no conflicts between diffuse benefits and specific costs — there would be no grounds for 'issue dissensus'. Similarly, smaller-scale decision-making might alleviate the problems leading to 'process dissensus'; it might enable us to avoid bureaucratization, to involve individuals directly in decision-making and so avoid the blinkered partisan nature of the representative political process, and pose simpler problems more suited to the limited capabilities of social science.

Simply to prescribe smaller-scale decision-making is of course no part of an answer to the problems I have identified. To do so in the absence of a change in the underlying techno-economics would simply be to deny the diffuse benefits because of the specific costs — just as arbitrary as the reverse, and, arguably, quite as coercive. But what if the techno-economic substructure is changing? A common theme among the 'post-industrial' school of futurologists is precisely the declining importance of *some* economies of scale. This does not immediately portend the wholesale withering-away of the modern state, because other economies of scale, particularly in the heartland of manufacturing industries, remain and increase. But this does, or may, mean that we might in the future be able to resolve some of the problems discussed here by disaggregating aspects of decision-making from the state to the regional or local level. In this sense the relationship between the political theorist and the forecaster assumed in this paper may be reversed. Instead of the forecaster looking to the philosopher for guidance as to his proper form of behaviour, the philosopher looks instead to the forecaster to predict the technical changes that will determine the appropriate structure for the political systems of the future.

But this is fantasy. The reality is that we, as technical participants in the public policy-making process, have no clear prescriptive role, and cannot realistically hope to find one.

NOTES

---

1. We might cite two cases. First, D. P. Moynihan; the process of disillusion with the possibility of rational social action may be seen by comparing his (1963) presidential report *The Negro Family: the Case for National Action* (reprinted in Rainwater and Yancey 1967) and his (1969) *Maximum Feasible Misunderstanding* in which he suggests that the social sciences have very little positive contribution to make to the formulation of public policy. Second, A. M. Rivlin once actively and enthusiastically involved in 'rational' educational planning, by the time she came to write *Systematic Thinking for Rational Social Action* (1971), had become quite pessimistic about its practicability.

2. See for example Simon (1957):

The task of rational decision is to select that one of the strategies (i.e. policy alternatives) which is followed by the preferred set of consequences...The task of decision involves three steps: (1) the listing of all the alternative strategies; (2) the determination of all the consequences that follow upon each of these strategies; (3) the comparative evaluation of these consequences. (page 67 — my parentheses.)

3. The statement of the incrementalist position in the following pages is drawn from Lindblom's (1965) *The Intelligence of Democracy*.

4. This direction is to be found in Lindblom (1965), 139-40.

5. See Lindblom (1965), 138-39.
6. This objection to incrementalism was made by Dror (1964), 154, 155.
7. An earlier version of this argument is to be found in Gershuny (1978), 301-03.
8. This model is to be found in Gershuny (1978), 308-11.

REFERENCES

Braybrooke, D. and C. E. Lindblom (1963) *A Strategy of Decision Policy Evaluation as a Social Process*, New York: Free Press.

Dahl, R. A. and C. E. Lindblom (1953) *Politics, Economics and Welfare*, New York: Harper and Row.

Dror, Y. (1964) 'Muddling Through — Science or Inertia?' *Public Administration Review*, Vol. 24: 153-63.

—— (1968) *Public Policymaking Re-examined*, Scranton, NJ: Chandler.

Etzioni, A. (1968) *The Active Society*, New York: Free Press.

Gershuny, J. I. (1978) 'Policymaking Rationality: a Reformulation', *Policy Sciences*, Vol. 9: 295-316.

Hirschman, A. (1970) *Exit, Voice and Loyalty: Response to Decline in Firms, Organizations and States*, Cambridge, Mass.: Harvard University Press.

Lindblom, C. E. (1965) *The Intelligence of Democracy*, New York: Free Press.

Moynihan, D. P. (1969) *Maximum Feasible Misunderstandings Community Action in the War against Poverty*, New York: Free Press.

Rainwater, L. and W. L. Yancey (1967) *The Moynihan Report and the Politics of Controversy*, Cambridge, Mass.: The MIT Press.

Rivlin, A. M. (1971) *Systematic Thinking for Rational Social Action*, Washington: Brookings.

Simon, H. E. (1957) *Administrative Behaviour*, New York: Macmillan.

10 Forecasting for Political Decisions

Lars Ingelstam
Secretariat for Futures Studies,
Stockholm

The present paper is a spin-off from a futures study project called Forecasting and Political Futures Planning. As a background to the project we would like to point out two factors. One is the mandate and mode of operation of the Secretariat for Futures Studies. It can be briefly described as working towards the political process in the broadest sense, mainly on the national level. For further elaboration of this we refer to Wittrock (in this volume). The second factor is a widely held suspicion about long-range forecasting, particularly numerical forecasts and formalized procedures of long-range planning. The suspicion is that these may, at least in a number of important cases, threaten the prerogative of political decision-makers and the democratic process. A very general goal of the project was from the beginning 'the raising of the forecast consciousness' of political decision-makers, civil servants, technocrats and the general public.

A paper containing a general discussion on the nature of decision-making with a long time perspective was presented at the workshop on Futures Studies and Policy Analysis in the Political Process (ECPR, Brussels, April 1979). Based on the discussions there, and our own subsequent work, the material has now been organized in six plus one numbered sub-sections.

Author's note: This paper was written in cooperation with Simon Andersson, Patrick Engellan and Mac Murray.

1. SOMETHING HAPPENED

During 1977 and 1978 we looked into the issues that subsequently became part of the project 'Forecasting and Political Futures Planning'. We found similar patterns in a number of different areas. Everywhere growth was forecast, but at a slower rate than had earlier been usual. Grand plans for expansion, including nuclear power plants, giant hospitals, super highways and industrial plants had shrunk to modest proportions.

Forecasts are scaled down and plans are pared. Sometimes this is a painful experience. But is not this basically something very undramatic? Is it not just a question of a reasonable adaption to the fact that economic growth does not any longer provide as much wind in the sails of the ship of society as it used to?

We believe there are reasons for trying to understand these changes in socio-psychological terms. When looking at forecasts and plans from the post-war era we seem to discover a fairly clear pattern. From the early 1950s to the late 1960s Swedish society has lived through a period characterized by security, harmony and, historically, an exceptionally high growth rate. Everybody was geared to growth, each in his particular field. Discussions on economic policies concerned what level of growth was 'reasonable'. Our society banked on technology, from electronics to nuclear power. All through the 1970s, however, the forecasts concerning e.g. energy consumption have been revised downwards. The changes are dramatic as far as nuclear power is concerned: from an installed capacity of 50 GW by the year 2000 (1970 plans) to 9.4 GW according to present (1979) plans.

And not only technologists and economists were affected by the comfortable spirit of progress of those days. Even among writers and environmentalists, only a small minority questioned the development of technology. The general atmosphere was bright and optimistic and bears witness to the climate of trustfulness that reigned in the mid-1960s. This atmosphere followed upon the legacy of insecurity and doubt left by the war. Since the beginning of the 1970s we seem to be back in a mood of insecurity and disharmony. Economic stagnation, environmental problems, the energy debate and understanding of the situation of the developing countries contributed to the disappearance of the unquestioned optimism of the 1960s. Of course, many forecasters and planners continued their old ways. But the politicians accused each other of 'lost years', the price of oil rose threateningly, nuclear energy was increasingly considered a problem. World famous economists advised us that a crisis could be averted by way of frugality and wise economic policies, whereas others, equally famous, confessed that their expertise could no longer help sort out the problems. 'Technology', which during the 1960s was looked upon as the engine of welfare, was increasingly denounced as an oppressor and a destroyer.

2. THE SPIRIT OF THE AGE

The very fact that prognoses seem to co-vary quite closely with each other over time, reflecting something that we might identify as the 'general mood' or 'the spirit of the age' is striking enough to set us in motion looking for understanding. We are led to believe that there in fact exist ways to understand, and that they have to be looked for somewhere in the intersection between systemic technology and social psychology.

The reasoning goes something like this. In a modern society, with its underlying technological structure, social change occurs as a result of a multitude, virtually thousands, of small and medium-size decisions. They are in fact coordinated, and have to be, if only for technical reasons. But this coordination does not come from dictate, nor from manuals to any large extent. It occurs by a whole host of mutual adjustments, resulting in a largely shared *perception* of the present and the future.

Every age has its own spirit which epitomizes and expresses its ambitions, fears and desires. The spirit of the age is closely shaped by the political manifestations of existing contradictions. It appears everywhere, in art, in educational policy, in social mores and so on. Everyone recognizes, at least in retrospect, the manifestations of a particular period.

The spirit of the age also determines what is regarded as possible and impossible. We believe that organizations — government agencies as well as multiorganizations — behave differently in periods characterized by different spirits. We have all experienced how ideas that were once considered impossible later became the height of fashion. But a common perception applies not only to the present but quite often also to the future. It is also fairly trivial to note that the generally held picture of the future in Western Europe and the USA in the 1950s and 1960s was: more of the same, better and bigger. Equally trivial is the counter-image, where environmental worries and other elements of 'consumer society hang-over' led to future images of gloom, even doom.

The deeper question is whether one can come to grips with a concept like 'the spirit of the age' in an intellectually defensible way. And if this is possible, can one observe any regularity in the future images emerging out of different spirits? There exists no straightforward relation between economic growth rates and the dominating spirit, as experience from the 1960s and the 1970s suggests. Also, there seems to be no clear-cut extension of a present spirit in to the future. Historical evidence suggests that gloomy and problematic times generally trigger an upsurge in utopianism.

3. ROOM FOR CHANGE

A standard assumption among planners is that the room for change, or the amplitude of possible variations, increases with the time horizon under which the planning is applied. The following figure, where the vertical axis represents a decision variable (such as a budget allocation), suggests a standard mode of thinking among planners:

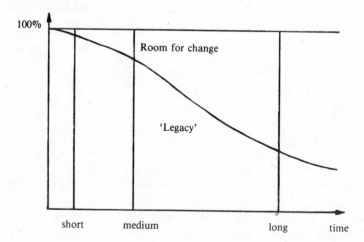

There is a great deal of truth in this. But there is an equally important piece of truth in the seeming opposite: only in the short range, and under rather exceptional circumstances, is there room for any genuine change. The potential for change (as depicted in the figure), is continually betrayed by the decision-maker, moving the lack of decision space closely ahead of his nose on his journey through time.

According to the less conventional view, the system is open to change only when it is out-of-kelter in some way. In 1957 Sputnik shook the US authorities so seriously that it was possible to change American research and educational policies almost overnight. The oil crisis in 1973-74 similarly seems to have opened up new avenues for change and rethinking, although these opportunities do not seem to have been very well turned to account.

Another hypothesis is that we can distinguish between periods of relative stability, when the spirit of the age is strong and unambiguous, and periods when doubts prevail and established patterns of action seem irrelevant. It may well be that hopes for strategic change should be pinned on to periods when resources are scarce and minds confused, rather than on self-gratifying epochs of growth and reassurance.

In any case, it seems probable that shocks and other extraordinary conditions open up wider margins for action than normal situations. This is a somewhat paradoxical fact, but nonetheless important. There are people who seriously suggest that once in a while we should create a crisis in order to force members of society to question their established beliefs. Perhaps they are right. But it seems sad if only some kind of shock therapy can achieve a general change of mind and a new direction of movement towards the future.

However, a period of uncertainty, an exceptional situation or a crisis can only be used as a vehicle for a real change of policies if ideas about alternatives are available. Nothing guarantees that this be the case. Maybe there exists no role that satisfies an organization's desires for stability and perhaps growth. Reality may have outgrown it. If there are no new ideas at hand an organization may easily be led to return to the old ones. The old role was secure, and the organization may very well be unwilling to realize that there is possibly no part for it in the new play that reality puts on the stage.

An organization's relapse into old patterns of thought and

behaviour may sometimes give an impression of stability. But such stability can only be temporary. The organization cannot play the old role convincingly. Sooner or later reality will break through and demand some sort of adaptation.

4. FORECASTING THE PRESENT

A standard objection, part of the 'folklore' around prognostication, is that forecasts tend to colonize the future. Some vested interest behind the forecaster is out to tie our hands. And it is true that a pure forecast does not concede the existence of choices. It depicts the future as inescapably determined by fixed laws. Sometimes it dons the garments of authority in order not to be faced with opposition. It appears in formulas that people do not understand, it refers to the ivory tower of science, where the general public are not admitted, it scorns all those who are distrustful but who cannot express their distrust in a respectable manner.

On the other hand, one cannot be so suspicious as to discern a plot in every diagram and a conspiracy behind each expert's opinion. And yet it is wise to be suspicious. There is always reason to question statements presented without proof. (Often it is wise to question statements with proof, too.)

And if we regard the decision-process as a search for a reasonable background material against which to make decisions, we discover, in fact, that those who are formally the decision-makers are highly dependent on those who prepare the decisions for them. In principle, the decision-maker in the government is the popularly elected parliament. But since the decisions are prepared by the cabinet, the ministries and the civil service one may well discuss whether the legitimate decision-makers have any chance of making decisions independently. The authorities that prepare the background material for decisions therefore have a very special position in the decision-making process. By choosing certain facts and avoiding others they are often able to influence the decision-makers. A comparable kind of influence is exerted by the civil service when the decisions are to be implemented. The civil service may interpret the decisions according to its own intentions. Government decisions therefore have to be acceptable to the civil service if they are to be well and rapidly implemented.

5. THE POLITICAL PARADOX

In Section 4 we touched on the problem of vested interests and bias in connection with forecasting. To the extent that forecasting activities enter into the political process proper, they take on a still more fundamental character. Gustavsson (in this volume) has studied questions related to research and evaluation of politically established programmes. He formulates the democratic paradox thus:

> What gives researchers and investigators, paid by taxpayers' money, the right to put into question, during working hours, the correctness of democratically made decisions?

We have come across a related difficulty of principle in our study. Political multi-party, parliamentary democracy requires a disciplined contest between different ideas and interests. Political democracy concedes that there are different interest groups and different opinions in society, but it gives the majority of the population the right to make the strategic decisions. However, its idea is not to give the majority the right to make decisions with such long-term effects that new majorities are not able to change the direction of movement. Parliamentarism makes high demands on future freedom of action. As a decision-making system it is of a short-term nature.

This observation raises a problem as far as the power and independence of the civil service is concerned. Many agencies make plans for five-ten years or even longer. Parliament is elected for three years and adopts one-year budgets. If the people are to be able to influence the policies of a three-year mandate period in the elections, one condition is that the future is not bound in advance when a new group of members of parliament enters office. If, in addition, the people by way of its representatives, are to exercise the right to determine their own taxes, it is necessary that expenditures are not raised automatically every time a new budget proposal comes before parliament. In this we discern a contradiction between the demands for democratic control of planning, on the one hand, and the reasonable ambitions on the part of the agencies to follow long-term and stable plans, on the other.

6. 'IT LOOKS BETTER FROM A DISTANCE'

It is fairly easy to establish that forecasts have generally become
more sophisticated methodologically than before, and have been
increasingly professionalized. Objectively, it is now more difficult
to check from the outside the assumptions and data underlying a
specific forecast. Whether this has increased or decreased their
credibility is a question that cannot, however, be answered in
general terms.

Finally, we have noted that forecasts are often used in chains.
One forecast builds on data from another, and so on. But in this
process, data tend to be more 'reliable' the further away from the
source we go. Uncertainties, reservations and ambiguities in the
basic forecast tend to be forgotten or suppressed, and this 'raw'
version is then passed on to the next consumer. Hence, for instance
in the field of GNP growth projections, a 'numerical example' may
in the next step be transformed to an 'alternative' and later to a
'forecast', and may eventually be read as a 'plan', carrying political
authority.

In the brief sections above (1-6) we have presented some observations on prognostication in general and its use for political and
public decision-making. When looking at economic forecasts, in
the long range, we have, however, wandered far astray from the
narrow methodological road. Part of the reason for this is the fact
that it is now clear that the problem is no longer one of 'fine-
tuning', or of taming a trend: it is much more fundamental. In the
following, last section of the paper we will very briefly outline our
approach.

7. INSIDE THE BLACK BOX

The machinery of economic policy collects data about all money
transactions (with some exceptions for the illegal, 'underground'
economy). The health of this 'formal' economy is measured in
various ways, but most typically by GNP growth. Most worries
about the ecnomic future are in fact closely tied to an unsatisfac-
tory GNP growth. At the same time, the 'social cost' in human,

non-monetary terms, for a high GNP growth is claimed by some observers to be unreasonably high. Also, trends indicate very clearly that services (offered to consumers and households) is a type of commodity that is gradually eased out of the market economy. The traditional therapy against this — expansion of the public service sector, seems to have fallen into disrepute and has perhaps reached a technical limit, lacking some fiscal innovation.

All this indicates that the *informal economy* merits a lot more attention both in research and policy. It is understood as the sum of all the work outside the market, ranging all the way from clearly illegal tax evasion (underground economy), over informal work exchange arrangements between persons, to the household economy. Already a rough estimate shows that the latter sector (in Sweden) contains an equal amount (6 billion hours/year) or slightly more of working time than the total labor market. (TV occupies 4 billion hours/year, as another comparison.) We are positive that a fuller understanding of the informal economy and its interlinking with the money economy carries important possibilities for social improvement. Some possibilities of this kind are related to the broad concept of a 'community action' economy.

11 Planning: Rational or Political?

Peter Self
London School of Economics

INTRODUCTION

This paper addresses the question of whether politics is in some sense 'irrational' in its treatment of policy problems. It discusses briefly some meanings of rationality, and the reasons for comprehensive attempts at governmental planning. It compares the tests of rationality that can be suggested for politicians with those applicable to experts. This leads to a comparison between political and bureaucratic styles of policy-making, and their influences upon how planning units approach their tasks. The main conclusion is the need for planning units which can escape both from the day-to-day pressures of the political agenda and from the bureaucratic or technocratic bias towards supposedly 'hard' or reliable data; and which can adopt instead a more imaginative and free-ranging but carefully objective approach to policy issues.

POLITICS AND RATIONALITY

It is often said and believed that politics is frequently 'irrational'. Politicians, it is said, are largely guided by short-run considerations of political and electoral advantage; they have a short time horizon;

they deal with issues ad hoc and seriatim, jump from issue to issue, and are unsystematic and inconsistent in their decisions.

By contrast the concept of planning is often associated with 'rationality'. Models of rational decision-making have often been described. While the details vary they all stress the need for a consistent and coherent set of objectives (goals matrix) and/or a consistent criteria of evaluation (as in the ideal version of cost-benefit analysis);[1] examination of the maximum feasible number of alternative policies (subject to time and information costs) and projection and evaluation of their consequences; scrutiny of policy constraints; all backed with adequate research that is as 'objective' as possible.

This paradigm of 'rationality' is generally agreed to be a counsel of perfection, unattainable in full, but (contrary to the arguments of some critics) that does not vitiate its prescriptive appeal. Much more to the point are the limitations of any purely logical devices for improving policy-making. Policy analysis cannot itself supply the value judgments which underlie decisions. What it can do is to provide information which will help a value judgment to be applied more efficiently to a given solution, and which will assist 'trade-offs' between conflicting value judgments. If more is known about the likely outcome of policy options, then it may (for example) seem possible to achieve a considerable gain in Goal B for a small sacrifice of Goal A. This may or may not be acceptable; that will depend upon the flexibility of a policy-maker's values, but even an inflexible policy-maker can gain from learning more about the impact of different decisions upon his own aims or values.

However, policy analysis is always and inevitably restricted in its coverage. It is structured by the way problems are perceived, and by the range of solutions considered to be feasible. It is set within a context of social beliefs and assumptions which can only partially and with difficulty be questioned. The 'information' about likely outcomes which an analyst can produce is in varying degrees speculative and uncertain (and much more attention needs to be given to the different types and meanings of uncertainty). Within this context 'rationality' stands for a high degree of objectivity and openmindedness directed towards the collection and assessment of evidence, and towards probing the basis and assumptions of various techniques for forecasting and evaluation. This work should improve the answers proposed to policy problems, but will not of course provide them. And whether there is an improvement or not depends less upon the logical framework that is utilised or upon special techniques than upon the general character of the approach employed.

The procedural meaning of rationality consists in familiar injunctions about the virtues of forethought, research, analysis. The critical questions concern how these injunctions are applied. Curiously, faith in policy analysis is often associated, irrationally, with an overemphasis (sometimes gross) upon those elements in the analysis that can supposedly be defined in 'hard' and quantified data — in respect both of forecasting and (still more erroneously) evaluation. There may also be some occupational tendency for analysts and researchers to overwork the concept of rationality just as political neglect of procedural rationality can be explained sociologically as the outcome of the politician's role of dealing with a constantly shifting agenda of issues and pressures.

Procedural rationality can be conceived not only as a mode of thought but as a *system of organization*. Mannheim views politics as a non-rational matrix interacting with a rationalized sphere of settled procedures (bureaucracy). But rational here means routinized and predictable, and just as these qualities are functional for bureaucracy (e.g. they both systematize and defend its operations), so they are dysfunctional for politics because politicians lose flexibility of response and power once committed to following a logical chain of coordinated decisions. The appearance of political issues cannot be routinized, almost by definition, although their handling within government can be to some extent. The confrontation of political and bureaucratic styles produces results which vary with the methods of recruitment and the power base of the two groups. European politicians generally adopt a more bureaucratic style than do American ones because they are sometimes drawn from and always closely dependent upon a bureaucratic élite which in the USA does not exist. Political dominance in the USA greatly reduces the practicality of systematic planning just as systematic economic planning could not have developed in France if the bureaucracy had not been powerful.

The necessarily erratic nature of the political agenda has certain consequences for government policy-making. Political and public attention is focused upon emerging problems and new policies to meet them but the implementation and effects of old policies get little attention save in exceptional or shocking individual cases. Thus the analysis of new policy problems is poorly related to evaluation of relevant ongoing policies or programmes. Bureaucracy has too little incentive to review its existing policies critically because of what is sometimes called 'the unimportance of being right in government'. Government gets polarized between a feverish concern with the current political agenda (the political matrix) and largely routinized implementation (bureaucracy).

The need for more attention to policy-making and planning within government can be argued for on several grounds. These include (a) the still growing pressures of public/political demands upon limited government capacities and resources (allocational overload); (b) increased systemic pressures (derivable from technological, economic and social changes) for comprehensive types of regulation (system overload); (c) growing politicization of social consequences (political overload); (d) increased vulnerability of all societies to world shortages of resources and ecological/economic chain reactions (international overload).

Of course even if one accepts the existence of these multiple 'overloads' it would be utopian to think that planning will enable governments to provide all the expected answers. In some cases the best response might be to reject or to reduce governmental responsibility. But even so the case for more effective methods of planning is powerful.

This is so not because there exist rational procedures waiting to be tapped whose more extensive use could greatly improve the content of policies (Dror 1968), but because it is necessary for governments to tackle societal problems on the scale on which they occur, difficult though this is. Another reason for new organs of policy advice is the wish of politicians to control bureaucracy more effectively. In recent years new organs for policy-making and planning have in fact increasingly emerged.

PLANNING AND POLITICS

Planning can be conceived as a 'backroom' activity concerned with the formulation of policies (policy planning). It can also be conceived as a framework for the coordination of particular policies and decisions. This is an ambitious activity whose focus is either specifically organizational (corporate planning) or else concerns a sector of the economy or society (sectoral planning) or some major aspect of total social behaviour (for example economic or environmental planning). While corporate planning accords with the concept of organizational rationality — so long at any rate as it is not too ambitious — these other forms of planning are often treated by 'incrementalists' as impracticable and undesirable, because of the enormous load of coordination and harmonization of decisions which they appear to require.

Certainly these broader forms of planning have many difficulties, but the theoretical objections often miss the mark. Thus the argument that comprehensive planning entails the centralization of authority and the erosion of a self-corrective process of 'partisan mutual adjustment' overlooks both the desirable character and the necessary limitations of such planning in Western democracies. The comprehensive plan is not usually a set of specific instructions, but of guidelines which influence the behaviour of numerous actors; and it may also function importantly as a guide to the ultimate arbitral decisions of government over the competing claims of dependent organizations. Moreover, the preparation of such a plan is more likely to incorporate than to reject a considerable degree of partisan mutual adjustment. In fact the main problem of comprehensive planning in Western societies is achieving enough leverage to be worthwhile, not achieving so much as to be dictatorial.

The justification for comprehensive planning is to achieve a better fit between public policy and the scale/structure of societal problems.[2] Some examples from sectoral fields may help:

(a) Transportation. The interests of users of public and private transportation modes are almost diametrically opposed in terms of access to facilities (concentration best in one case; diffusion in the other) and of the usage of highways. Partisan mutual adjustment has led to the dominance of one group, to mutual frustrations within the dominant group (congestion costs) and to a serious loss of facilities available to the weaker group. This may be a good example of the theory that for everyone to follow his own first (egoistic) preference will often lead eventually to most people not even achieving their second preference — which they would settle for if others would do likewise. Thus in cases like the transportation dilemma a satisfactory synthesis of interests may be impossible

without a comprehensive plan — which is not of course to argue that any plan would produce such a synthesis.

(b) Energy, Defence are familiar cases of production planning where the outputs of different organizations or divisions are closely substitutable or complementary. This is a case of the taxpayer's interest in 'resource rationality', which gets more leverage in cases where costs are high and outputs closely interrelated even when allowing for enormous problems of uncertainty. In both these cases, though in different ways, the case for overall policy goals is also strong. Thus energy policy-making can hardly ignore any longer the evidence about likely future shortages and about the many though different undesirable side-effects (ecological, political, etc.) of existing major energy sources.

These examples of broad-brush 'integrative' planning (e.g. integrating an objectively interrelated policy field) should be distinguished from broad-brush 'allocative' planning. Budgeting comes in the second category as does economic planning where the objective is to parcel out the products of economic growth among claimants. Budgeting is close to corporate planning because it is an organizational imperative, and economic planning of an allocative kind can be regarded as setting guidelines for budgeting activity. Allocative planning is concerned more with the worth or justice of claims (priorities) than with the integration of policies — hence it may be politically hard but it is organizationally much easier than the latter type of planning. Where, however, the concern of economic planning is to produce economic growth, or other specific objectives, it entails a very difficult form of policy integration.

The political problems of comprehensive planning are:

(a) Consultation with interests may be biased towards the stronger groups and organizations — a familiar problem with economic and industrial planning. But attempts to get broader participation may also fail because it is largely the strongest groups who 'participate' — a familiar problem with urban plans.

(b) Parliament and even political leaders may feel isolated from the planning process. The inability of parliaments to offer constructive comments upon economic plans or public expenditure plans is well known. If they have the political right and the technical support to unstick and remake the plan, as the American Congress does the budget, they can shift its political priorities. But since a comprehensive plan has to integrate a large number of variables into a decision-making framework, it is difficult to take apart and remake without elaborate study and it has to be tested for organizational feasibility and at least minimal cooperation. Undoubtedly governments (and planners) sometimes make too much of these difficulties so as to keep their legislative critics at bay. But the difficulties do tend to confine even parliamentary committees to at best the rôle of useful critics rather than initiators or rewriters of plans.

(c) Politicians frequently neglect planning until there is a controversial issue of implementation. They may accept planning on technical grounds as a necessary background exercise, which should not, however, predetermine (or even strongly influence) particular decisions. In English local government, the preparation of structure plans is largely left to professional planners, whereas 'implementation' arouses much more political interest.

To some extent this list of problems simply describes the characteristics of modern democratic governments. Some power has moved from elected politicians to corporate interests, and to some small extent to populist groups. Some groups are disproportionately powerful (the inequalities of pluralism) and the only possible corrective is elective leadership based upon latent majorities and/or a generalized social welfare ethic within government. This latter criterion may suggest the desirability of strengthening the rôle of elective political leadership within the planning process.

Planning is often pictured as potentially too powerful or dominant a process, but the greater danger is that it will become increasingly ritualistic. Growing distributional conflicts slow up the processes of plan making and approval, and dilute the plans' content and bite. Exercises in participation involve further delays. Plan-making and 'monitoring' is becoming an increasingly esoteric technique or art, whose latent political function sometimes seems to be to draw off the steam of public protest against decisions which de facto are reached in different arenas — or else get postponed indefinitely.

POLITICAL AND ECONOMIC RATIONALITY

The goodness or worth of policies is not a function of the methods by which they are made or the data on which they are based, although there is of course a relationship. What is the nature of this relationship and in what sense is it or could it be more or less 'rational'?

To this big question there are a number of possible answers, some conventional and some less so. I will not go through all these theories here. The truth with most of them is that they are either simply rationalizations of how the policy process works or is supposed to work in a democracy — usually some version of a pluralist idyll — or else rest on a narrow view of the 'rationality' of some function performed within that policy process. Consider briefly two theories of the latter kind as affecting politicians and experts.

(a) Is political behaviour in a democracy 'rational'? If it is then the policies and decisions which flow from such decisions will also presumably be rational, however erratic or shortsighted they appear to observers — provided of course that the democratic process is itself functioning properly (and if it is not, the solution would be procedural or institutional changes in the process — not in the ultimate criterion of good policy-making which will remain political behaviour).

Now it is true enough that it is 'rational', e.g. in accordance with democratic concepts, for politicians to reckon political opportunity costs and to pursue electoral success. The argument that 'political rationality' in this sense is as meaningful and valid as the concept of 'economic rationality' (with which political behaviour is sometimes unfavourably contrasted) is true as far as it goes — but subject to the extremely limited nature of *both* concepts of rationality. If the political entrepreneur is to be compared with the economic entrepreneur, it must be recognized that he deals in 'futures' of a very different kind. For the latter it may be unimportant (though not actually so much so as textbooks assert) whether he produces ships or sealing wax so long as profits are adequate. But the politician cannot so easily switch from a peace to a war policy, or to and from racial equality, capital punishment and a compulsory incomes policy, according to his perceptions of electoral success. This is not just a question of sunk commitments, but of the sociological difficulty of 'selling' policies in which one has no personal belief or interest. It can be done but not too easily. It is probably, though not universally, a paradox of politics that to win one must be keen on other things besides winning.

Politics does not present a consumers' market of rational egoistic choice, but an arena in which ultimate individual costs and benefits are distributed according to complex patterns of group action and interaction, and in which individual voters — partly because of high information costs but also for other reasons — generally allocate a trustee rôle to leaders to look after their interests. Moreover, these interests often seem to be perceived on a different basis (societal or group cooperation) and in a more prudential way (more attention to the long term) than would be suggested by examination of the same individuals' market behaviour and preferences.

A theory of politics which claims that the self-interest of politicians will produce politics that are rational in the sense of according with the 'will of the people' is therefore seriously deficient. Moreover, this egoistic theory conflicts with another of the same type which says that since politicians are always imposing costs which they bear only fractionally (if at all) themselves, they will have a superficial view of the resulting costs and benefits. In the end one cannot dispense with some kind of 'public interest' philosophy, however vague — and one that must extend also to the rôle of the bureaucracy. If one believes, for example, that future societal problems should be anticipated and forestalled, or that a more harmonious and equal society should be forged, then it is true that no political action is possible without some supportive public opinion — that is the 'price' of democratic rationality. But the supportive opinion has to be nourished and led. There is an ineluctable need for political vision and leadership — for the old-fashioned concept of statesmanship in fact.

(b) Is the authority of knowledge (expertise) 'rational'? The answer is that it is so only to a limited extent and within a broader context of social norms and processes. It is not so hard to show this in relation to 'deep but narrow' forms of expertise which are primarily instrumental in a policy sense. For example, knowledge of how to construct motorways does not give an engineer any logical claim to say whether or not a motorway should be built — unless one accepts a technological determinism which would anyhow make the issue redundant. But this logical truth does not imply that the government engineer should have no say whatever in the issue, but should function absolutely as a technical surbordinate. Sociologically this is impractical — for the engineer has always de facto some influence — and normatively it is undesirable — for individuals are entitled and ought (as rational beings) to have some influence over the uses to which their special knowledge is put. To suppose otherwise is to fall into the same narrow and mechanical view of social rôles that characterizes some theories of the politician. The only way out is to educate the engineer to think about his expertise in the context of social behaviour, social problems, social issues.

The case is clear with the engineer but seems more obscure in the case of 'policy experts' such as economists — indeed particularly with economists since (i) they are the most frequently consulted and influential type of policy adviser in modern societies; (ii) they are themselves potent critics of 'technocracy' in virtue of their subordination of technical claims and arguments to generalized tests of 'economic efficiency' or of the distribution of costs and benefits; and (iii) they possess a formidable battery of theories which in some branches such as welfare economics introduce their own criteria of rational policy-making. By contrast other policy experts in such subjects as town planning, systems analysis and operations research are without any similar theoretical rationale and bite.

Yet the concept of 'welfare' as deployed by economists itself represents a particular policy position, even if one sets aside the seemingly insoluble internal theoretical debates about its application. Thus welfare is conceived as deriving from the 'preferences' exhibited in the behaviour of individuals in their use of and claims upon available resources and individual preferences as thus revealed provide the touchstone for welfare. Welfare economists usually assume that the aim of public policy should be to maximize the sum of individual satisfactions as conveyed by individuals' willingness to pay for some good or other satisfaction, or for the avoidance of some bad (such as pollution). They may temper the analysis with theories about distribution but the essential basis remains the individual's willingness to pay for what he wants (or does not want). In theory this looks highly democratic and even 'populist' in the sense of pitting a direct enquiry into individual costs and benefits against the claims of pressure groups or politicians who claim to know what these effects will be.

Political and social debate does not usually conceive 'welfare' in the economists' terms. If individuals spend increasing sums upon drink and gambling that brings increases of welfare in the economist's sense though the conclusion seems perverse to ordinary people. It might indeed be suspected that the economist is really talking about freedom of choice rather than about welfare. Economists would indeed concede that too much drink might produce 'adverse externalities' which could presumably justify some taxation subject to the usual problem of the highly uncertain relationship of such a measure to individuals' costs and benefits. But the more welfare economic theories are bent (as they can be in many directions), the less their theoretical leverage as a normative test of policy.

Those concerned with future studies must carefully consider economic treatments of the discount rate. A high discount rate virtually abolishes (within the economist's welfare calculus) any concern for the future beyond a relatively few years. But how is the discount rate to be derived? If by generalization from existing practices then the economist is merely accepting that neglect of the future which is in fact embodied in current institutional and social behaviour. He may of course do useful analytic work in explaining how economic markets have produced this situation. But how can he justify a lower discount rate from his own theoretical foundations? Future generations are in no position to express their 'willingness to pay' to prevent some prospective harm that may be done to them. Of course it is true that even if we ascribe to government some significant rôle of trustee for the future it is clear that this rôle cannot be sustained in a democratic society without the support of public opinion. In this sense the individual preferences appealed to by the economist are unassailable. The point is that he has no way of applying his theories to future welfare except by stepping into the rôle of a 'concerned citizen'.[3]

Our conclusion is that the idea of rationality within the social process is a complex and comprehensive phenomenon, incapable of being reduced to tests of the interest (political) or knowledge (expert) of the participants — though such tests have a limited utility within any evaluation of the total system.

POLITICAL AND BUREAUCRATIC PLANNING

A polarization between political and bureaucratic orientations towards policy-making and planning has already been posited. Both orientations may seem rational within the limited criteria of prescribed rôles, but much less so on any broader view of social needs. Moreover, the gap between the two orientations is hard to close. Politicians attend to political expediency and bureaucracy to some technical factors and to consistency of administration. But the middle ground of more imaginative, necessarily more speculative social analysis is weakly cultivated.

Of course the uses of expert knowledge cannot be equated with bureaucratic inputs into the policy process. Experts function both as political advisers (usually temporary) and as regular members of the bureaucracy. To some extent these rôles are self-selected, and depend upon the expert's political beliefs (or lack of them) and view of his own knowledge and its possible use. Experts take on much of the 'style' of political or bureaucratic policy-making with which they are associated. But the numbers of experts within bureaucracy are far greater than those in political (or even semi-political) appointments. Bureaucracy has much the greater resources.

But how are the resources used? We can distinguish between those planning units or policy advisory groups which function primarily as 'staff assistance' to ministers or cabinets, and those which are bureaucratized. In the former case the work of the unit will be heavily concerned with the current political agenda. There will be rather little if any time for 'forward looks' unless relevant to immediate legislation or decisions. There will be a frequent and rapid turnover of issues. There will be only erratic attention to policy coordination or implementation. The methods and concerns of the unit will be responsive to those of its political chief or 'chiefs'. (In Urwick's sense it will function, anyhow to some extent, as an extension of the chief's persona.)[4] Some differences will occur with the size and composition of the unit; a larger unit, and one staffed to a greater extent from career civil servants, will be relatively more routinized and bureaucratic. But the same tendencies will be there. For example, most of the above observations would apply to the Central Policy Review Staff (CPRS) attached to the British Cabinet even though the CPRS was originally intended to help plan and supervise a coordinated strategy (or corporate plan) for government as a whole. It has not functioned in that way, partly because cabinets find difficulty in maintaining a comprehensive general strategy, partly because a small advisory unit cannot really coordinate on such a vast organizational scale. What the CPRS and similar policy advisory units can do is to give politicians the benefit of an alternative opinion to departmental submissions, which even if superficial has a certain organizational independence and novelty (Urwick 1931).

Planning units sunk within departments function differently. Their tendencies are towards political and social caution, and the avoidance of speculation; towards reliance upon 'respectable' professional techniques, preferably using supposedly 'hard' numerate data (even if its derivation is obscure). Their well-known difficulty is that of achieving any leverage in the policy process. Sometimes such a unit may be almost invisible at the political level but play a considerable part in the detailed construction of a programme. For example, once the money has been allocated (somewhat arbitrarily) for a road programme, the planning unit may plan the network according to esoteric technical and economic calculations — to be modified later in the light of political or social objections. Sometimes such units are seriously underused or underemployed, unless diverted to current chores. Often too it is hard to define the units and persons within a department specifically concerned with policy analysis (for example, a 'planning' or research unit may simply be feeding in statistical data to line administrators who will be making their own policy evaluations).

Exercises in social forecasting within bureaucracies tend to be heavily based upon the historical extrapolation of existing trends, and confined to those trends which can be plausibly demonstrated by existing techniques. Most respectable probably is demographic forecasting; next comes economic forecasting to the extent that growth in demand can be plausibly predicted or associated with other variables, e.g. car ownership with income levels or energy consumption with the growth of GNP. Most such forecasts assume certain constraints about social behaviour which may not be closely investigated. For example forecasts of housing demand assume a falling average size of household, a trend which might not (for social and economic reasons) continue indefinitely in its present form. There may be some attention to new technological possibilities, but much less to their social implications. The analysis of possible social change — and still more of possible political change and movements of public opinion — is muted within bureaucratic planning units for fairly obvious reasons. It may seem to be challenging politicians' judgments on their own ground, as well as to offend professional norms about the reliability of techniques and data. But the effect is to add to the 'communications gap' and to increase the influence of those techniques which purport to be tolerably reliable and dependable.

The tendency of modern democracies to plan for 'more of the same' under conditions of economic growth (or expected growth) has often been remarked upon. Often these plans come badly unstuck if the growth does not materialize; for example the British educational plan of 1973, prepared after extensive consultation within — but not beyond — educational circles, assumed a large increase in the demand for secondary and university education which has not materialized because fewer students than expected stayed on at school and fewer of those qualified wished to go to university; and assumed a much enhanced need for teachers which has been vitiated by fewer pupils than expected and by less mobility among teachers (for job security and other reasons), as well as by diminished public funds. Some of the teacher training colleges that had been quickly built were still more quickly declared redundant. These results were not just the outcomes of declining economic growth but of subtle social influences. Doubtless no forecasting exercise as such could have been anywhere near right. But if the frailty of 'hard' techniques of forecasting had been fully realized, and if the yardstick of evaluation had questioned the 'more of the same' assumption, policy analysis would have been forced into more original research and more imaginative formulations.[5]

Politicians have a strong interest in how issues are posed for investigation; for the posing of an issue has — however unintentionally — a potent effect upon subsequent research and analysis. For this they need the help of their policy staffs. Politicians also need to make sure that research and analysis is not dominated by technocrats or even 'econocrats'. To do this they need to encourage bureaucratic planning units to make more use of 'soft' data and to be more venturesome and imaginative.

There are of course ways of trying to bridge the gap between political and bureaucratic attitudes towards planning, and of escaping from the limitations of a conventional government system. Some important experiments consist in policy advisory units which are designed so as to be independent of short-run political and bureaucratic pressures, but yet able to draw on government information and to bring their findings to the attention of decision-makers in an authoritative manner. Such experiments as the Scientific Council for Government Policy in the Netherlands and the Future Studies Secretariat come in this category in different ways, and their work is evaluated elsewhere in this volume. Another way of following the same goal in respect of a particular issue is to set up an independent commission with adequate powers of research and investigation. It needs to be insulated as far as possible from both organizational and technical forms of bias, and to have its own sources of both expert data and informed opinion. But the recipe may not work.

Even in the case of such a comprehensive and costly enquiry as that of the 'Roskill' Commission on the Third London Airport, most of the desiderata of policy planning were breached.[6]

(a) The terms of reference specified the need for a four-runway airport to serve London. These terms required assumptions about the treatment of substantial traffic from the English Midlands that was currently using London airport. Assuming as the Commission did that the new airport should cater efficiently for such traffic — save to the extent that it might be drawn north to Manchester — and by combining this requirement with that for a single giant airport, the terms of reference could be said to point strongly towards the Commission's actual conclusion — a giant airport north of London. The terms of reference were both dogmatic and somewhat obscure.

(b) The members of the Commission were strongly selected for their technical and economic skills. This led them to place great faith in technical forecasting combined with an elaborate cost-benefit study which (transplanting techniques from other transportation contexts) incorporated the 'time costs' as well as the money costs of passengers' journeys to the airport. All quantified costs were pooled in a comprehensive equation, regardless of differences in their assumptions, reliability, and techniques of measurement. Various techniques were used to cost environmental 'spillovers' but their obvious unreliability led to this part of the analysis being eventually scrapped. The damage had been done, however. The

Commission was left in a position of striking a balance between supposedly 'objective' quantified data and its 'subjective' judgments — a quite false dichotomy when one reflects that some of the 'subjective' views had a more reliable factual basis (e.g. crude data about environmental impacts) than the value assumptions behind the economic techniques.

(c) Commitment to these techniques went with little imagination or foresight in other directions. For example, failure to assess the growing importance of environmental opinion led the Commission to propose a site which was promptly rejected as politically impossible by the government.

Could these failures of the Roskill Commission have been avoided? They would at least have been less likely if firstly the terms of reference had been more carefully and imaginatively considered, and secondly there had been less technocratic bias in the selection of its members. These defects occurred partly because of the gap between political impulsiveness (shown by the immediate rejection of the Commission's findings as well as its hasty appointment) and the bureaucratic and technical bias towards the supposedly hard ground of quantified forecasting and evaluation techniques.

CONCLUSIONS

Some possible prescriptive inferences from this paper may be briefly suggested in conclusion:

(a) Planning staffs should be designed to reduce the political/bureaucratic polarization by including a mixture of career civil servants and political appointees. This should apply within departments as well as in central agencies.

(b) Staff should also include a broad spectrum of skills and capacities. There is particularly room for more use of people with social and scientific imagination.

(c) There should be more effort spent upon broadening professional forms of education, so that dialogues among experts and between experts and politicians become more meaningful. Such education should have a broad humanitarian orientation and concern with social issues. In particular there should be more attention to the normative assumption of economists and other groups of policy experts.

(d) The case for various forms of comprehensive planning points to the creation of an interrelated network of planning cells within both central coordinating agencies and line departments.

(e) Much more analysis is desirable of the meanings and problems of 'comprehensive planning', in particular of the relations between corporate planning and framework planning across organizational lines, and between resource planning and policy integration.

(f) Planners and policy advisers working in different fields should have some education in common, dealing with general methods and issues of planning and with the interrelation of different kinds of planning and policy-making. But this should go with deep knowledge of policy-making in a particular substantive field, in which the planner will specialize.

NOTES

1. An ideal form of cost-benefit analysis in which the benefits of government policies were evaluated and preferably quantified on a uniform basis is the concept of 'rational decision-making' advocated by Herbert Simon in his well-known *Administrative Behaviour* (New York, 2nd edition 1957, Ch. 2). For a comment see Self (1977), 29-38.

2. The intellectual, political and organizational conditions of planning are discussed in Self (1974).

3. For a full analysis of the welfare economists' position see Self (1975).

4. See the contribution by William Plowden to *Public Administration Bulletin*, June 1974, based on a longer unpublished paper.

5. See *Education: A Framework for Expansion* (London: HMSO 1973). Comments by Sir Toby Weaver are in *Planning, Forecasting, and Frustration in the Public Services* (Yorkshire & Humberside Regional Management Centre 1978).

6. Report of the Commission on the Third London Airport, London: HMSO 1971. For discussion see Self (1975), Ch. 7.

REFERENCES

Dror, Yehezkel (1968) *Public Policymaking Re-examined*, San Francisco.
Self, Peter (1974) 'Is Comprehensive Planning Possible and Rational?', *Policy and Politics*, Vol. II, No. 3: 193-293.
—— (1975) *Econocrats and the Policy Process: The Politics and Philosophy of Cost-Benefit Analysis*, London.
—— (1977) *Administrative Theories and Politics*, London, 2nd edition.
Urwick, L. F. (1931) 'Organization as a Technical Problem', in L. F. Gulick and L. F. Urwick (eds.), *Papers on the Science of Administration*, New York.

Notes on Contributors

Peter R. Baehr, born 1935, is executive secretary and staff director of the Scientific Council for Government Policy in the Hague. From 1969-76 he was professor of international relations at the University of Amsterdam.

Sverker Gustavsson, born 1940, is assistant professor in the department of government at Uppsala University. He is also associated with the National Swedish Institute of Building Research. His dissertation, *Debatten om forskningen och samhället* (Stockholm, 1971), is a study of various approaches to adopting a conscious public policy towards research and development. He is currently conducting a study of Swedish housing policy from a decision theory point of view together with a study of the more general problem of how corporatism should be explained within the context of the modern welfare state.

Jonathan I. Gershuny, born 1949, is a fellow of the Science Policy Research Unit of the University of Sussex. He is author of *After Industrial Society* (London 1978).

Andries Hoogerwerf, born 1931, is professor of policy studies in the department of public administration, University of Twente, Enschede. He has published extensively in social science and policy studies.

Lars Ingelstam was professor of mathematics at the University of Uppsala from 1966-73 and since then has been director of the Secretariat for Futures Studies, Stockholm.

Juliet Lodge is lecturer in politics at Hull University, having previously lectured in European politics at Auckland University, New Zealand and been visiting fellow at the London School of Economics.

Simon Miles is a development consultant working with governments and international organizations world-wide on many aspects of policy and programme planning, institutional development and decision-making. He is author of *Metropolitan Problems, International Perspectives* and *Developing a Canadian Urban Policy*.

William Plowden has been director-general of the Royal Institute of Public Administration, London, since 1978. He was previously a lecturer in government at the London School of Economics (1965-71), a member of the Central Policy Review Staff (1971-77) and under-secretary in the Department of Industry (1977-78). His publications include *The Motor Car and Politics in Britain* (1971).

Peter Self is professor of public administration at the London School of Economics. His previous positions have included a visiting professorship at Cornell University (1958 and 1967) and at the Australian National University (1976). His publications include *Cities in Flood: The Problems of Urban Growth* (1957/61), *The State and the Farmer* (1962/71), *Administrative Theories and Politics* (1972/77), and *Econocrats and the Policy Process* (1976), as well as articles and contributions.

Daniel Tarschys is a Liberal member of the Swedish parliament and chairman of the Swedish Government Commission on Public Policy Planning.

Björn Wittrock is associate professor of political science at the University of Stockholm. His recent publications in English include contributions to *The Uses and Abuses of Forecasting* (1979), *Internationale Dimensionen in der Wissenschaft* (1979), *Politics as Rational Action* and to such journals as *Futures*, *West European Politics* and *Journal for the General Philosophy of Science*.